HOLOCAUST AND HOME
THE POETRY OF DAVID FRAM FROM LITHUANIA TO SOUTH AFRICA

LEGENDA

LEGENDA is the Modern Humanities Research Association's book imprint for new research in the Humanities. Founded in 1995 by Malcolm Bowie and others within the University of Oxford, Legenda has always been a collaborative publishing enterprise, directly governed by scholars. The Modern Humanities Research Association (MHRA) joined this collaboration in 1998, became half-owner in 2004, in partnership with Maney Publishing and then Routledge, and has since 2016 been sole owner. Titles range from medieval texts to contemporary cinema and form a widely comparative view of the modern humanities, including works on Arabic, Catalan, English, French, German, Greek, Italian, Portuguese, Russian, Spanish, and Yiddish literature. Editorial boards and committees of more than 60 leading academic specialists work in collaboration with bodies such as the Society for French Studies, the British Comparative Literature Association and the Association of Hispanists of Great Britain & Ireland.

The MHRA encourages and promotes advanced study and research in the field of the modern humanities, especially modern European languages and literature, including English, and also cinema. It aims to break down the barriers between scholars working in different disciplines and to maintain the unity of humanistic scholarship. The Association fulfils this purpose through the publication of journals, bibliographies, monographs, critical editions, and the MHRA Style Guide, and by making grants in support of research. Membership is open to all who work in the Humanities, whether independent or in a University post, and the participation of younger colleagues entering the field is especially welcomed.

ALSO PUBLISHED BY THE ASSOCIATION

Critical Texts
Tudor and Stuart Translations • *New Translations* • *European Translations*
MHRA Library of Medieval Welsh Literature

MHRA Bibliographies
Publications of the Modern Humanities Research Association

The Annual Bibliography of English Language & Literature
Austrian Studies
Modern Language Review
Portuguese Studies
The Slavonic and East European Review
Working Papers in the Humanities
The Yearbook of English Studies

www.mhra.org.uk
www.legendabooks.com

STUDIES IN YIDDISH

Legenda *Studies in Yiddish* embrace all aspects of Yiddish culture and literature. The series regularly publishes the proceedings of the International Mendel Friedman Conferences on Yiddish Studies, which are convened every two years by the European Humanities Research Centre of the University of Oxford.

PUBLISHED IN THIS SERIES

Managing Editor
Dr Graham Nelson, 41 Wellington Square, Oxford OX1 2JF, UK
www.legendabooks.com

Holocaust and Home

*The Poetry of David Fram
from Lithuania to South Africa*

HAZEL FRANKEL

LEGENDA
Studies in Yiddish 18
Modern Humanities Research Association
2021

Published by Legenda
an imprint of the Modern Humanities Research Association
Salisbury House, Station Road, Cambridge CB1 2LA

ISBN 978-1-83954-007-3

First published 2021

Copy-Editor: Dr Marie Isabel Matthews-Schlinzig

CONTENTS

This study is dedicated to my parents,
Benny and Sylvia Eidelman (née Slayen) z''l;
and to my grandparents,
Benyomin Hillel Eidelman z''l, Sarah Hinde Eidelman (née Peres) z''l,
Morris Slayen z''l, and Leah Slayen (née Wainstein) z''l,
who left Lithuania before the Holocaust, bringing Yiddish
with them to South Africa, the land far off;
and to the members of my extended family
who perished in Lite and Latvia;
to my great-aunt,
Henna Pogrund (née Peres) z''l,
for whom I am named;
and as a legacy for my dearest children and grandchildren.

ACKNOWLEDGEMENTS

I would like to thank Jack and Naomi Friedman, as well as the Editorial Board of Legenda Press, for their generosity in support of the unique academic book series, Studies in Yiddish, of which this book forms a part. I am also most grateful to the University of the Witwatersrand, my alma mater, and ANFASA (The Academic and Non-Fiction Authors of South Africa) for their generous funding awards, which enabled me to pursue my research.

I am deeply indebted to Professor Joseph Sherman z"l, whose extensive writings on Fram inspired me, providing me with the rich foundation for my own endeavours; it is also due to Sherman's foresight that Fram's legacy is preserved in the Benson Latin American Collection at the University of Texas in Austin.

I would like to offer my sincerest thanks to Shifrah Mina Fram for permission to translate and transliterate her father's poems.

I am ever grateful to Cedric Ginsberg for his thoughtful input and commitment; Linda and Grant Katzeff for their gracious care and beneficence; Steven Earnshaw for believing in the worth of the work from its outset, and for his insightful mapping of the path; Mikhail Krutikov for his positive assessments, and for suggesting meaningful avenues of exploration; Gennady Estraikh for his interest in and affirmation of the value of my manuscript, and for his sense of urgency; Merle Williams for her wisdom, and for her understanding of the length and breadth of the terrain; Michael Titlestad for his ongoing encouragement and guidance; Beruriah Wiegand for her focused assistance; Astrid Starck-Adler who provided me with useful support; Kenneth Moss for his invaluable pointers; Justin Cammy who shared informed ideas; and Ber Kotlerman who alerted me to worthwhile possibilities.

I would especially like to acknowledge the work of my copy editor, Marie Isabel Matthews-Schlinzig, for her acute focus, meticulous eye for detail, sense of synchronicity, and dedication that enabled me to complete the book.

It is due to acute sense of direction and skill of Graham Nelson, managing editor of Legenda, that the volume has found a safe haven. Thank you.

My thanks are also due to the publishers for permission to include material from the following articles: 'David Fram: Yiddish Poet of the South African Diaspora', *Jewish Affairs*, 65.1 (Pesach 2013), 26–35; 'Journey with Two Maps: Longing and Belonging in the Yiddish Poetry of David Fram', *The English Academy Review*, 32.2 (October 2015), 222–37; 'From Steppe to Veld: The Landscape Poems of the Yiddish Poet David Fram', *Journal for Semitics*, 25.1 (2016), 235–52; 'A Panorama of Portraits: Elements of Empathy in the Yiddish Poems of David Fram', *Literator*, 37.1 (2016), 1–10; 'Stones in the Landscape: Memory and Postmemory in the Yiddish poems of David Fram', *European Journal of Jewish Studies*, 11.1 (2017), 148–73; 'From the Outside Looking in: The Yiddish Poems of the Lithuanian South African Poet David Fram (1903–1988)', *Journal of Literary Studies*, 35.2 (2017), 20–34; 'Home and the Holocaust in Selected Paintings of Marc Chagall and Yiddish Poems of David Fram', *Soundings: An Interdisciplinary Journal*, 101.4.3 (2018), 341–59.

H.F., January 2021

INTRODUCTION:
BIOGRAPHY AND OVERVIEW

This study responds to the Yiddish poetry of David Fram written in a critical era in world history, before, during, and after World War II.[1] Set between Lithuania[2] and South Africa, part of a cultural continuum, his poems contribute a record of an obliterated culture in the old country and its surviving offshoots in the new.

Celebrating diversity, the research also sheds light on the symbiotic process in which the outsider from the icy steppes enriched South African literature, and Yiddish was enriched in turn by the infusion of veld and thorn bush. Fram viewed Lite through the prism of South Africa, and South Africa through the memory of Lite. Rich in Jewish history, culture, and tradition in juggling conflicts of belonging and not belonging, the poems evoke his early family life, and the effects of migration.

As the project explores the Yiddish narrative through the trajectory of a specific individual, it establishes interconnections where transformations took place.[3] Making a significant contribution to the understanding of the impact of the loss of home through a single immigrant's journey, these interconnections may also shed light on the experiences of other exiled, migrant communities. Highlighting some outcomes for a minority language and community in the diaspora, they provide vehicles for a deeper understanding of contemporary concerns. With reference to Holocaust representation, they 'may be considered valuable for providing evidence'.[4] Bearing witness for the Jewish victims in their *mameloshn* [mother tongue], they keep the memory of the Holocaust in Lithuania alive and visible.

As Fram's memories of *di alte heym* [the old home], his depictions of life in South Africa, and the personal impact of the Holocaust deepen our understanding and illuminate larger issues, the particular may be used as a catalyst for further scholarly insights. By placing the poems at the forefront of literary consciousness beyond purely Yiddish and Jewish cultural interests, and across other disciplines, they are made available to a wider audience.

The interconnected chapters of this book highlight Fram's themes, concerns, and world view through close textual analysis of language, imagery, and style.[5] The YIVO ['Yidisher visenshaftlekher institut', Yiddish Scientific Institute] trans-literation system is used throughout, except where the 'ch' is more familiar than 'kh', as in 'cheder'. Although Yiddish does not have capital letters, it has become the custom to capitalize the first word of a sentence, proper nouns, and the first word of a title when transcribing Yiddish into the Roman alphabet. I have also chosen to capitalize the first words of lines in Fram's transcribed poems in some instances.

Eastern European place names are given in their current form, thus Panevezys (Ponevezh), Kaunas (Kovno), Vilnius (Vilna). Southern African place names are stated as Fram would have known them, thus Transvaal (now Gauteng), Rhodesia (now Zimbabwe), Salisbury (now Harare). Where known, dates of first publication are noted in brackets after the titles of the poems.

All translations of Fram's poems are my own unless otherwise indicated. They remain faithful to the originals' imagery and implications but dispense with rhyme to avoid contorting the rhythms and linguistic structures of English. Together with my transliterations of a selection of poems from his two published collections, two pamphlet poems, and uncollected works from various literary journals, these provide the source material for the discussions.

Biography

David (Dovid) Fram was born in 1903 in Krekenava (Krakinove), in the district of Panevezys, Lithuania, in the Russian Pale of Settlement.[6] Jews in the *shtotn* and *shtetlekh*[7] were distinguished from their gentile neighbours by religion, occupation, language, and culture. Defined by their interlocking economic and social networks, they used their *mameloshn* in their interactions in the marketplace, for communal and religious functions, and to continue relationships with emigrants abroad.

Fram attended a traditional Jewish *cheder* [Hebrew school] and *yeshive* [institution for religious studies], and also received secular private tuition.[8] In 1915, for security reasons, Fram, his family, and many other members of the Jewish community were relocated from the Pale to Samara on the Volga River in the Russian interior. His displacement before bar mitzvah age, when he experienced hunger and witnessed pogroms and death, was the first of many times that Fram endured the vicissitudes of migration.

Fram attended the Lomonosov Russian *gimnazye* [high school] and matriculated at a Soviet trade school. On returning to Panevezys in 1921, his Russian qualifications were unacceptable in the newly independent Lithuanian Republic. In order to avoid military service, he attended the Ukmerge[9] Yidisher *gimnazye*. He boarded with the linguist and lexicographer, Yudl Mark, who became his tutor and lifelong mentor, providing him with the foundation for his flowing, 'flisendiker yiddisher shprakh'.[10] In 1926, Fram spent time in Paris with three of his four sisters in the vibrant Yiddish-speaking community of writers and artists that included Marc Chagall.[11] He then attended the agricultural school in Toulouse for three months. Fram left Europe permanently in 1927 for economic reasons, to join an uncle who paid for his ticket.

After the assassination of Czar Alexander II in 1881, the Russo-Japanese War fought during 1904–05, the failed revolution of 1905, the Kishinev pogrom in 1903, the Russian Revolution, and World War I, the 'great traumatic events in Jewish history'[12] before World War II, thousands of Jews left Eastern Europe to escape antisemitism, poverty, and persecution. A further incentive was 'the existence of pre-established Jewish communities elsewhere',[13] so that emigrants followed family and friends. Fram became one link in a 'chain of immigration',[14] an exodus that included a 'flood of Yiddish immigrants from Lithuania to the shores of the Cape of Good Hope',[15] when the South African government permitted a fresh wave of immigrants from Eastern Europe to join the already sizable Yiddish-speaking community established there.

Thus, the secular Jewish culture spread to the far-flung diaspora, *a goldene medine* [land of gold]. In the Transvaal, Fram worked variously as a travelling salesman, a 'smous', going from house to house selling goods, and as a 'trayer',[16] surviving on bread and ginger beer,[17] as a pharmaceutical salesman,[18] and from November 1927 as a teacher at the Mayfair Hebrew Congregation Talmud Torah.[19] His first poetry collection, *Lider un poemes* [Songs and Poems] was published in 1931.[20] He became the Yiddish editor of *Der afrikaner yidishe tsaytung* [The African Yiddish Newspaper] with Arthur Markowitz, the English editor, and then the Yiddish editor of the weekly *Der yidisher ekspres* [The Yiddish Express] with Abel Shaban.

In December 1934, he left for London where he worked at the Imperial War Museum and saw Michael Balcon's philosemitic film *Jew Süss*.[21] He spent the years of World War II in Johannesburg, where he wrote his epics *Efsher* [Perhaps] (1947)[22] and *Dos letste kapitl* [The Last Chapter] (1947).[23] During 'a four-month trip in 1946–7 to Paris,[24] Basel, Antwerp, and New York he met with other Yiddish writers to discuss his writings'.[25] After another stay in Whitechapel, London, in the late 1940s, and with the publication of the two epics,[26] his poetry became better known.[27]

During this time, also Fram dealt in carpets and diamonds, and went farming in the seclusion of Hekpoort, Transvaal. Once 'Chantecler' was sold, he relocated to Rhodesia[28] to be close to his brother, and became a food producer in Salisbury.[29] He returned to Johannesburg in the 1960s where he opened a pickling and canning factory. He remained in Johannesburg until the end of his life.

Overview: I. Yiddish in Eastern Europe and South Africa

Chapter 1: Tundra and veld: The landscape poems

Landscapes in Fram's poems exemplify his 'romantic choice of subject matter',[30] and reveal his 'abiding emotional concern'[31] with nature. This chapter examines his responses to the differences between home and abroad. The early lyrics 'Shney' [Snow] (1925), 'Shkiye' [Sunset] (1924), 'Harbstik' [Autumnal] (1928), 'Shotns' [Shadows] (1924), and 'Shtilkayt' [Silence] (1925), as well as 'Es hot a blaykhe hant getsundn di ikone' [A Pale Hand Touched the Icon] (1926)[32] and 'Ikh hob shoyn dem vinter, dem vinter dem tsveytn' [This Winter, this Second Winter, I have Already Written] (1928–29)[33] are 'traditional landscape poems',[34] which indicate his attachment to the icy steppes. Fram's romantic subject matter and imagery link him to his contemporaries, Dovid Eynhorn, Leyb Naydus, Dovid Hofshteyn, and Moyshe Kulbak.

In contrast, 'In an afrikaner baginen' [In an African Dawn] (1927)[35] and 'Oyf transvaler erd' [On Transvaal Earth] (1930)[36] evoke the heat of the veld and the exotic luxuriance of its flora. However, his style remained within the Yiddish folk song and ballad tradition.

II. Traditionalism, Neo-Romanticism, and Modernism

Chapter 2: Poems of loss and longing: A journey with two maps

Where the 'archaeology of a culture'[37] is embedded in the poems, Fram's close connection to his Litvak roots is apparent in 'Mayn opfor' [My Departure] (1928),[38] 'Mayn mame hot mir tsugeshikt a kishn' [My Mother Sent Me a Cushion] (1928),[39] 'Iz vos?' [So What?] (1929),[40] *Efsher*, 'Nokh vos zol ikh forn?' [Why Should I Leave?] (1930),[41] 'In tsveyen' [Twofold] (1928),[42] and 'Ikh benk' [I Long] (1929).[43]

Chapter 3: Looking inward, looking out: From the outside, looking in

Because language provides a place for collective memory, there can never be 'a rounded picture of the growth and development of the South African Jewish immigrant community without a thorough knowledge of what was written about it in Yiddish'.[44]

The physical 'translation of [Jewish] identity [...] always entails gains as well as losses'.[45] Fram's 'Fun tate-mames yidishe' [From Jewish Parents] (1929)[46] and 'Ikh bin a Yid' [I Am a Jew] (1971)[47] emphasize the author's continuing commitment to his Jewish identity and traditional Jewish life; 'Tsu di shvartse' [To the Black Man] (1929)[48] and 'Matatulu' [Matatulu][49] respond to his South African encounters, incorporating this cross-cultural dynamic.

Where once Fram was a victim of discrimination himself, having been part of the oppressed minority in Europe, in South Africa he found himself in a place of privilege being white. Since the impact of migration and the effects of multicultural conflicts remain sadly contemporary, and conflict continues to flare around issues of race and colour locally as well as globally, the poems provide a useful prism through which to imagine the lives of others.

Chapter 4: A panorama of portraits

Illustrative of Fram's acculturation in his new homeland, this series of multicultural portrait poems reflect his 'double consciousness'.[50] His absorption of a South African viewpoint also enriches Yiddish study by challenging monolingual and homogeneous views of national identity and local literary history, opening a 'doorway to understanding'.[51]

The extended lyrics, 'Baym zeydn' [At Grandfather's] (1925–26),[52] 'In a zunikn tog' [On a Sunny Day] (1930),[53] as well as 'Reb Yoshe un zayn gortn' [Reb Yoshe and his Garden] (1928),[54] all written in South Africa, emphasize the richness of both the Litvak people and his homeland. In doing so, these poems engage the notion of 'empathic unsettlement'.[55]

Steeped in the vernacular and local customs of South Africa, and showing his compassion for the underdog, Fram's 'Fun shop tsu shop' [From Shop to Shop] (1984)[56] and 'Matumba' [Matumba][57] describe the predicament of Blacks in a hostile environment, highlighting Fram's 'liberal inclinations'[58] and his 'strong belief in human equality and brotherhood'.[59] 'Burn' [Farmers and/or Afrikaners] (1971)[60] focuses on the local Afrikaners surrounded by their abundant crops. 'Dimantn'

[Diamonds] (1953),[61] and 'Vert den gringer derfun?' [Where Lies the Comfort?],[62] show how the miners' travails impact on the poet's social conscience.

III. Holocaust Memory and Representation

Chapter 5: Holocaust poetry of memory and postmemory: David Fram, Sarah Aisen, Leah Benson-Rink, and Hayah Fedler

Although little poetry about the Holocaust specifically was written or published in South Africa, Fram's *Dos letste kapitl*, 'An entfer der velt' [An Answer to the World] (1971),[63] 'Lesterung' [Blasphemy] (1969),[64] and 'Undzere kedoyshim' [Our Martyrs] (1969),[65] provide historic and symbolic reflections. This discussion references Theodor Adorno's proscription that there could be no poetry after Auschwitz,[66] Marianne Hirsch's notions of memory and postmemory,[67] and Brett Ashley Kaplan's elaborations on the value of Holocaust representation.[68]

Poems by three other Yiddish poets who were Fram's contemporaries and who also left Eastern Europe before the genocide are included: 'Leb ikh nokh' [I Live Still] in *Geklibene lider un poemes* [Selected Songs and Poems] (1965) by Sarah Aisen (1910–1980),[69] 'Mayn kholem' [My Dream] in *Oysgetunkt in trern* [Dipped in Tears] (1954) by Leah Benson-Rink (1892–1974), and 'Mayn heym' [My Home] in *Bleter-fal* [Falling Leaves] (1953) by Hayah Fedler (d. 1953). Written in the mother tongue of the victims, they are a stark reminder of the ever-present dangers of genocide, and its accompanying destruction of culture and language.

Chapter 6: The place of witness: Representations of the Holocaust in David Fram and Abraham Sutzkever

A selection of David Fram's Holocaust poems is contrasted with those written in the Vilna Ghetto by Abraham Sutzkever (1913–2010). The discussion notes how both poets wrestle with the issues of belief, prayer, blame, action, and revenge, as they strive to 'give form to chaos',[70] and 'broaden [...] the archive of memory'.[71] Fram's *Dos letste kapitl* calls attention to Lithuania's once-beautiful landscape, and the subsequent fate of its Jewish population.[72]

Sutzkever's 'Der tsirk' [The Circus] (June–July 1941),[73] describes what he considers his own inadequate reaction to a life-threatening incident; 'Tsum kind' [To my Child] (18 January 1943)[74] encompasses soul-searching after he fails to save his child; and 'A vogn shikh' [A Wagonload of Shoes][75] describes the murder of his mother. By individualizing and memorializing his family members, they become representative of the murdered millions. 'Glust zikh mir tsu ton a tfile — veyst ikh nit tsu vemen' [I Feel Like Saying a Prayer — But to Whom?] (1942)[76] grapples with the poet's inability to pray thereafter, while 'Di blayene platn fun roms drukeray'

[The Leaden Plates of the Rom Printing Press] (1943)[77] proposes fighting back against the invaders. In his statement at the Nuremberg Trials in 1946,[78] Sutzkever proffers an alternative mode of testimony.

Chapter 7: Yellow crucifixion, yellow star: Home and the Holocaust in selected paintings by Marc Chagall and poems by David Fram

Where Yiddish is 'informed by other bodies of literature, languages, cultures, and perspectives [...] it lends itself to more comprehensive and panoramic studies'.[79] Going beyond a purely Yiddish focus by adopting an integrative and comparative approach, this chapter engages and interacts with other cultural fields and contemporary concerns.[80]

As comparative methodology[81] has led current Yiddish scholarship to the creative 'fragmentation of the field',[82] a dialogue is set up between Fram's poems 'Ikh benk', 'Oyf mayn dakh hot amol gesvistshert a shvalb' [Once a Swallow Twittered on my Roof],[83] as well as *Dos letste kapitl*, and Marc Chagall (1887–1985) paintings *I and the Village*[84] and *The Blue House*,[85] in which Fram and Chagall evoke their memories of home in different ways.

In addition, juxtaposing Chagall's paintings *White Crucifixion* (1938)[86] and *Yellow Crucifixion* (1943)[87] with Fram's poems 'An entfer der velt' and 'Lesterung' within Holocaust narratives offers alternative and unexpected conjunctions:[88] with reference to their perception of mankind's indifference to the tragedy, God's abandonment of the victims, their subsequent reproach of God, and/or their direct rejection of observance and faith.

Conclusion: Revitalization, preservation, and memorialization

Yiddish was the linguistic homeland in which Fram could best recover, reconstruct, and memorialize a world lost in the *khurbn*;[89] a mark of his Jewish and literary identity, it reinforced his connection with his heritage. By placing the poetry of one of very few significant South African Yiddish poets within an Eastern European–South African framework, this study argues for its ongoing relevance. Given 'how little is known about the South African Yiddish culture and its literary production',[90] the present book offers some pioneering work in the field. Through the processes of retrieval, recuperation, extension, and inclusion, this project also serves remembrance.

Notes to the Introduction

1. Hazel Frankel, 'David Fram: Lithuanian Yiddish Poet of the South African Diaspora, and "Illuminating Love"' (doctoral thesis, University of Sheffield Hallam, 2013), p. 1 <http://shura.shu.ac.uk/4914/1/frankel_david_fram.pdf> [accessed 2 November 2020].
2. Yiddish: Lite, which included today's Belarus, Lithuania, and parts of eastern Poland.
3. Anna Lipphardt, 'Yiddish after the Holocaust: A Case Study', *Europa Ethnica*, 3–4, special issue on Jewish Diaspora (2011), 80–87 (p. 80).
4. Gary Weissman, 'Questioning Key Texts: A Pedagogical Approach to Teaching Elie Wiesel's Night', in *Teaching the Representation of the Holocaust*, ed. by Marianne Hirsch and Irene Kacandes (New York: Modern Language Association of America, 2004), pp. 324–37 (p. 326).
5. For a chronological discussion see Dovid Wolpe's, 'Dray periodn in shafn fun Dovid Fram' [Three Stages in the Work of David Fram], *Dorem Afrike* (July–August 1963), 16–20.
6. This was the frontier area between the Austro-Hungarian Empire and territories of the Russian

Empire, the only area where the czars permitted Jews permanent legal settlement. It included the Lithuanian provinces of Vilna, Kaunas, and Grodno, and parts of the Ukraine, Moldavia, Courland, and the Crimea, see John Klier, 'Pale of Settlement', *YIVO Encyclopedia of Jews in Eastern Europe* (14 September 2010) <https://yivoencyclopedia.org/article.aspx/Pale_of_Settlement> [accessed 21 November 2020].

7. The Yiddish terms *shtotns* and *shtetlekh* commonly refer to larger and smaller market towns in pre-World War II.

8. J. M. Sherman, '"David Fram": On the Occasion of his 50th Birthday', *Jewish Affairs*, 13.3 (October 1953), 25–27 (p. 25).

9. Formerly Vilkomer.

10. Zalman Levy, 'Dovid Frams arayntrit in der yidish-dikhtung un zayn shpeterdiker gang' [David Fram's Entry in Yiddish Poetry and his Later Progress], *Dorem Afrike* (July–September 1983), 38–40 (p. 40).

11. Marian De Saxe, 'Sing Me a Song of History: South African Poets and Singers in Exile, 1900–1990' (unpublished doctoral thesis, University of Sydney, 2010), p. 210.

12. J. Simon, 'Jewish Identity in Two Remote Areas of the Cape Province: A Double Case Study', in *Place and Displacement in Jewish History and Memory*, ed. by David Cesarani, Tony Kushner, and Milton Shain (London: Mitchell, 2009), pp. 114–28 (p. 114).

13. M. Langfield, 'Lost Worlds: Reflections on Home and Belonging in Jewish Holocaust Survivor Testimonies', in *Place and Displacement*, ed. by Cesarani, Kushner, and Shain, pp. 29–42 (p. 30).

14. Simon, 'Jewish Identity', p. 114.

15. David Fram, 'Yerushe un hashpoes in yidishn vort-tsushtayer fun Dorem Afrike' [Heritage and Influences on the Yiddish Contribution of South Africa], in *Antologye: Dorem Afrikanish. Fragmentn fun forshavetn tsu der karakteristik un zikhroynes* [South African Anthology: Characteristic Fragments and Memories], ed. by Shmuel Rozhansky (Buenos Aires: Ateneo Literario en el Iwo, 1971), pp. 296–313.

16. The term 'trayer' was used by the Yiddish immigrants to describe someone who tried to earn a living in any way he could. Richard Feldman, 'David Fram at Fifty', *South African Jewish Times*, 23 October 1953, n. p.

17. Feldman, 'David Fram at Fifty'.

18. Stephen Davimes, 'Hillbrow's Yiddish Poet Drinks to Life', *Sunday Express*, 24 June 1984, n. p.

19. The University of Texas at Austin, University of Texas Libraries, Benson Latin American Collection, *David Fram Papers* (1920s–1984), Folder 1, p. 22. Further referred to as *David Fram Papers*.

20. Fram's collection *Lider un poemes* was published in Vilna, which was part of Poland at the time. Publication opportunities for such collections were unavailable in South Africa.

21. Joseph Sherman, 'David Fram Centenary Tribute', *The Mendele Review: Yiddish Literature and Language*, 140 (2004), 1–17 <http://yiddish.haifa.ac.il/tmr/tmr08/tmr08001.htm> [accessed 21 November 2020].

22. *Efsher* (London: Narod Press, 1947), pp. 1–81 <https://www.yiddishbookcenter.org/collections/yiddish-books/spb-nybc211771/fram-david-efsher> [accessed 21 December 2020]; 'Efsher' (extract), *Dorem Afrike* (August 1949), 21; *Antologye*, ed. by Rozhansky, pp. 199–200.

23. *Dos letste kapitl* (London: Narod Press, 1947), pp. 1–65; 'Dos letste kapitl' (excerpt), *Dorem Afrike* (January–March 1984), 12.

24. He may have seen his surviving sisters, Nekhele, Rochel, and Miriam in Paris. Rivke had gone to Israel, and his brother Motel (Max) to Rhodesia (Zimbabwe).

25. Sherman, 'David Fram Centenary Tribute', p. 1.

26. Leonard Prager, *Yiddish Culture in Britain: A Guide* (Frankfurt a. M.: Lang, 1990), p. 254; Avram Stencl, 'Dovid From' in *Loshn un lebn* [Language and Life] (November 1947), p. 48; (August 1949), pp. 49-50.

27. Barry Davis, 'David Fram, Yiddish Poet', *The Jewish Quarterly*, 35.4 (Winter 1988), 45–49. For this article, Davis interviewed S. J. Goldsmith (Goldschmidt), a journalist who had been a close friend of Fram.

28. Now Zimbabwe.

29. Now Harare.

30. Y. R. Brinman, 'Dovid Fram — Lider, un poemes' [David Fram — Songs and Poems], *Der veg* [The Way] (30 July 1938), 5–6 (p. 5).

31. Joseph Sherman, '"What Balm for the Heart...?" The Yiddish Poetry of David Fram (1903–1988)', *Midstream*, 52 (July–August 2006), 7–11 (p. 7).

32. 'Es hot a blaykhe hant getsundn di ikone', *Lider un poemes* [Songs and Poems], (Vilna, Poland: Krejnesa, 1931), p. 28. From now on, this collection will be referred to as *Lider*.

33. *Lider*, p. 11.

34. Brinman, p. 6.

35. *Lider*, p. 74; *Antologye*, ed. by Rozhansky, pp. 77–78.

36. *Lider*, pp. 263–74; (extract), *Antologye*, ed. by Rozhansky, pp. 29–37.

37. Benjamin Harshav and Barbara Harshav, *American Yiddish Poetry: A Bilingual Anthology* (Berkeley: University of California Press, 1986), p. 9.

38. *Lider*, p. 14.

39. *Lider*, p. 18.

40. *Lider*, pp. 16–17.

41. *Lider*, p. 24.

42. *Lider*, p. 7.

43. *Lider*, p. 89.

44. Joseph Sherman, 'Between Ideology and Indifference: The Destruction of Yiddish in South Africa', in *Memories, Realities and Dreams*, ed. by Milton Shain and Richard Mendelsohn (Johannesburg: Ball, 2000), pp. 28–49 (p. 48).

45. Ranen Omer-Sherman, *Diaspora and Zionism in Jewish American Literature* (Hanover: Brandeis University Press, 2002), p. 268.

46. *Lider*, p. 77; *Antologye*, ed. by Rozhansky, p. 293.

47. 'Ikh bin a Yid', *A shvalb oyfn dakh: Poemes un lider* [A Swallow on the Roof: Poems and Songs] (Johannesburg: Kayor, 1983), p. 69; *Dorem Afrike* (July–August 1971), 23. From now on, this collection will be referred to as *A shvalb oyfn dakh*.

48. *Lider*, pp. 19–21.

49. *A shvalb oyfn dakh*, pp. 89–92; *Dorem Afrike* (December 1953), 17–19.

50. Carol Zemel, 'Diasporic Values in Contemporary Art: Kitaj, Katchor, Frenkel', in *The Art of Being Jewish in Modern Times* ed. by Barbara Kirschenblatt-Gimblett and Jonathan Karp (Philadelphia: University of Pennsylvania Press, 2007), pp. 176–92 (p. 177).

51. David Cesarani, Tony Kushner, and Milton Shain, 'Introduction', in *Place and Displacement in Jewish History and Memory*, ed. by David Cesarani, Tony Kushner, and Milton Shain (London: Mitchell, 2009), pp. 1–14. (p. 4).

52. *Lider*, pp. 147–209.

53. *Lider*, pp. 123–32.

54. *Lider*, pp. 91–100; *Der oyfkum: khodesh-zshurnal far literatur un kultur-inyonim* [The Rebirth: Monthly Journal for Literature and Art] (1929), n. p.

55. Dominick LaCapra, *Writing History, Writing Trauma* (Baltimore: John Hopkins University Press, 2001), p. xi.

56. *Dorem Afrike* (July–September 1984), 29.

57. *A shvalb oyfn dakh*, pp. 85–88; *Dorem Afrike* (November 1953), 16–17.

58. Davis, 'David Fram, Yiddish Poet', p. 46.

59. Ibid.

60. (extract), *Dorem Afrike* (May–June 1971), 13; *Lider*, pp. 210–49.

61. *A shvalb oyfn dakh*, pp. 60–64; (extract), *Dorem Afrike* (September 1953), 17–18. Fram shortened the original of 200 to 135 lines. Numerous versions are located in the *David Fram Papers*, Folder 13, pp. 407–11.

62. *Lider*, pp. 5–6; translation by Amelia Levy in L. Goodman, 'David Fram: A Study in Growth', *Jewish Affairs*, 8.1 (January 1949), 28–31 (p. 28).

63. *Dorem Afrike* (July–August 1971), 50.

64. *A shvalb oyfn dakh*, pp. 127–29; (extract), *Dorem Afrike* (May–June 1965), 3.

65. *Dorem Afrike* (March–April 1969), 17.

66. Theodor Adorno, *Negative Dialectics*, trans. by E. O. Ashton (London: Routledge and Keegan Paul, 1973); Lawrence Langer, *Admitting the Holocaust* (Oxford: Oxford University Press, 1996).

67. Marianne Hirsch, *The Generation of Postmemory: Writing and Visual Culture after the Holocaust* (New York: Columbia University Press, 2012), p. 107.

68. Brett Ashley Kaplan, *Landscapes of Holocaust Postmemory* (New York: Routledge, 2011), p. 5.

69. Sarah Aisen, *Geklibene lider, un poemes* [Selected Lyrics and Poems] (Johannesburg: Farlag fun der Dorem-Afrikaner Kultur-federatsye, 1965) <https://www.yiddishbookcenter.org/collections/yiddish-books/spb-nybc213583/aisen-sarah-geklibene-lider-un-poemes> [accessed 21 November 2020]; Leah Benson-Rink, *Amol un haynt* [Once and Today] (stories) and *Oysgetunkt in trern* [Dipped in Tears] (poems) (Cape Town: Kinder, 1963) <https://www.yiddishbookcenter.org/collections/yiddish-books/spb-nybc201844/benson-rink-leah-amol-un-haynt-dertseylungen-oysgetunkt-in-trern-lider-oyf-dem-keyver-fun-a-zun> [accessed 21 November 2020]; Hayah Fedler, *Bleter-fal* [Falling Leaves] (Cape Town: Fedler & Co., 1954) <https://www.yiddishbookcenter.org/collections/yiddish-books/spb-nybc204669/fedler-hayah-bleter-fal> [accessed 21 November 2020].

70. Heather Valencia, *Avrom Sutzkever: Still my Word Sings* (Düsseldorf: Düsseldorf University Press, 2017), p. 265.

71. Marianne Hirsch and Leo Spitzer, 'Holocaust Studies/Memory Studies', in *Memory: Histories, Theories, Debates* ed. by Susannah Radstone and Bill Schwarz (New York: Fordham University Press, 2010), pp. 390–405 (p. 404).

72. Several English translations by Joseph Leftwich are located in the *David Fram Papers*, Folder 17, pp. 1, 2, 3, 15. Brief selections of these appear in *The Golden Peacock*, ed. by Joseph Leftwich (New York: Yoseloff, 1961), pp. 631–32.

73. Abraham Sutzkever, *Di ershte nakht in geto* [The First Night in the Ghetto] (Tel Aviv: Farlag Di goldene keyt, 1979), 1–34 <https://www.yiddishbookcenter.org/collections/yiddish-books/spb-nybc203216/sutzkever-abraham-di-ershte-nakht-in-geto> [accessed 21 November 2020]; Jan Schwarz, *Survivors and Exiles: Yiddish Culture after the Holocaust* (Detroit: Wayne State University Press, 2015), p. 30.

74. Valencia, pp. 95–99.

75. Abraham Sutzkever, *Lider fun yam ha-moves fun Vilner Geto, vald un vander 1936–1967* [Poems from the Dead Sea of the Vilna Ghetto, Forest, and Wandering] (Tel Aviv: Farlag Bergen-Belzen, 1968), p. 41. <https://www.yiddishbookcenter.org/collections/yiddish-books/spb-nybc213587/sutzkever-abraham-lider-fun-yam-ha-moves-fun-vilner-geto-vald-un-vander> [accessed 21 November 2020]

76. Valencia, p. 95.

77. Abraham Sutzkever, *Poetishe verk* [Poetic Works], 2 vols (Tel Aviv: Yoyvl-Komitet, 1963), p. 35 <https://www.yiddishbookcenter.org/collections/yiddish-books/spb-nybc208866/sutzkever-abraham-poetishe-verk-vol-1> [accessed 9 November 2020].

78. Nuremberg Trial Proceedings, VIII, 69th day, Wednesday, 27 February 1946, pp. 300–07, in *The Avalon Project: Documents in Law, History and Diplomacy* <http://avalon.law.yale.edu/imt/02-27-46.asp> [accessed 27 July 2020]. Sutzkever gave testimony at the Nuremberg Trials as a member of the Russian delegation, and when cross-examined by Chief Councillor Lev Smirnov, he was referred to as a Soviet citizen. Obliged to give his account in Russian, not in Yiddish as he had requested, he stood throughout his delivery, as if he were saying *kaddish*, the Jewish mourners' prayer, to honour the dead, his mother, newborn baby, and his Lithuanian Jewish community.

79. Hana Wirth-Nesher, 'Tradition, the Individual Talent, and Yiddish', *In geveb* (December 2015), 1–8 (p. 8) <https://ingeveb.org/articles/tradition-the-individual-talent-and-yiddish> [accessed 1 December 2020].

80. See also Jan Schwarz's *Survivors and Exiles*; *Memories, Realities and Dreams*, ed. by Shain and Mendelsohn; *Place and Displacement in Jewish History and Memory*, ed. by Cesarani, Kushner, and Shain; and David Roskies, *The Jewish Search for a Usable Past* (Indiana: Indiana University Press, 1999).

81. Mikhail Krutikov, 'Yiddish Studies from a New Perspective', trans. by Saul Noam Zaritt,

In geveb (December 2015), 1–3 <https://ingeveb.org/articles/yiddish-studies-from-a-new-perspective > [accessed 18 November 2020].

82. Krutikov, 'Yiddish Studies from a New Perspective'.
83. *A shvalb oyfn dakh*, p. 67; *Dorem Afrike* (October 1953), 6. The first line of the poem is used as the title.
84. *I and the Village*, 1911, oil on canvas, *Marc Chagall: Paintings, Biography, and Quotes* <https://www.marcchagall.net/i-and-the-village.jsp> [accessed 7 December 2020].
85. *The Blue House*, 1917, oil on canvas, *Marc Chagall: Paintings, Biography, and Quotes* <https://www.marcchagall.net/the-blue-house.jsp> [accessed 7 December 2020].
86. *White Crucifixion*, 1938, oil on canvas, <http://www.artic.edu/artworks/59426/white-crucifixion> [accessed 7 December 2020].
87. *Yellow Crucifixion*, 1943, oil on canvas, *pneuma* <http://www.pneuma.org.uk/art/marc-chagall-the-yellow-crucifixion/> [accessed 7 December 2020].
88. Other studies include Gennady Estraikh, *Yiddish in the Cold War* (London: Legenda, 2008); *Yiddish in the Contemporary World: Papers of the First Mendel Friedman International Conference on Yiddish*, ed. by Gennady Estraikh and Mikhail Krutikov (Oxford: European Humanities Research Centre, University of Oxford, 1999); *The Shtetl Image and Reality: Papers of the Second Mendel Friedman International Conference on Yiddish*, ed. by Gennady Estraikh and Mikhail Krutikov (Oxford: European Humanities Research Centre, University of Oxford, 2000); Tamar Lewinsky, *Displaced Poets: Jiddische Schriftsteller im Nachkriegdeutschland, 1945–1951* (Göttingen: Vandenhoeck & Ruprecht, 2008); Joseph Sherman, *Yiddish after the Holocaust* (Oxford: Boulevard Books, 2004).
89. Yiddish for Holocaust, catastrophe, devastation.
90. Astrid Starck-Adler, 'Multilingualism and Multiculturalism in South African Yiddish', *Studia Rosenthaliana*, 36: *Speaking Jewish — Jewish Speak: Multilingualism in Western Ashkenazic Culture* (2002–03), 157–69 (p. 158).

PART I

Yiddish Language and Literature in Eastern Europe and South Africa

Yiddish emerged in the Rhine area around 1000 CE.[1] An inclusive language, it was spoken by people 'of different ideologies, education and commitment, as much the language of gangsters and shopkeepers as that of poets and intellectuals'.[2] Hebrew is the *lashon hakodesh* [Holy Tongue],[3] the language of the Torah, the Bible, the prayer book, and religious education.[4] Thus, as a nation's culture is 'embedded in words',[5] the Jewish culture is vested in both Yiddish and Hebrew, 'the two eyes of Jewish life; take one away and we are blind.'[6] Taking advantage of the interconnection between them, the 'great early Yiddish writers, Aizik Meyer Dik, Mendele Mokher Sforim, Yitskhok Leib Peretz, and Sholem Aleikhem, [as well as] the secular Yiddishists, the Lubavitcher *Rebbe* and a faction of the Zionist movement'[7] switched from Hebrew to Yiddish to reach a larger potential audience; the Bund[8] also promoted Yiddish in Eastern Europe, using it as the most effective way of communicating with the masses.

However, Yiddish literature was not part of 'any authorized curriculum in Lithuania',[9] so Yiddish poets were in the unusual situation of not having studied their language formally. Almost no poet learned Yiddish literature in school (most Yiddish schools were founded after World War I — after the major writers and poets appeared, using their authority for validation). Naturally, they imbibed a vivid Yiddish language spoken in their homes and environment, but only in rare cases did they acquire knowledge of Yiddish literature from their parents.[10] Instead, students who 'went to *yeshives*[11] would have studied in Hebrew, while those who attended the *gimnazye*[12] would have learned Russian, German and English and been influenced by those literatures'.[13]

Fram's first published poem, 'Zima' [Winter], was written in Russian and appeared in a Russian journal, but thereafter he always wrote in Yiddish.[14] His debut occurred in 1923 when his poems appeared in the journals *Kvaytn* [Blossoms] (Panevezys), *Yidishe shtime* [Yiddish Voice] (Zionist; ed. by Ruven Rubinshteyn) and *Folksblat* [People's Paper] (Kaunas[15]) (Folkist,[16] then pro-communist; ed. by Mendl Sudarski). Later poems written between 1924 and 1931 were published in a wide range of literary journals and papers that display no particular party line: *Der Velt* [The World] (Kaunas), *Literarishe bleter* [Literary Pages], and *Haynt* [Today] (Warsaw); Kaunas' *Nayes* [News], *Kovner tog* [Kaunas Day], *Mir aleyn* [Myself Alone],

Shlyakhn [Paths],[17] *Dem shtral* [The Beam] (Liepaja,[18] Latvia), and *Der vokh* [The Week] (Riga, Latvia); and *Zuntog* [Sunday] as well as *Oyfkum* [Rebirth] (New York).

Literarishe bleter was the leading Yiddish literary journal in the interwar period and published work of various aesthetic sorts but saw itself as a bastion of literary quality. Its editor, Nakhman Mayzl, was a careful reader and a fan of Modernism broadly speaking.[19] Fram was in frequent contact with Mayzl at the time,[20] and acknowledged his support.[21]

On the other hand, the Kaunas' *Nayes* was a 'Yiddishist-Folkist paper that identified with non-socialist, diaspora-nationalist Yiddishism and was opposed to the pro-Communist, pro-Soviet ideology of the Lithuanian *Kultur-lige*'.[22] The same was also true of the *Folksblat*, a continuation of *Nayes*. Kaunas' *Yidishe shtime* and Warsaw's *Haynt* were Zionist papers, while *Folksblat, Yidishe shtime*, and *Mir aleyn* were 'local and provincial publications, unlikely to be too avant-garde'.[23] Thus, had Fram elected to publish only in 'literary journals that were congruent with his political stance, he would probably not have been able to publish much'.[24]

In South Africa, Yiddish was not accepted as a fully-fledged European language at first, and prospective immigrants were turned away if it was the only language they knew.[25] However, after the publication of a pamphlet *Yiddish — Is It a European Language?* (1903), by journalist David Goldblatt, and the representation made to the South African Immigration Department by Morris Alexander, President of the Cape Jewish Board of Deputies, immigration of Eastern European Jewry was permitted. Native speakers were then allowed to continue to 'speak, read and write in their mother tongue'.[26] Thereafter, despite the initial lack of linotype machines, trained compositors, and loose type, Yiddish newspapers such as *Der Afrikaner* [The African] appeared as a regular weekly from November 1911.

Fram's poems appeared in *Dorem Afrike* [South Africa], *Yidishe tribune* [Yiddish Tribune], *Foroys* [Onward], and *Der yidisher ekspres* [The Yiddish Express], all based in Johannesburg, and the *Fri-Stayter baginen* [Free State Dawn] (Bloemfontein). These publications represent different literary and political outlooks, and so Fram's readership would have been equally varied. His first collection *Lider un poemes* [Songs and Poems] (1931),[27] 'the first such collection based in part on South African experiences',[28] was published in Vilnius, which suggests that Fram had kept up some ties with the literary establishment there. Fram expressed his search for a 'loss of identity'[29] as did so many immigrant poets and writers. Their poems illuminate the consequences of dispersal and fragmentation, asserting 'recollections and recordings of deep, consequential collective feelings [...] the memory of the past'.[30]

Fram also scripted a play for children *Lili un Bliling: A vald maysele in eyn akt* [Lili and Bliling: A Forest Tale in One Act] (1929).[31] Two plays for adults, *A tsegayner fantasie* [A Gypsy Fantasy] (1932),[32] and *Fun Fordsburg biz Parktown* [From Fordsburg to Parktown] (1933),[33] a satire of upward Jewish mobility in four acts, were performed by the Yiddish Drama Circle at the Jewish Guild, Johannesburg. Hirsch Ichilchik and Francis Boehr composed the music.[34] Sponsored by Rachmiel Feldman and Leon Behrman, the productions enabled Fram to support himself and travel to London (1934–39).[35]

Fram's epic poems, *Efsher* and *Dos letste kapitl*, were published separately by the Narod Press[36] in 1947. They were internationally acclaimed.[37] He also published critiques of the artists Gerard Sekoto[38] and Herman Wald,[39] as well as reviews of Yiddish writers Nathan Berger[40] and J. M. Sherman.[41] A prolific letter writer, Fram kept copies of much of his correspondence with B. J. Byalostotsky,[42] Jacob Glatshtayn,[43] Chaim Grade,[44] Hyman Ehrlich,[45] his friend Fayvl Zygielbaum,[46] as well as his Vilkomer teacher and mentor Yudl Mark.[47] Some of these letters were reproduced and published on the 100th anniversary of his birth.[48] Fram's second collection *A shvalb oyfn dakh: Poemes un lider* [A Swallow on the Roof: Poems and Songs] was issued through the South African Kultur-lige [Culture League] imprint *Kayor* in 1983, but much of his oeuvre remains uncollected and unpublished.[49]

In his poetry, bridging the old world and the new, perpetuating the cultural and linguistic heritage of both the historical and personal past, 'a fertile tension exists between these two linguistic layers, [which] meet in a symbiosis between the former homeland, *di alter heym*, and the new reality, *a heym oyf dos nay*.'[50] Fram also provides one example of '[the] Yiddish-speaking Jew, [whose] fear of physical and spiritual effacement [commits him to a] desperate effort to sustain the values and languages of his history'.[51] Further, as the Jewish immigrants' experiences and views of life in Africa differed considerably from those of other immigrant groups, these became fertile territory for Yiddish writers.

Hence, Jewish secular literature made its mark on the reconstituted communities, and became part of the literary culture of South Africa. N. D. Hoffmann's *Sefer Hazikhroynes* [Book of Memoirs] (1916) was the first book-length Yiddish volume of prose to be published there. Contrasting his home country with South Africa, it set the tone of much future, local writing, portraying the hardships and moral dilemmas in a nation predicated on institutionalized racial discrimination. Rachmiel Feldman published a volume of short stories, *Shvarts un vays* [Black and White] (1935). This included 'Gold un dimantn' [Gold and Diamonds], in which the narrative decries local racist policies against the Black population. His brother Leibl Feldman wrote *Yidn in Dorem Afrike* [Jews in South Africa] (1937) and *Yidn in Yohanesburg* [Jews of Johannesburg] (1961). Morris Hoffmann, a scholar who became a shopkeeper in De Aar in the Karoo, published an anthology, *Voglungs-klangn* [Songs of a Wanderer] (Warsaw, 1935), and his short stories appeared posthumously in *Unter afrikaner zun* [Under the African Sun] (1951). He expressed a 'realistic, unsentimental view of immigrant Jewish life',[52] which compared the difficulties of the Jew with those of the Afrikaner in rural areas during the Depression. It also evoked the destructive effects of Nazi ideology and antisemitism. Hyman Polsky's short story collection *In Afrike* [In Africa] (1939) consists of monologues of struggling immigrants who felt perpetually alien, filled with the sense of loss of and longing for their birthplace from which they had escaped with their lives. Their Yiddish texts contrast their longing for the values, climate, and rootedness of the old home with their new world experiences.[53] Thus, immigrant writers transposed their history and background onto new soil, through the lens of their 'particular history, circumstances, and tradition'.[54]

By the 1930s, Yiddish was the third-largest European language in the Transvaal after English and Afrikaans, and there were thirty to forty *landsmanshaftn*[55] in Johannesburg alone. South Africa, therefore, came to be regarded as a 'colony of Lithuania',[56] and numerous publications confirm their commitment to the continuation of the Yiddish language and Lithuanian culture far from its original locus. In 1933, *Der Afrikaner* amalgamated with another paper as *Afrikaner yidishe tsaytung. Dorem Afrike*[57] was published intermittently in the 1920s, and regularly after 1948.

Thus, 'a multicultural Yiddish literature emerged encompassing both the known and the foreign',[58] preserving their own Jewish, Eastern European concepts of difference,[59] and perpetuating Yiddish close to its original form. Transposing Yiddish onto new soil, the revolutionary and ideological ideas that were very much part of Eastern European Yiddish poetry were superseded by descriptions of personal experiences.[60] Though linked to the literary and political developments in their home country, the writers also found a particular and individualistic South African tone.[61]

Once 'the victims of racial discrimination in Eastern Europe, they found themselves in a role reversal in racist South Africa'.[62] Ostracized by other whites but socially and politically privileged over Blacks, their themes were often interracial contacts or tensions. Disturbed by political injustice and racial inequality, Fayvl Zygielbaum, Rachmiel Feldman, Shmuel Leibowitz, Mendl Tabatchnik, Chaim Zaks, and Nehemia Levinsky[63] aimed to alert readers to the pervasive injustice and inequalities, offering an enlarged view of the white immigrant experience.[64] However, they also encountered numerous obstacles in choosing to maintain Yiddish.

Although the immigrants felt themselves to be insiders because of their new status, they became vulnerable because of the import of Nazi antisemitism, which fuelled the Grey Shirts, a group of local Afrikaner Nazi supporters, and was endorsed as early as 1930 when Jewish immigration was restricted. This 'external pressure'[65] from the gentile community, and the 'animosity of an alien world towards the image of the Jew, was projected upon their language'.[66]

The 'rejection of Yiddish amongst Jewish immigrants particularly in the English-speaking world was also a function of acculturation';[67] by using English — the language of empowerment — as their lingua Franca, they hoped to achieve upward mobility. Highly cultured, well-settled Germans Jews kept themselves apart from Yiddish-speaking Lithuanians; second-generation immigrants separated themselves from the first generation because of their desire to fit in and belong. Many of the new arrivals jettisoned the language of *di alte heym* as they became part of the dominant culture.

Of those who continued to 'speak, read and write in their mother tongue',[68] most knew little of its literature. Because there was a lack of interest in cultural expression, there was only a very small intelligentsia and readership. Few Yiddish writers saw their work in print. Even when it did appear, it was given little space, unlike in the international journals such as *Literarishe bleter* and *Forverts* [The Forward] that actively promoted all Yiddish literature, including that of South Africa.

Further, the conflicts among the various Yiddishist groups themselves, the Geserd [Gezelshaft far erderbetendike yidn; Jewish Agricultural Workers Association], the Yidisher arbeter klub [Jewish Workers Club] — which was strongly Bundist, and culturally active before World War II — , and the Po'alei Zion [Workers of Zion],[69] which was pro-Zionist, were self-destructive as they tried to establish (themselves and their) rival publications in a small community.[70]

In addition, non-religious Zionists and the orthodox religious communities had no interest in Yiddish. 'Both Yiddishist and Zionist educators instituted Jewish instruction policies for South African children that consciously cut them off from half their heritage.'[71] Thus, Yiddish became a casualty of the conflicting ideologies of Hebrew and Zionism, which prevented its education among the younger generation. As marginalization occurred within the minority group itself,[72] by the 1940s 'most contemporary Jewish organisations were hostile to Yiddish and Yiddish culture'.[73] Unlike in Argentina, for example, there was no group for whom Yiddish would have been the language of choice and education, and who would therefore have sought it out. These 'conflicting ideologies and communal indifference threw Yiddish writing in South Africa into almost-total neglect'.[74]

Consequently, there is little archived material of its literature. Regarded as being on both the 'general and Jewish periphery',[75] it became almost entirely erased from the collective memory of South African Jewry, as did 'a vigorous body of work about the Jewish experience'.[76] One significant exception is Shmuel Rozhansky's unique *Antologye: Dorem Afrikanish* [South African Anthology] (1971),[77] which made a representative range and variety of local Yiddish literary writing available for the first time to the international reading public. Most of the works included had previously been published in Johannesburg or Cape Town, Vilna or Warsaw; providing a benchmark of Yiddish writing as world literature, the anthology's thematic and geographical framework forms part of the multilingual literary impulse of South Africa.[78]

Yet, 'very little research has been undertaken to evaluate the extensive body of South African Yiddish literature listed in three progressively enlarged bibliographies'.[79] While several journal articles about individual writers by scholar Joseph Sherman[80] and others[81] have appeared, there are no intensive, in-depth or book-length studies of South African Yiddish literary writing as yet.[82] With so few readers of Yiddish, the need to translate the rich holdings of material into English is urgent in order that it be further interpreted.[83] This literature, a 'noteworthy addition to the body of general South African culture'[84] has been neglected for too long, to the 'great injury of our fullest self-awareness as an ethnic minority'.[85]

As his themes remain extensively contemporary, Fram's responses also have far-reaching resonance for a wider audience. Recuperating his work sheds light on the understanding of the South African Jewish community as a particular and significant representative of its original *kehile* [congregation]. Where various *landsmanshaftn*[86] did perpetuate their *mameloshn*, and were 'strongly committed to it as a living language and as a culture',[87] these groups of Yiddish-speaking *landslayt* [compatriots] provided a safe space in which Fram could express himself freely.

Re-evaluation through the study of homegrown Yiddish is essential, especially at this decisive time in our history, as a duty to our forebears and ourselves.[88]

Post-1994, with the recognition of the history of every ethnic minority,[89] what was once 'taboo has now been recovered [and] valorized'.[90] Although Yiddish is not an integral part of South African literature, and is not one of the eleven official languages, its presence continues today in contemporary South Africa, actively promoted by the Yiddish Academy in Johannesburg and Cape Town. This study traces the trajectory of Yiddish and the transformation of a community through the lens of Fram's poetry.

Notes

1. See Max Weinreich's *History of the Yiddish Language*, 2 vols (Yale: Yale University Press, 2008).
2. Maeera Shreiber, 'The End of Exile: Jewish Identity and its Diasporic Poetics', *PMLA*, 113.2 (1998), 273–87 (p. 280).
3. Yiddish: 'Loyshn koydesh'.
4. *American Yiddish Poetry*, Harshav and Harshav, p. 10.
5. Omer-Sherman, p. 111.
6. Sherman, 'Between Ideology and Indifference, p. 43.
7. Cedric Ginsberg, Email to the author, 29 July 2011.
8. Founded in Vilnius (Vilna), Poland, by groups of young Jewish intelligentsia and the new working class, the Bund was influenced by Marxism and the emergent Russian revolutionary movement. Daniel Blatman, 'Bund', *YIVO Encyclopedia of Jews in Eastern Europe* (30 July 2010) <http://www.yivoencyclopedia.org/article.aspx/Bund> [accessed 13 November 2020].
9. Gennady Estraikh, Email to the author, 11 November 2010.
10. *American Yiddish Poetry*, Harshav and Harshav, p. 21.
11. Boys' schools for Torah learning.
12. Secular high schools.
13. Estraikh, Email.
14. Sherman, 'What Balm for the Heart...?, p. 7.
15. Yiddish: Kovno.
16. Focusing on Jewish cultural and political autonomy.
17. This publication only appeared in 1932. It also included poems by Sarah Aisen, who was also born in Panevezys and settled in South Africa.
18. Yiddish: Libau.
19. Kenneth Moss, Email to the author, 3 January 2011.
20. *David Fram Papers*, Folder 2, pp. 64–69, 72, 73, 77.
21. 'Bagrisung fun Dovid Fram' [Greetings from David Fram], *Dorem Afrike* (July–December 1987), 36.
22. Moss, Email, 3 January 2011.
23. Ibid.
24. Ginsberg, Email, 29 July 2011.
25. Because it was not written from left to right, it was not considered a legitimate European language.
26. Joseph Sherman, 'Introduction', in *From a Land Far Off: A Selection of South African Yiddish Stories*, ed. by Joseph Sherman (Cape Town: Jewish Publications, 1987), pp. 1–15 (p. 6).
27. Chief Rabbi J. L. Landau headed the committee, and five editions were published between 1931 and 1999.
28. Solomon Liptzin, *The Maturing of Yiddish Literature* (New York: John David, 1970), p. 251.
29. Stuart Hall, 'Cultural Identity and Diaspora', in *Identity, Community, Culture, Difference*, ed. by Jonathan Rutherford, (London: Lawrence and Wishart, 1990), pp. 222–37 (p. 224).
30. David Bleich, 'Learning, Learning, Learning: Jewish Poetry in America', *Jewish American Poetry*,

ed. by J. N. Barron and E. M. Selinger (Hanover: Brandeis University Press, 2000), pp. 117–94 (p. 181).

31. Published by Grinike beymelekh, Vilnius, 1936, <https://www.yiddishbookcenter.org/collections/yiddish-books/spb-nybc212454/fram-david-lili-un-bliling> [accessed 6 December 2020].

32. Joseph Sherman, 'David Fram Centenary Tribute' (' "Singing with the Silence": The Poetry of David Fram'), *The Mendele Review*, 08.001 (14 January 2004), 1–17 (p. 5) < http://yiddish.haifa.ac.il/tmr/tmr08/tmr08001.htm> [accessed 5 December 2020]; no publication details of the script are available.

33. Sherman, 'David Fram Centenary Tribute', p. 5; no publication details of the script are available.

34. Ibid.

35. Ibid.

36. Narod Press also printed and published Avram Stencl's *Loshn un lebn* [Language and Life].

37. Sherman, 'Between Ideology and Indifference', p. 28.

38. 'Sekoto' [Sekoto], *Dorem Afrike* (January 1949), 19–21.

39. 'Herman Wald' [Herman Wald], *Dorem Afrike* (March 1949), 22–23.

40. 'Natan Berger. A poeme vegn Yohanesburg' [Nathan Berger: A Poem of Johannesburg], *Dorem Afrike* (March–April 1969), 25.

41. 'Ayndrukn vegn a bukh: *Land fun gold un zunshayn*, Y. M. Sherman' [Impressions of a Book: *Land of Gold and Sunshine*. J. M. Sherman], *Dorem Afrike* (March 1957), 19–20.

42. *David Fram Papers*, Folder 3, p. 118.

43. *David Fram Papers*, Folder 3, p. 126, 128.

44. *David Fram Papers*, Folder 3, pp. 115, 147–48.

45. *David Fram Papers*, Folder 6, p. 342, and Folder 7, pp. 350–51.

46. *David Fram Papers*, Folders 3, 4, and 5. After the Nazis crushed the Warsaw Uprising, Fayvl's brother Shmul Zygielbaum committed suicide to protest against the inaction of the Western Allies.

47. These include letters written from Johannesburg to Mark in Vilkomer and in Canada. *David Fram Papers*, Folders 1, 2, 3, 4, and 5.

48. 'Brivn fun Dovid Fram Tsu Yidishe Shrayber, 1947–1949' [Letters from David Fram to Yiddish Writers, 1947–1949], *Di tsukunft* [The Future], 107.4 (December 2002), 5–12.

49. Eli Rosenblatt, 'Enlightening the Skin: Travel, Racial Language, and Rabbinic Intertextuality in Modern Yiddish Literature' (unpublished doctoral thesis, University of California, Berkeley, 2017), p. 77.

50. Ibid.

51. Isaac Bashevis Singer cited in Omer-Sherman, p. xii.

52. Joseph Sherman, 'South African Literature in Yiddish and Hebrew', *The Mendele Review*, 03.012 (31 July 1999), 1–11 (p. 5) <http://yiddish.haifa.ac.il/tmr/tmr03/tmr03012.txt> [accessed 5 December 2020].

53. Sherman, 'Between Ideology and Indifference', p. 49.

54. Wirth-Nesher, 'Tradition, the Individual Talent, and Yiddish', p. 8.

55. Community groups, compatriot groups, and self-help associations formed by people from the same town or surrounding areas *in der heym* [at home] on their arrival in the new country.

56. Nahum Sokolow in Veronica Belling, 'A Slice of Eastern Europe in Johannesburg: Yiddish Theatre in Doornfontein, 1929–1949', in *Place and Displacement in Jewish History and Memory*, ed. by Cesarani, Kushner, and Shain, pp. 169–80 (p. 170).

57. South African Journal of the Yidisher Literarisher Farayn [Yiddish Literary Association].

58. Starck-Adler, 'Multilingualism and Multiculturalism in South African Yiddish', *Studia Rosenthaliana*, 36, 'Speaking Jewish-Jewish Speak: Multilingualism in Western Ashkenazic Culture' (2002–2003), 157–69 (p. 158).

59. Joseph Sherman, 'Serving the Natives: Whiteness as the Price of Hospitality in South African Yiddish Literature', *Journal of Southern African Studies*, 26.3 (September 2000), 505–21.

60. Dovid Wolpe, 'Dray periodn in shafn fun Dovid Fram', p. 21.

61. Astrid Starck-Adler, 'South African Yiddish Literature and the Problem of Apartheid', *Jewish*

Affairs, 65.1 (Pesach 2010), 6–12 (p. 6); first published, trans. by Karen-Anne Durbach, in *Jewish Affairs*, 49.2 (Winter 1994), 39–45.

62. Sherman, 'Between Ideology and Indifference', p. 49

63. See *Antologye*, ed. by Rozhansky.

64. Sherman, 'Between Ideology and Indifference', p. 31.

65. Ginsberg, Email, 29 July 2011.

66. Omer-Sherman, p. 5.

67. Ginsberg, Email, 29 July 2011.

68. Sherman, 'Introduction', p. 6.

69. This Marxist-Zionist Jewish workers' movement developed in Poland, Europe and the Russian Empire at the turn of the 20th century.

70. Sherman, 'Between Ideology and Indifference', p. 41.

71. Ibid., p. 35.

72. German Jews in South Africa followed the patterns of British Jews, and the Lithuanians found their customs 'fancy and pretentious' (Ginsberg, Email, 29 July 2011).

73. Cesarani, Kushner, and Shain, 'Introduction', p. 10.

74. Sherman, 'Between Ideology and Indifference', p. 28.

75. Belling, 'A Slice of Eastern Europe in Johannesburg, p. 170.

76. Sherman, 'Between Ideology and Indifference', p. 28.

77. *Antologye*, ed. by Rozhansky.

78. Starck-Adler, 'South African Yiddish Literature and the Problem of Apartheid', p. 6.

79. Sherman, 'Between Ideology and Indifference', pp. 28–29.

80. See Bibliography for Sherman's numerous articles on Fram and Yiddish in South Africa.

81. Some examples include Veronica Belling, 'Yiddish Writing in South Africa: Leibl Feldman's Radical History of Johannesburg Jewry', *Journal for the Study of Religion*, 19.2, special issue: *Echoes of Religion in Minority Literatures* (2006), 63–75; Dov Ber Kotlerman, 'South African Writings of Morris Hoffman: Between Yiddish and Hebrew', *Journal of Semitics*, 23.2i (2014), 569–82; Astrid Starck-Adler, 'These Two Autobiographical Books are my Identity Document: David Wolpe', in *Selves in Question: Interviews in Southern African Auto/Biography*, ed. by Judith Luther Coullie and others (Honolulu: University of Hawai'i Press, 2006), pp. 357–65; Astrid Starck-Adler, 'Old Home vs Land of Opportunity: Interrogating "Home" and "Exile" in Rakhmiel Feldman's *Trayers* [Tryers]', *Jewish Affairs: Literature*, 52.3 (Spring 1997), 79–84.

82. Starck-Adler, 'South African Yiddish Literature and the Problem of Apartheid', p. 6.

83. Sherman, 'Between Ideology and Indifference', p. 48.

84. Ibid., p. 49.

85. Ibid. The diasporic tradition continued into the next generation of Jewish writers. These include Nadine Gordimer, Dan Jacobson, and Sarah Gertrude Millin, and poets Ruth Miller, Bernard Levinson, Karen Press, Helen Segal, Lewis Sowden, and Olga Kirsch, but they wrote in English, not Yiddish.

86. Immigrants from the same area in Europe.

87. Lipphardt, p. 80.

88. Sherman, 'Between Ideology and Indifference', p. 49.

89. Ibid., p. 48.

90. Cesarani, Kushner, and Shain, 'Introduction', p. 4.

CHAPTER 1

Tundra and Veld:
The Landscape Poems

Fram was strongly influenced by the upsurge of neo-romanticism in Eastern Europe as a young poet in Lithuania and during his first years in South Africa. Highlighting the bond between themselves and their environment, Yiddish poets developed a particular sensitivity to nature as a mark of their local identity.[1] Filled 'with lyric and the love of cultural heritage',[2] they invented fresh metaphors for rural and urban landscapes. Situating Fram's poetry within a traditional literary context, this chapter suggests its value and relevance to a modern Yiddish canon.

As 'a Yiddish reader in Lithuania, he would have been able to find some Romanticism (German, Russian, English) [...] original, translated and in Yiddish'.[3] Further, 'given Fram's cultural and literary education, he would have been well-read in these areas.'[4] As Fram himself noted: 'Un kh'ver nokh oft baroysht fun likhtik-hele zaln; | Un trog zikh nokh arum mit pushkinen un sheln' [And still I often long for the brightly lit halls, | As I carry Pushkin and Shelley with me] (9–10).[5] These and other Russian and English Romantic poets would have appeared in some of the same journals as his own work.[6]

Hence, reminiscent of Percy Bysshe Shelley in 'Ode to the West Wind', William Wordsworth's 'Evening on the Beach', and John Keats' 'Ode to a Nightingale', Fram too wrote as 'a man speaking to men, [through] the sincerity of his personal vision and experience',[7] so that, for example, 'Reb Dovids lider-gortn [...] shmekt in toyznt temen, vi di yagdes vos yoshe tsekert ayn mit branfn' [David's song-garden is steeped in the tastes of a thousand themes, like Yoshe's berries in brandy].[8] Displaying his 'abiding emotional concern'[9] with the landscape and heightened pleasure in the natural world, his 'outpourings of a man coming to terms with universal suffering'[10] may be considered to be in the Romantic tradition.

Like David Eynhorn, Dovid Hofshteyn, and Moyshe Kulbak, who were popular in the 1920s, and Leyb Naydus, who explored the metaphorical potential of nature to celebrate the changing seasons,[11] Fram reveals his Romantic inclinations, looking at the landscape through a nostalgic lens. Praised by Chaim Nachman Bialik,[12] Fram's traditional mode epitomizes 'freedom of individual self-expression, sincerity and spontaneity',[13] and characteristically exhibits the 'emotional intensity often taken to extremes of [...] nostalgia for childhood or the past, melancholy'[14] as well as 'joy'.[15]

Y. R. Brinman described Fram's poetry as 'fun litvishn landshaft un litvishn umet un troyer' [of Lithuanian community and Lithuanian loneliness and sadness].[16] As a result, Brinman aligned Fram's traditional, lyrical, Romantic, and classical form, and choice of subject matter with the Lithuanian Eynhorn.[17] Shmuel Niger, in his review of *Lider un poemes*,[18] confirmed that Fram's descriptions of town and countryside show Eynhorn's influence. David Wolpe[19] and Peretz Markish[20] also placed Fram's early output within that existential, anti-modernist arena.

The title and first line of 'Es hot a bleykhe hant getsundn di ikone' [A Pale Hand Touched the Icon] (1926),[21] as well as the subsequent line 'blaser bleykher sheyn' [pale, pale beauty], link him directly to Eynhorn.[22] Fram's poems also suggest the influence of the traditional landscape poems of Kulbak, whose first collection, *Shirim* [Poems] (1920), 'characteristically romantic in tone',[23] confirmed his place in that tradition.[24]

Hence, a section of Fram's *Lider un poemes* entitled 'Idilyes' [Idylls] includes his early series of 'traditional landscape poems',[25] such as 'Shney' [Snow] (1925),[26] 'Shkiye' [Sunset] (1924),[27] 'Shotns' [Shadows] (1924),[28] and 'Shtilkayt' [Silence] (1925).[29] Illustrating the poet's ongoing affinity for and close bond with nature, they exemplify a 'romantic choice of subject matter';[30] influenced by the local landscape, he wrote 'simple, melodious quatrains and traditional stanza forms about [...] timid longings', of 'romantic nature far removed from urban abodes'.[31] Zygielbaum also noted that Fram's lyrics, both simple and dense, were marked by his sincerity and graceful language, as well as his musicality.[32]

Fram's choice of language and descriptions of landscapes and towns, summers and winters also show the Romantic influence of Bialik's 'Mayn gortn' [My Garden].[33] His regular rhyme schemes, a/b/a/b, the stanzas of four lines, and 'regular musical rhythm of traditional Yiddish verse'[34] are suggestive of the folk ballad.[35] Zaramb also drew attention to Fram's classical and regular iambic or dactylic rhythm, rich similes and metaphors, and his variety of themes.[36] In addition, the musicality of his lyrical nature and pantheistic poems contain undertones of the liturgy.

'Shney' combines Fram's 'romanticism and realism'.[37] As his imagination takes flight, his 'extensive use of metaphoric language'[38] implies rather than describes the details of the frozen, whitened landscape. Thus, the image of the '[...] bloye vaytn | In bazilbert-vayse hiles' [...] blue distance | In silvery-white slipcovers] (1–2) suggests how the blanket of snow lights up the terrain, and also becomes a protective covering.

Fixed in place, the poet sees, or imagines he sees, other specific images, the 'white doves of innocence' [umshuld-vayse toybn] (3), and 'Blonken elnt vayse shifn' [White ships [that] stray forlornly] (12). While the birds fly purposefully, and the ships seem to have lost their way, they may presage his own future — the doves fly away from the cold, the ships are uncertain of their destination. For Fram, the natural world reflects 'emotional intensity [...] taken to extremes of rapture'.[39] At one with the universe, he senses the 'vaytn vayse tfiles' [distant white prayers] (4) emanating from the quietude of the vista itself: 'Zingt di shtilkayt haleluye, | Shotns vayse zingn halel' [The silence sings halleluja, | White shadows sing Hallel.] (5–6).

Inspired by the beauty around him, the poet feels uplifted, 'Kh'bin in nakht aleyn mispalel' [I am in the night alone praying] (8), in songs of praise: 'halleluja' (5) and 'Hallel' (6). As he is in tune with nature, so nature is attuned to him: 'Bloye tropns zilber trifn. | In der nakht, vi mayne tfiles.' [Blue drops of silver drip. | In the night, like my prayers] (10–11). The sound repetitions of 'vayse' [white] (3, 4, 12), 'vaysn' [white] (16), and 'vaytn' [distant] (1, 12) echo eerily, heightening the atmosphere of pervasive emptiness. Within the silence, the poet is overcome with emotion:

> Vil ikh zingn mit der shtilkayt
> In mayn soydes-fuln hekhl,
> Efsher vet di nakht mir shenkn
> Far mayn lid a vaysn shmeykhl... (13–16)

> [I want to sing with the stillness
> In my secret-filled palace.
> Perhaps the night will grant me
> For my song, a white smile...][40]

Absorbed in and by the silence, longing for happiness, Fram's lyrical use of rhyme and regular rhythm is similar to that of Kulbak's 'Raysn' [Byelorussia],[41]

> Un s'hot zikh gehert: oyfn himl es rirn zikh shtern,
> A roykhele to lyres zey ayn, vi a varme nigun;
> A tsiterike nets hot farnumen dem himl dem lern
> Un shvimen dort fishlekh, finklen un vign zikh, vign... (4–8)

> [And what could be heard were the stars in the sky now in motion,
> And if smoke in a wisp had enclosed them in music;
> And the sky that was empty now gleamed in a network
> Of light in which fish were gleaming and bobbing...]

The influence of these Lithuanian landscapes and poetics continued once Fram had left, in 'Ikh hob shoyn dem vinter, dem vinter dem tsveytn' [This Winter, this Second Winter, I Have Already Written] (1928):[42]

> Ikh hob shoyn dem vinter, dem vinter dem tsveytn
> Mit atsves un elnt in hartsn fartseykhnt —
> On shtile, farshleferte, shneyike breytn,
> — mit tife un bloye un zunike heykhn...   (1–4)

> [I have already this winter, this second winter,
> With sadness and loneliness written down in my heart —
> About the quiet, dreamy, snowy expanses
> — with deep and blue and sunny heights...]

Thus, although aware of the gifts of clear air and bright sunshine bestowed by his new country, Fram nevertheless finds them burdensome:

> Ikh hob shoyn dem vinter dem tsveytn farshribn
> Mit flisikn zilber fun klore fartogn,
> Un gold hob ikh reynem in oytsres geklibn,
> Az shver iz mir, shver itst dos gold shoyn tsu trogn. (5–8)

[This winter, the second, I have already written
With the flowing silver of clear dawns,
And the pure gold treasures I have gathered
So that now it is heavy for me to bear.]

Fram's poem emphasizes the weight of his sadness through the repetition of 'dem vinter, dem vinter' in line 1 and 'dem vinter' in line 5, as well as by starting both lines, 1 and 5, with 'Ikh hob shoyn [...]'.

Filled with yearning for what has passed, for the precious times that he once knew, Fram's poem echoes Hofshteyn's 'In vinter-farnakhtn...' [In Winter's Dusk...]:[43]

In vinter-farnakhtn oyf rusishe felder!
Vu ken men zayn elnter, vu ken men zayn elnter?
A ferdll an altinkes, a skripnder shlitn,
A shliyakh a farshnayter — un ikh bin in mitn. (1–4)

[Russian fields on winter evenings!
Where can one be more lonely, where can one be more lonely?
An old horse wheezing and a sleigh creaking,
A snow-covered road — and I half-way along.]

As can be seen here, Hofshteyn also responds to the icy, empty expanse, using regular rhythm and rhyme. To emphasize the state of mind the view evokes in him, the poem is framed by the anaphora of lines 1–2 and 19–20, 'In vinter-farnakhtn oyf rusishe felder! | Vu ken men zayn elnter, vu ken men zayn elnter?':

Fun untn, in eyntsikn vinkl in blasn,
Nokh leshn zikh troyerik tliende pasn.
Fun fornt farshpreyt zikh a midber a vayser,
Un vayt dort tsezayt iz a tsendlikhl hayzer —
Dort dremelt a kutor, farzunken in shneyen... (5–9)

[Below, in the only pale corner of twilight,
Sad streaks of light dying and smoldering.
Before us stretching a desert of whiteness,
And sown in its vastness a scatter of houses.
Sunk in its snow-depths a farmhouse dreaming...]

Similarly, in 'Ikh hob shoyn dem vinter, dem vinter dem tsveytn', looking with longing into the distance, Fram hopes to catch a glimmer of the places and spaces he once knew. Even the sunshine around him brings him no solace. Instead, it is the memories of what he left behind that prevail:

Iz hefkerdik vel ikh di oytsres tsevarfn
Un vern in leydike vaytn gelaytert,
Kdey mit a veytog a topltn-sharfn
Nokh gilderne vintern benkn shoyn vayter. (9–12)

[So freely I will scatter the treasures
And become purified in the empty distances,
So that with a pain doubly sharp
Long once more for gilded winters.]

Thus, for Fram, the memories of his homeland remain full of 'sweet melancholy',[44] highlighted by references to 'benkn' [to long for] (12) and 'elnt' [loneliness] (13): 'Un dan vel ikh vider mayn elnt farbindn | Mit tife un klore un zunike breytn' [And then I will once again link my loneliness | With deep and clear and sunny expanses] (13–14). The final description 'dimyen tsetsindn | Di fayerlekh kalte fun steps bashneyte' [fantasy kindles | The cold little flames of the snowy steppes] (15–16) confirms Eynhorn's influence on Fram[45] in its melancholic meditation.

'Unlike so many moderns, [Fram] does not shroud his work in symbolism and is easily understandable, not because he is shallow but because he is direct and this directness mirrors his every mood.'[46] Hence, 'S'iz beser...' [It's better...][47] straightforwardly evokes his feelings of heavy resignation and sadness,

> Es bleybn dokh tomid farshvign di verter
> Vi nakete tsveygn in harbst in dem shotn.
> Shoyn beser avekgehen mit eygenem umet,
> Ungornisht-not monen, un keyn zakh nisht betn... (5–8)

> [They stay always speechless and silent, the words —
> Like naked, small branches in autumn in the shadows.
> Far better to leave with one's own lonely heart,
> And lay claim to nothing, and stilly depart...] [48]

Thus, Fram's poems about Lite carry his sense of loss on leaving behind the muddy farmlands, the ice and snow. Even when his geographic location alters, he remains 'a dikhter fun litvishn landshaft un natur, fun litvishn umet un troyer, der kleyne lite iz im nokh alts nenter fun der zunike afrike' [a poet of Lithuanian community and nature, of Lithuanian sadness and sorrow, small Lithuania is still close to him in the sunny Africa].[49] Inwardly and outwardly divided between his two homelands, he interlaces nostalgia with Africa's 'pulsating vibrancy'[50] and 'stony soil and scorching skies'.[51]

Maintaining his traditional style, 'In an afrikaner baginen' [In an African Dawn] (1927)[52] and 'Oyf transvaler erd' [On Transvaal Earth] (1930)[53] both signal the stark contrasts he became aware of between the old and the new. The prevalence of metaphoric language in 'In an afrikaner baginen' visually evokes the bright landscape and people in a joyful ballad of praise:

> S'iz zunik un s'iz loyter der frimorgn.
> Ekh, vos hele, shtralndike zun!
> Un azoy bafrayt fun dayges un fun zorgn —
> Kvatshket ergets-vu a leygedike hun. (1–4)

> [It's a sunny and clear early morning.
> Oh, what a radiant, full-rayed sun!
> And so, free of worries and cares —
> A laying hen clucks nearby.]

As can be seen here, Fram continues to use the regular quatrains and rhyme schemes of 'Shney' and 'Ikh hob shoyn dem vinter, dem vinter dem tsveytn'. However, the South African veld evokes optimism in the summer joy rather than melancholy or introspection.

Zygielbaum further highlighted how Fram's clear form and content supported his 'bildlekhkayt',[54] his pictorialization; responding with all his senses, he gives his emotions free rein. The repeated references to the sun emphasize brightness and light: 'zunik' (19), 'zunen' (27), in 'A shmir, a shot, a glants fun toyzent zunen' [A smudge, a shadow, a radiance of a thousand suns] (28), and 'Tsegisht zikh klarer shayn oyf felder gantse emers' [Full buckets glow and pour out on the fields] (28). The inclusion of sensory images intensifies the poet's experience: the tactility of 'Fun tsarte flaterlekh, fun babelekh, fun flign' [From soft butterflies, from beetles, from flies] (11), the aromatic, 'stoygn shmekedikn hey' [fragrant haystacks] (13), and the piquant, 'Oy, s'iz gut! S'iz zunik-hel. S'shmekt in vayse epel' [Oh, it's good! It's sunnily bright. It tastes of white apples] (19). Under the 'bloyen himl-shayn' [blue heaven-splendour] (45), the glowing sunshine, the clucking hen, the white doves in flight, the wind blowing, and the songs spreading widely amidst the smell of the sweet hay, the green grass, and the yawning fields, fill the earth with nature's abundance; as a result, 's'kvelt a hele freyd in tsapldike brustn' [bright joy and delight well up in quivering breasts] (31).

Incorporating 'the new, wild and beautiful African world around him',[55] the poem's rich references to fruit and vegetables further affirm the land's fertility, in 's'gist zikh on der vayn in grine troybn' [wine pours from green grapes] (7), as the 'royte kavones in feld dergeyen' [red watermelons ripen across the field] (8); this richness is also emphasized in the phrases 'korn baykhikn' [potbellied rye] (15) and 'kupes hey, oyf shmekedike felder' [heaps of hay, over sweet-smelling fields] (48), so that 'shiker iz di luft fun tsaytikdike peyres' [the air is drunk with ripening fruits] (9) in 'di zunike, di loytere fartogn' [the sunny, the clear dawns] (50).

Humanity is nurtured by the bounty of 'mame-erd' [mother earth] (41) a sensual and close bond engendering 'a freyd an erdishe' [an earthy joy] (25). As a result of 'zikh durkhmishn mit erd, mit leym, mit royte gruntn' [wallowing in the earth, with clay, with red soil] (43), the poet becomes drunk with delight, 'A tsetumelter, farshikert begilufn' [Confused, intoxicated with joy] (42).

The poem's lyricism enhances links between the visual the aural senses, as in the synaesthetic 'klingt zikh op in gold mit kishefdikn zemer' [ring out in gold, in enchanted melody] (30), so that the warmth of the sun's beams become part of nature's song. Sound matches sense in the springing rhythm of 'shtiklekh shtraln brekln zikh un zipn zikh un zipn' [bits of sun-rays shred and screen and sift ...] (18), as well as in 'A klung, a shprung, a tants oyf feste gruntn' [A ring, a jump, a dance on firm ground] (23). Endorsing his high spirits, the poet's body 'aroysshrayen mit ale dayne glider' [shouts out with all [his] limbs] (39), so much so that one 'zikh aleyn mit eygenem geshray fartoybn!' [deafens oneself with one's own cry!] (46).

Around him, the cacophony of other creatures fills the air: 'Kvoktshet ergets-vu a leygedike hun' [A laying hen clucks nearby] (4) and 'A fokh, a patsheray, un fligl shotndike veyen' [A flap, a beating, and shadowy wings fanning the air] (6). Intensifying the tumult, the alliteration in the lines 'Trikenen zikh shtil oyf grine lonke-lipn' [Drying lightly on green lips of the fields] (17) and 's'shpreyt zikh oyset vayt a nign' [And melody spreads far and wide] (12), heightens the contrast with the 'shvaygenish fun velder' [silence of the forests] (49). The imagery and rhythm go hand in hand with the earth's richness in 'A lid, a brumeray, a shire farn boyre' [A poem, a hum, a song of praise for the Creator] (10).

As Fram transfers his 'intense (even religious) identification with nature from the soil of Lithuania [in 'Shney'] to that of Africa'[56] in 'In an afrikaner baginen', the poems as well as the landscape become ' — A shire, a geveyn, a loybgezang dem boyre' [— A song of praise, a lament, a hymn for the Creator] (32). By offering 'regn un toy batrifte tfiles' [rain- and dew-spattered prayers] (16), it seems to the poet as if the world itself 'Frum mispalel zayn un davenen un benshn | In di oysgehelte vayles!' [Pray[s] piously and worship[s] and blesses | In the sunny brightened moments!] (37–38).

Similarly, the epic 'Oyf transvaler erd' also incorporates his responses to the strange and foreign landscape through the accretion of sensory imagery. Similar to Kulbak's 'Raysn' in its simplicity of expression, the disparity between the icy steppes and the sunny veld is evident in the descriptions: 'es varemt zikh teg azoy shtile in Transvaal' [the days are quietly warm in the Transvaal] (89), as the spanned oxen trudge across the field, 'trot bay trot' [step by step] (3). Dragging their ploughs over the hard, dry earth, there is no easy fodder for them as the sun,

> Mit a fuler hant tseshit es un tseshpreyt,
> Farshmirt dem gantsn step mit flisedike shtraln,
> Un aza bloye vayt iz durkhzikhtik un breyt. (97–99)

> [Shoots and spreads with full hands,
> Smearing the whole steppe with flowing rays
> And blue distance is transparent and broad.]

The poet also alerts us to the clear, fragrant air, the variety of trees and plants, and the bright, abundant fruit:

> S'zetikt zikh in zun zayn leymik royter bodn.
> Di luft iz trunk heys. Es shmekt in ekaliptus.
> In zislekhn gerukh fun frayikn baginen.
> A yam mit klorn likht — glaykh emetser tsezipt es
> Mit gilderdiker farb fun rayfe apelsinen. (92–96)

> [The red ground saturates itself with sun.
> The air drinks heat. It tastes of eucalyptus.
> In the sweet smell of the fresh dawn
> A sea of clear light — as if someone has sieved it
> With the golden colour of ripe apples.]

All the tastes and smells of the bright veld, with its abundance of fruit and flowers affirm the land's fertility,

> Un s'dakht[57] zikh, az se fleytst di zun fun toyznt kvaln,
> Fun toyznt mit amol tserint zi un tsekvelt,
> Vi s'rint-arop a taykh fun berg iz oyf harte gruntn.
> Un ot azoy mit shayn bagosn a velt... (100–03)

> [And it seems that the sun surges from a thousand springs,
> From a thousand that at once dissolves and revels,

As if a river gushes over from the mountain onto hard ground,
And pours onto the world like this...]

The sweet aroma, the warmth of sun, and the ripe fruit are new to him, and he drinks in the sounds and tastes of his exotic surroundings,

Un do tsvishn feld un shtot, in bleter fun bananes,
In shtiler, oysgeshpreyter ru un fleytsendiker tekheyles —
Tseleygn zikh vu a shtetl nokh mit shtiblekh un parkanes. (161–63)

[And here between veld and town, in leaves of bananas,
In quiet, spread-out peace and surging skyblue —
A town lies, set out with little houses and palisades.]

The richness of nature also manifests in the vibrant flowers, which the poet had never encountered before,

Baflokhtn un bahangen zikh mit 'haybiskes' un 'daylis',
Un s'blit zikh shoyn der 'krismas-blum', di tunkele 'fintsetas',
Mit groyse, royte kvaytenkep, vi bekhers fule ofn,
Az s'vert dos oyg tsetumelte farkisheft, ven es zet es. (164–67)

[Stained and hung with hibiscus and dahlias,
And the Christmas flowers flash, the dipped poinsettias,
With huge, red bloom heads, fully open like chalices,
So the eye is confusedly bewitched when it sees this.]

The inclusion of the profusion of site-specific fruits and plants using Yiddish versions of their English names,[58] 'watermelon' (36), 'cactus' (64), 'peaches' (76), 'dahlias' and 'hibiscus' (164), 'eucalyptus' (93), 'Christmas flowers' and 'poinsettias' (165), and the Afrikaans 'burijan' [dry grass] (9), seems to suggest the poet's adaptation. However, as he later designates the veld using the European term 'steppes' (84); in this nuanced way, the poet captures his continuing conflict.

Similar to Kulbak in his early poetry, Fram 'placed nature's pantheistic aspects at the centre of his concerns'.[59] Euphoric and filled with wonder, 'idyllic [in] referring to an innocent past and an idealized future',[60] Fram's poems reflect his surroundings, mood, and state of being. Viewing the natural phenomena as 'a means of divine revelation',[61] Fram's 'Reb Yoshe un zayn gortn' [Reb Yoshe and his Garden][62] acknowledges the Creator for his bounty, 'A dank Got' [Thank God] (29). In 'Ikh benk' [I Long],[63] the poet feels a similar reverence, 'Dan gloyb ikh ... dan gloyb ikh mit hertser, vos gloybn emunedik-frum, | Vos zaynen mit heylike tfiles vi harbstike kelers gepakt' [Then I believe ... then I believe with an observant heart, | Packed like autumn cellars with holy prayers] (17–18). Here, the poet also makes specific reference to the Jewish Sabbath, 'Vos shlepn aheym zikh oyf shabes durkh osyendik-vintike nekht, | Un garn nokh ruiker shalve fun shverer farmatete vokh' [Who drag themselves home for Sabbath through windy autumn nights | Craving tranquillity from the exhausting weekday gloom] (7–8). Rather than using the generalized term *boyre* for the Creator, the poem refers to Him as the Almighty, as the poet's experience of the magnificence of His world evolves into belief in Him, 'Tsevakst dan in vareme hertser a groyse, derbarmiker Got, | Un shpreyt aza mekhtikn gloybn oyf groyer, farshvigener velt' [And growing then in warm hearts, a great, merciful God | Spreads a mighty belief on a grey silent world] (15–16). In this way, man's spirit is restored by the abundance of nature, which then becomes 'a responsive mirror of the soul'.[64]

While Fram retained Yiddish as his linguistic homeland, a language of memory, recovering the world of the steppes, it also became one of discovery, featuring South African elements.[65] Adapting to accommodate his new, vibrant reality in brief lyrics and expansive epics,[66] the poet thus incorporates 'two worlds [...] the world he brought with him and the new, wild and beautiful African world around him'.[67]

Connected to Eynhorn, Hofshteyn, and Kulbak, Fram's style remained rooted in East European Yiddish poetics, which profoundly shaped his literary identity. However, in this novel, exotic environment, his images of the ever-bright sun, stark sky, the lush fruit and flora, scattered mine dumps, and the ochre veld developed into a personal iconography. 'Like an African pineapple with juicy Lithuanian Yiddish speech, his Yiddish language as rich as a pomegranate',[68] his poetry enriched Yiddish 'with an entire continent'.[69] By embracing the paradoxes of old and new, Lithuania and South Africa, possibly idealizing both, Fram contributed to a deeper understanding of a particular immigrant experience.

Notes to Chapter 1

1. Mikhail Krutikov, 'Raysn: The Belarusian Frontier of Yiddish Modernism'. A Festschrift in honor of David Roskies, *In geveb: A Journal of Yiddish Studies* (June 2020), 1–11. <https://ingeveb. prg/articles/raysn-the-belarusian-frontier-of-yiddish-modernism> [accessed 15 July 2020].
2. Liptzin, p. 150.
3. Kenneth Moss, Email to the author, 4 January 2011.
4. Gennady Estraikh, Email to the author, 11 November 2010.
5. 'Fareltert' [Obsolete], *Lider*, pp. 85–86.
6. Eliezer Niborski, 'Dovid Fram', *Mendele: Yiddish Literature and Language*, 20.004 (11 September 2010), 1–4 (p. 3) <https://mailman.yale.edu/pipermail/mendele/2010-September/000420.html> [accessed 6 December 2020].
7. *The Concise Oxford Companion to English Literature*, ed. by Margaret Drabble, J. Stringer, and D. Hahn (Oxford: Oxford University Press, 2007) <https://www.oxfordreference.com/ view/10.1093/acref/9780199214921.001.0001/acref-9780199214921> [accessed 8 December 2020]
8. Wolpe, 'Dray periodn in shafn fun Dovid Fram', p. 19.
9. Sherman, 'What Balm for the Heart...?', p. 7.
10. Susan Tumarkin Goodman, *Chagall: Love, War and Exile* (New York: Yale University Press, 2013), p. 28.
11. Ibid.
12. In C. Gershater, 'The Triumph of David Fram', *Zionist Record* (30 October 1953), 5.
13. *The Oxford Companion to English Literature*, ed. by Dinah Birch (Oxford: Oxford University Press, 2009) <https://www.oxfordreference.com/view/10.1093/acref/9780192806871.001.0001/ acref-9780192806871> [accessed 9 December 2020], n. p.
14. Ibid.
15. *The Concise Oxford Companion to English Literature*, ed. by Drabble, Stringer, and Hahn, n. p.
16. Brinman, p. 5.
17. Ibid.
18. Shmuel Niger, 'Naye Dikhter: Dovid Fram un Moshe Dovid Giser' [New Poets: David Fram and Moshe Dovid Giser], *Di tsukunft* [The Future] (October 1934), 615–18 (p. 615).
19. David Wolpe, 'Yidishe literatur in Dorem Afrike' [Yiddish Literature in South Africa], *Dorem Afrike* (December 1956), 21–23.

20. Gennady Estraikh, 'Hofshteyn, Dovid', *YIVO Encyclopedia of Jews in Eastern Europe* (12 August 2010) <https://yivoencyclopedia.org/article.aspx/Hofshteyn_Dovid> [accessed 3 July 2020].

21. Fram, *Lider*, p. 28. Where the poem was published elsewhere before it appeared in his collections, the original publication date is given in brackets.

22. Melech Ravitch, 'A por khaverishe araynfir-verter' [A Few Friendly Introductory Words], in *Lider*, n p.; this review also appeared later as 'Dovid Fram un zayn lider' [David Fram and his Songs], *Literarishe bleter*, 4.403 (4 November 1932), 59.

23. Avraham Novershtern, 'Kulbak, Moyshe', *YIVO Encyclopedia of Jews in Eastern Europe* (19 August 2010) <https://yivoencyclopedia.org/article.aspx/Kulbak_Moyshe> [accessed 3 July 2020].

24. Novershtern, 'Kulbak, Moyshe'.

25. Brinman, p. 6.

26. *Lider*, p. 43.

27. *Lider*, p. 29.

28. *Lider*, p. 48.

29. *Lider*, p. 267.

30. Brinman, p. 5.

31. Liptzin, p. 132.

32. Fayvl Zygielbaum, 'Tsu Dovid Frams avekforn' [On David Fram's Departure], *Dorem Afrike* (August 1949), 22–23 (p. 23).

33. in Niger, p. 615.

34. Brinman in Niger, p. 615.

35. Brinman, p. 5.

36. S. Zaramb, 'The Poetry of David Fram', *The Zionist Record* (9 November 1934), p. 20; translation of his article in *Literarishe bleter*, 27 (1934).

37. Brinman, p. 6.

38. Frieda Aaron, *Bearing the Unbearable: Yiddish and Polish Poetry in the Ghettos and Concentration Camps* (New York: State University of New York Press, 1990), p. 57.

39. Birch, n. p.

40. 'In the stillness and seclusion | I will sing my secret song. | Maybe that the night will lend it | Flying wings for which I long', from 'Snow' (Shney), trans. by Jacob Sonntag, *Jewish Literary Gazette*, 6 April 1951, p. 2; 'I will sing alone with silence | In my deep and hidden temple, | In the hope the night might grant me | For my song a smile of favour', in Sherman, 'What Balm for the Heart...?', p. 11.

41. Moyshe Kulbak, 'Raysn' [Byelorussia], trans. by Leonard Wolf in *The Penguin Book of Modern Yiddish Verse*, ed. by Irving Howe, Ruth Wisse, and Khone Schmeruk (New York: Penguin, 1987), pp. 388–93.

42. *Lider*, p. 11.

43. Dovid Hofshteyn, 'In vinter-farnakhtn...' [In Winter's Dusk...], trans. by Robert Friend in *The Penguin Book of Modern Yiddish Verse*, ed. by Irving Howe, Ruth R. Wisse, and Khone Shmeruk, (New York: Penguin, 1987), pp. 260–61.

44. Liptzin, p. 134.

45. Brinman, p. 5.

46. Fayvl Zygielbaum, 'David Fram's 60th Birthday in Salisbury', *Zionist Record and S.A. Jewish Chronicle* (23 August 1963), n. p.

47. *Lider*, pp. 9–10.

48. Zalman Levy, 'A Premier Yiddish Poet in South Africa', *Jewish Affairs*, 36.9 (September 1983), 32–35.

49. Brinman, p. 6.

50. Sherman, 'David Fram Centenary Tribute', p. 14.

51. Ibid., p. 7.

52. *Lider*, p. 74; *Antologye*, ed. by Rozhansky, pp. 77–78.

53. *Lider*, pp. 263–74; line references to *Antologye*, ed. by Rozhansky, pp. 29–38.

54. Fayvl Zygielbaum, 'Dovid Fram's yuvil: Tsu zayn 50stn geburtog' [David Fram's Jubilee: To his Fiftieth Birthday], *Dorem Afrike* (October 1953), 3–5 (p. 3).

55. Ravitch, 'Dovid Fram un zayn lider', p. 59.

56. Davis, p. 46.
57. This word appears as *s'dukht* (90) in the version in *Lider*, p. 268.
58. Yiddish versions of the English names were placed in scare quotes by the poet.
59. Novershtern, 'Kulbak, Moyshe'.
60. Liptzin, p. 134.
61. Novershtern, 'Kulbak, Moyshe'.
62. *Lider*, pp. 91–100; *Der oyfkum: khodesh-zshurnal far literatur un kultur-inyonim* [The Rebirth: Monthly Journal for Literature and Art] (1929), n. p.
63. *Lider*, p. 89.
64. Birch, n. p.
65. Wolpe, 'Yidishe literatur in Dorem Afrike', p. 21.
66. Levy, 'Dovid Frams arayntrit in der Yiddish-dikhtung un zayn shpeterdiker gang', p. 38.
67. Ravitch, 'Dovid Fram un zayn lider', p. 59.
68. Ibid.
69. In Joseph Sherman, 'Singing with the Silence: The Poetry of David Fram', *Jewish Affairs*, 44.5 (September–October 1988), 39–44 (p. 41).

PART II

Traditionalism,
Neo-Romanticism, and Modernism

As discussed in Chapter 1, Fram's Yiddish oeuvre was in dialogue with the aesthetics of his time. His lyric, epics, and folk ballads may be located in the continuum of traditional poetry and the early romanticism and pantheism of Dovid Hofshteyn and Moyshe Kulbak. However, his choice of language and his commitment to Yiddishism were not indicators of his political or religious affiliations, but registered a diasporic, secular identity. Invested in commitment to the richness of the culture as 'an end in itself',[1] this dedication to Jewish traditional practices and communal values and culture can be described as a form of 'culturalism'.[2]

In South Africa, Fram was a founder member of the Unicorn, a society of artists, including (Isaac) Lippy Lipschitz,[3] Irma Stern,[4] and Alexis Preller, as well as writers Uys Krige and Vincent Swart.[5] They met every afternoon in the East African Pavilion, a well-known upmarket café, but as they had all been born in South Africa, and had Afrikaans- or English-speaking backgrounds, their outlooks were different from Fram's. They intended to start their own journal and form a club based on the model of the Moscow Stoila Pegasa [The Stall of Pegasus];[6] however, the venture was short-lived for lack of funds.[7]

In addition, Fram was part of a group of Yiddish immigrant writers that included J. M. Sherman and Rachmiel Feldman.[8] They played cards, smoked, and talked radical politics, decrying the treatment of the Blacks, and expressing themselves freely in Yiddish at Feldman's home. There were also get-togethers of poets, musicians, and artists held at David's home in Johannesburg and later in Hekpoort.[9] Through their common language and similar experiences, the close bond among these Eastern European Jews in Johannesburg extended to New York, Buenos Aires, London and Paris, where Yiddish poetry was widely published.[10]

Neither observant nor Zionist in inclination, Fram did not subscribe to the socialist theories of the Bund, which in any case had very little influence in South Africa. There is also no evidence that he was a member of the Jewish Workers' Club,[11] though he was in correspondence with the South African Cultural Federation and a member of Pen South Africa.

He was much influenced by the Yiddish renaissance in Lithuania after World War I, 'Yiddishe mitlshuln hobn zikh arumgetrogn mit Avraham Raizens un Moyshe Kulbaks lider-bikher un hobn zey geleynt oyf di griner benk in di parkn, in shotns fun ayngevortstelte kashtanbeymer.' [Students read Avraham Raizen's and Moyshe Kulbak's poems on the grass of green parks in the shadows of cherry trees].[12] In addition, 'men hot geshlungen Yosef Opatashus "Poylishe velder" un H. Leivicks "Golem" un "Sibirer lider".' [The students were 'enthralled by Joseph Opatoshu's 'Polish Forests', H. Leivick's 'Golem' and 'Siberian Poems', and works by Manye Leib, Melech Ravitch and Uri-Tsvi Grinberg].[13]

Traditional Yiddish poetry reverberates with themes and images of Hebrew-Aramaic religious, mythological, and cultural traditions, figures of Jewish history and Slavic folklore and literature.[14] Its style also draws on the 'homely verse of nineteenth-century troubadours travelling from shtetl to shtetl, and the Romantic poetry of Heine and Pushkin, Byron and Lermontov'.[15] Using regular rhyme and metre and equal-length stanzas, it was amenable to the absorption of expressions from other spoken languages, thriving on colloquial expressions, proverbs, anecdotes, quotations, and stories from other sources.

Thereafter, modernists searched for new forms of mimesis and expression. The literary groups *Di yunge* [The Young], *Yung Vilne* [Young Vilna], *Di khalyastre* [The Gang], and *In zikh* [The Introspectivists] blossomed, and the standards of their journals — *Literarishe bleter, Albatros, Folkshrift far literatur, kuns un kultur* [Weekly Journal for Literature, Art and Culture] and *Di khalyastre* — were comparable to those of publications in America and Europe. Nevertheless, although Fram's oeuvre did not grow out of their radical break with the Lithuanian Jewish literary or historical past, he may have been influenced by their approach and attitudes.

Di yunge emerged in the United States in 1907–08. It rejected the rigidity of 'traditionalism, political propaganda, didacticism and chauvinism' combining 'Yiddish literary conventions, traditional values of Yiddishkayt and Romanticism with Expressionism and Symbolism'.[16] Instead of having a political agenda, these poets promoted art for art's sake in an impressionist poetry of mood and atmosphere,[17] emphasizing 'individuality, subjectivity and unhampered — sometimes audacious — methods of expression'.[18] Similarly, Fram's personal poems 'Mayn opfor' [My journey] and 'Mayn mame hot mir tsugeshikt a kishn' [My Mother Sent me a Cushion] have no political agenda, but their style, form, and imagery remain traditional.

Di khalyastre published poetry in Warsaw in the 1920s, aiming to popularize Yiddish and widen its audience by making the transition to modernism. The major avant-garde movement in Poland between 1919 and 1924, it brought together poets, novelists, and artists who were modern secular Jews determined to construct a new lay culture in Yiddish. Unlike *De yunge, Di khalyastre* poets emphasized the 'primacy of individuality and experimental forms and showed unmistakable expressionistic tendencies; proclaiming a form of anarchy they denounced the *Haskalah*,[19] religion and politics'.[20] Member-poets Melech Ravitch, Peretz Markish, and Uri-Tsvi Grinberg 'divined from historical events not only the crisis of the individual in the western world but of the entire world'.[21] They consciously strove for art in their choice of language, drawing on cultural density, Jewish lineage, Hasidic[22] tales, and historical disasters, and they favoured expressionist themes as well as violent clashing imagery. Although they shared the desire for aesthetic innovations, their ideological differences later led to the group's demise.

Although sections of Fram's 'Baym zeydn' [At Grandfather's] appeared in *Literarishe bleter* in 1926, attesting to the poem's quality, it 'does not exhibit Modernist tendencies [such as] unusual patterns of versification and grammatical structures [or] punctuation'.[23] However, since Fram's poems 'Ikh bin a Yid' [I Am a Jew], 'Iz vos?' [What if?], and 'Mayn opfor' assert the primacy of the self, the group may have influenced him. Ravitch praises and supports Fram's work in his introduction to *Lider un poemes* [Songs and Poems].[24]

The American modernist group *In zikh* consisted of older poets, including Jacob Yankev Glatstein who helped to launch it in New York in the 1920s. In opposition to *Di yunge*, *In zikh* championed Yiddishkayt and the poet's presence in the modern world. Embracing Yiddish as their creative language of choice, their subject matter encompassed politics, personal relationships, Jewish and universal issues, while their free-verse forms favoured modern principles and stream-of-consciousness techniques. In these ways, they hoped to capture the multidimensional nature of contemporary life. They were the first Yiddish poets to make free verse a cardinal rule, 'promoting a chaotic composition, avoiding any continuity of line and space, showing defiance to coherence and closure, and constructing a random collage of discordant elements in one text'.[25] This was a revolutionary transformation 'for a poet raised on metrical verse to free himself from [...] automatized scansion'.[26] Although Fram's 'In an afrikaner baginen' [In an African Dawn] is written with varying line lengths — like *In zikh* poems — it still retains his characteristic regular rhyme scheme. While his poems 'Fun shop tsu shop' [From Shop to Shop][27] and 'Tsu di shvartse'[28] [To the Black Man][29] *do* react to local political and social issues, there is no proven link.

Yung Vilne [Young Vilna] was a Yiddish literary group of independent writers, poets, and artists who came of age creatively in the 1930s[30] in *Yerushalayim de Lite*, the 'Jerusalem of Lithuania', the centre of Jewish cultural life and learning at the time. These poets were 'highly politicized by poverty and antisemitism, Zionism, territorialism and socialism [but did not] provide unified poetic principles'.[31] Though they were united by generation, place, and leftist, humanistic orientation, they had no artistic manifesto. Principal members included the poets Chaim Grade, Abraham Sutzkever, and Leyzer Volf. They experimented with language rather than with form, playing upon the infinite flexibility of Yiddish vocabulary in a way that no earlier poets had dreamed of doing,[32] transforming the generic and impersonal 'I' into a distinct and personal one, as did Fram.

Fram's inclusion of indigenous terminology from the Afrikaans and Zulu vernaculars also suggests '[e]xpressionist trends, [with an] opening up of the poetic language to all possibilities and intonations of the spoken idiom, including dialects'.[33] In a swing between his old and new homes, involving a 'linguistic geographical and human border-crossing',[34] numerous poems in *Lider un poemes* and *A shvalb oyfn dakh* [A Swallow on the Roof], and single poems published elsewhere incorporate African themes. Thus, while the forms of 'Fun shop tsu shop', 'In an afrikaner baginen', 'Tsu di shvartse', 'Burn' [Farmers and/or Afrikaners], 'Matumba' and 'Matatulu' remain conventional, their innovatory cultural layering and multilingual usage display 'Modernist tendencies'.[35] Thus, in exile, 'he clung to poetry to provide stability and a sense of place in South Africa, [and] forged a connection between Eastern Europe and South Africa'.[36]

Further, Fram's Holocaust poems 'Lesterung' [Blasphemy],[37] *Dos letste kapitl* [The Last Chapter], and *Efsher* [Perhaps] added new dimensions to the South African Yiddish literary pantheon. By doing so, 'South Africa's finest Yiddish poet [...] who began in 1923 with idyllic poems of Jewish life in Lithuania',[38] broke new ground. As he was not part of any international, Eastern European, or South African literary movement with a specific agenda or single ideology, Fram may be considered to be an individualist, a group of one.[39]

Notes

1. Moss, Email to the author, 5 January 2011.
2. Ibid.
3. Lipschitz's bust of David Fram is in the permanent art collection of University of the Witwatersrand.
4. Stern, who was a frequent guest at Feldman's home, provided reproductions of five of her landscapes and a portrait of Fram as illustrations for *Lider un poemes*. She painted his portrait numerous times.
5. Sherman, 'David Fram Centenary Tribute', p. 4.
6. Ibid.
7. Marcia Leveson, 'Introduction', in Vincent Swart, *Collected Poems*, ed. by Marcia Leveson (London: Donker, 1981), pp. 7–24 (p. 11).
8. De Saxe, p. 210.
9. Zygielbaum, 'Tsu Dovid Frams avekforn', p. 23.
10. De Saxe, p. 210.
11. Ibid, p. 211.
12. Fram, 'Yerushe un hashpoes in yidishn vort-tsushtayer fun Dorem Afrike', in *Antologye*, ed. by Rozhansky, pp. 313–28 (p. 315).
13. Ibid.
14. Harshav and Harshav, *American Yiddish Poetry*, p. 10.
15. *A Treasury of Yiddish Poetry*, ed. by Irving Howe and E. Greenberg (New York: Holt, Rinehart and Winston, 1969), p. 8.
16. Aaron, p. 3.
17. Harshav and Harshav, p. 30.
18. Aaron, p. 3.
19. Meaning: Enlightenment.
20. Aaron, p. 4.
21. Ibid., p. 21.
22. Hasidism [Chasidism]: A religious and social revival movement, which appealed to the masses as well as the elite, it followed the teachings of the Ba'al Shem Tov, which include folk elements and structured thought, enthusiastic commitment to their leader, and the energetic worship of God. The term derives from the Hebrew *chesed* [kindness] and *chasid* [pious].
23. Aaron, p. 9.
24. Ravitch, 'A por khaverishe araynfir-verter', n. p.
25. Harshav and Harshav, p. 40.
26. Ibid., p. 43.
27. *Dorem Afrike* (July–September 1984), 29.

28. The use of the term *shvartse* [black] is now regarded as racist and offensive.
29. *Lider*, pp. 19–21.
30. Jack Kugelmass and Jonathan Boyarin, 'Introduction', *From a Ruined Garden: The Memorial Books of Polish Jewry*, ed. and trans by Jack Kugelmass and Jonathan Boyarin (New York: Schocken Books, 1983), pp. 1–19 (p. 7).
31. Aaron, p. 4.
32. *A Treasury of Yiddish Poetry*, ed. by Howe and Greenberg, p. 28.
33. Harshav and Harshav, p. 15.
34. Starck-Adler, 'Multilingualism and Multiculturalism in South African Yiddish', p. 169.
35. Aaron, p. 9.
36. De Saxe, p. 209.
37. *A shvalb oyfn dakh*, pp. 127–29.
38. Liptzin, p. 251.
39. Moss, Email, 5 January 2011.

CHAPTER 2

A Journey with Two Maps:
Poems of Longing and Loss

Fram's poems resonate with the warm atmosphere of traditional Jewish life, drawing on a 'rich store of memories of place [...] evok[ing] in some small measure the familiar environment of the old country'.[1] This chapter highlights how 'place matters in understanding the immigrant experience',[2] focusing on the manifestations of home and the impact of exile in 'Mayn opfor' [My Departure] (1928),[3] 'Mayn mame hot mir tsugeshikt a kishn' [My Mother Sent Me a Cushion] (1928),[4] 'Iz vos?' [So What?] (1929),[5] 'In tsveyen' [Twofold][6] and 'Nokh vos zol ikh forn?' [Why Should I Leave?].[7] Fram's 'knowledge of and sensitivity to the Yiddish language are everywhere apparent [in] his distinguished verse'.[8] The tone and mood of the poems in the section entitled 'Mit eygene laydn' [With my Own Suffering] in *Lider un poemes*, and in his epic *Efsher* [Perhaps],[9] demonstrate the poet's continuing attachment to his Litvak roots, and Russia and Lithuania were always *di heym* — home.

Since 'nomadism [is] a source for Jewish text',[10] it is useful to explore Fram's poems through the rootlessness of the Jewish people, who have been characterized as a 'scattered and diverse phenomenon'[11] for more than 2000 years.[12] The term 'Hebrew' itself denotes a crossing–over, as contained in the command given to Abraham, 'Lech Lecha' [Get you gone from your country and your birthplace and from your father's house].[13] Moses' passage through the Red Sea to Sinai, Joshua's crossing of the Jordan River into Canaan, and the Israelites' journey from Babylon to Zion are Jewish narratives of wanderings and homecoming, which may be physical and/or spiritual.[14]

Moreover, diaspora[15] signifies exile away from the land of one's birth, or in the cases of religious Jews and modern Zionists, living outside the original homeland, the Promised Land, *Eretz Yisroel*. Many religious or Zionistic Jews request burial there if they do not achieve the goal of return in their lifetime, endorsed by the final declaration of the annual Pesach Seder,[16] 'Next year in Jerusalem'. These repetitions of the latter form part of the 'collective cultural memory of wandering and dislocation',[17] which may be considered the Jewish 'paradigmatic experience'.[18]

However, home does not simply exist as physical manifestations, and may be as much about embracing its imagined 'intellectual, emotional, and metaphysical dimensions'.[19] The loss of home may therefore evoke a continuing sense that 'something essential to being and identity is missing, [in which] what completes the individual is still present but only as memory'.[20] When viewed from a distance, 'nostalgia [may be] the only mode in which [the idea of home] could be explored',[21] and there may be an idealization of

> activities, or a satisfaction in simple living, or an absence of negative emotions, of the joy of being in or cultivating a garden, of children growing up, of particular trees and shrubs, [and] associations with particular people or special sites. Some of these elements [of home] are not portable because they are conceptual and intangible.[22]

Where location plays a significant role in Fram's poetic choices, home becomes a substantial presence, as much a psychological as a geographical state, and his journeys provide an illustrative example of the travails of wandering Jew,[23] a 'central image of Jewish historical consciousness'.[24] Hence, he was not alone in his use of the 'leitmotif of diasporic cultural expression of physical and existential rootlessness, and a ubiquitous image in literature'.[25]

Thus dispossessed as they settle in places with no traces of their past to locate them, immigrants may remain outsiders who are flaneurs rather than participants. Moyshe Kulbak evoked a poetic persona of a Jewish vagabond traversing the fields and forests of his native Belarus and the landscape near Vilna[26] in his poetic cycle 'Raysn' [Byelorussia],[27] and the urban setting of his long poem *Shtot* [City] (1920) is also mediated through the perspective of a wanderer.[28] Leyb Naydus nostalgically depicted his hero's wanderings through the landscape,[29] and many of the poems of Elkhonen Vogler are set in the Lithuanian and Belorussian countryside, their Romantic themes influenced by Kulbak. In this tradition, Fram's poems record 'the old home in beautiful pictures because the young sentimental Fram found it difficult to part with his home, with his Lite'.[30]

This kinship between absences and 'the writer's situatedness'[31] may shape both individual and literary identity, and may even become like a 'Jerusalem-of-the-mind where dreamscapes, as opposed to real landscapes, provide the symbolic and material dimension for the poet'.[32] Recollecting family and former lifestyle, Fram's 'Mayn opfor', is intimate, introspective, and emotional. Touching his shirt, sewn for him by his sister, triggers memories of close relationships with her and his parents in finely drawn vignettes:

> Dos hemd — atstind gedenk ikh nokh — mayn shvester hot geneyt.
> Derken ikh ire kleyne shtekh, di forzikhtike net.
> Zi hot mit shtiler hartsikayt un benkshaft es baveyt
> In lange, lange oventn farzesn zikh biz shpet. (1–4)

> [The shirt — I still remember — sewn by my sister.
> I know her tiny stitches snug and neat,
> Made while sitting in quiet diligence alone
> For long, long evenings until late.]

This simple, everyday object, the handmade shirt, provides a concrete, visual focus for the expression of an imaginative crystallization of memory; although the physical link with his family has been broken, the emotional connection remains.

The second stanza describes the sweetmeats his mother packed for his journey, and the memory of the tastes of the 'pomerantsn' [oranges] and 'tsukerlekh' [sweets] (6) evoke both his close bond with her, and the bitterness of his departure: 'Gedenk ikh, aza kleyninke in harbstikn farnakht | Fardayget mikh aroysbagleyt tsum breyt-tseleygtn trakt' [I remember, such a tiny woman in the autumn evening, | As she anxiously escorted me to the wide, far-reaching road] (7–8). Just as the pair clung to each other physically, the poet holds on to the memory. Similarly, he recalls how he also tore himself away from his father,

> Mayn tate iz geshtanen mid mit dine, lange hent,
> Dem vaysn kop aropgelozt, on verter un on reyd.
> A shkiye hot a blutike in hartsn zikh tsebrent,
> Un s'hot a nakht a finstere unz alemen tsesheyd. (9–12)

> [My father stood wearily with thin, long hands,
> His white head bowed, without words and silent.
> A bloody sunset burned in [our] heart,
> As a dark night separated us all.]

His departure ripped the fabric of his family apart, so that the firmament itself seemed seared with blood. In stanza four, the descending darkness emphasizes the anguish together with the adjectives 'tseshnitn' [severed] (14) and 'sharfer' [sharp] (14).

> Un kh'hob in nakht in harbstiker farlozn zey aleyn,
> Tseshnitn hot mayn shtume harts a trukn-sharfer vey,
> Un s'hot a vildn shpar geton mit trern a geveyn —
> Farshtikt in triber elntkayt an elntn geshrey. (13–16)

> [And in the autumn night I left them on their own,
> My quiet, severed heart is full of pressing, sharp pain,
> And many lonely tears we moan —
> Pierced with dismal loneliness we cry out desolately.]

Stanzas one and five frame the poet's current existence and longing for a past that is shaped by familiar places, family, and community.

> Un do, in vayter Afrike, iz veytogdik un shver,
> Durkh benkenish geleyterter farvoglt in der fremd...
> Mayn shvester hot mikh oysgeputst mit shmekedikn hemd,
> Un mame hot aroysbagleyt in veg mikh mit ir trer. (17–20)

> [And here, in far-off Africa, in pain and hardship
> I am an exiled stranger filled with pure longing...
> My sister dressed me in a sweet-smelling shirt,
> And mother accompanied me along the path, crying.]

In addition, the final couplet, 'in vayter Afrike, iz veytogdik un shver, | Durkh benkenish geleyterter farvoglt in der fremd' | 'in far off Africa, in pain and hardship | I am an exiled stranger filled with pure longing' (21–22), endorses the poet's extreme loneliness expressed in lines 13 and 16. Now, in an alien land, severed from his loved ones, the poet treasures the wholeness of his shirt, as his sister's careful stitches and the memory of his mother's tears continue to connect him to them.

As in 'Mayn opfor', Fram once more employs a concrete object for a central image in 'Mayn mame hot mir tsugeshikt a kishn'. In advancing the sonnet's narrative, the cushion becomes a symbol of loss, a container of memories of his mother's feelings for him and his for her. Writing far away from the hub of Yiddishism, Fram embeds his yearning for Lithuania and his adaptation to his new circumstances in this choice of imagery.

The tenderness with which his mother sends him the gift reminds him of his home, 'A grus a heymisher fun benkendiker Lite!' [A homemade greeting from yearning Lithuania!] (2). Applying the adjective 'benkendiker' [yearning] to his homeland rather than to himself, emphasizes the enormity of their longing and also highlights its opposite — the harshness of his current circumstances: 'Do in Afrike, in enger kaferite.[33] | Oy, ven zi volt epes fun dem visn!' [Here in Africa, in the crowded concession store. | Oy, if she only had an inkling about it!] (3–4). The expression 'oy' (4), encapsulates his mother's regret and disbelief that her dreams for him had not materialized.

The 'kaferite'[34] [kaffir-eating houses] were established by concession on mine property for the Black miners during the gold industry's boom. They also provided the newly arrived, Yiddish-speaking immigrants with what was often the only employment available to them. These 'kafereatniks' were badly treated, underpaid, and looked down on by other whites. While they worked, they learnt English, Afrikaans, and *fanagalo*, 'a simplified, artificial mixture of words from various Bantu languages',[35] and slept either on or underneath the counters. In their turn, the Black migrant labourers, as dislocated as the Jewish waiters, were served execrable food in filthy conditions. Thus, having worked in a mining concession store when he first arrived, Fram's own experiences of hardship coloured his views, and enabled him to 'identify with [...] other oppressed people'.[36]

Illustrative of the change of circumstance, he describes how 'hakhnoedik, tsufridn un farlitn, | Kafers muz ikh shmutsike badinen' [servile, content and patient | I must serve dirty Black customers] (7–8), and the necessary adjustment to the differences between past and present. Although Fram expresses deep regret at what he forfeited, here he also indicates some acceptance, acknowledging the pleasantness of Africa's 'lange teg un zunike baginens' [long days and sunny dawns] (5). With his current surroundings being so different from Russia's 'vayse vintern' [white winters] (16), the immigrant may thus evolve by overcoming 'spatial and temporal barriers'[37] between himself and the majority resident community, and by engaging with different cultures.

Through these interactions, despite gruelling hours of work, the poet begins to feel a degree of closeness to those he serves. Thus, they become 'Glaykh vi oreme un leydndike brider' [Just like poor and suffering brothers] (10), became, like them, 'farshvigener un mider' [silent and tired] (11), he is counting the length of time of his suffering, 'Tseyl ikh oventn tsuzamen shoyn in yorn' [I already count my nights in years] (12). Through repetition, 'Tseyl ikh glaykhgiltik a shtumer yedn ovnt' [Indifferent I count each night in silence] (13), the tedium and the slow passage of time for both himself and the labourers become apparent.

In the final stanza, the image of flower petals 'fun gertener gerisn' [torn from the gardens] (14), contrasts with the feathers, so tenderly 'gekhovet' [gathered] (16) to fill the cushion:

> Tseyl ikh glaykhgiltik a shtumer yedn ovnt
> Vi blumen harbstike fun gertener gerisn;
> Mayn mame hot mir tsugeshikt a kishn —
> Durkh vayse vintern di federn gekhovet. (13–16)

> [Indifferent I count each night in silence,
> Like autumn flowers torn from the gardens;
> My mother sent me a cushion —
> The feathers gathered through winters white.]

The feathers remind him of the beauty of his home, as opposed to his current degraded circumstances, where like 'blumen harbstike fun gertener gerisn' [autumn flowers torn from the gardens] (14), he too has been torn away. The metonymic scattered feathers and shredded petals reinforce the opposite, the memory of his mother's endurance and stability.

Epitomizing the wandering Jew as a perpetual outsider, Fram's poem 'Iz vos?' highlights the legendary figure condemned to wander without rest,[38] and the nomad-poet links himself to the biblical Hebrews:

> Iz vos, oyb gelebt kh'hob amol in der vayter un shtiler Samare[39]
> Un nokhdem megulgl gevorn aleyn tsu di breges fun Lite,[40]
> Un itst — shoyn in Afrike fremder, vu s'shmekt mitn zamd fun Sahare,
> Mit trukene zunen farbroynte un shteynerne felzn tseglite? (1–4)

> [So what, if I once lived in distant and silent Samara,
> And after that, transformed, I landed up alone on the shores of Lite,
> And now — a stranger in Africa, which smells of the sand of Sahara,
> Browned by the dry sun and stony glowing cliffs?]

Using concrete images, Fram captures his feelings of insecurity and vulnerability caused by his migration, contrasting the aridity of the desert with the fertility of home and the sweetness of old lullabies.

> Iz vos, oyb es hobn gehodevet mikh ven der Volges tsegosene breges
> Un s'hobn farvigt mikh di lider fun berdike, mide 'batrakes'?
> Az s'hot mikh mayn gorl farbundn mit troyer fun blutike reges
> Vos zaynen gerunen in khoyshekh, vi ayeter fun ofene makes. (5–9)

> [So what, if I was raised where the Volga overflowed its banks,
> And the songs that lulled me to sleep were those of bearded weary farm
>   labourers?
> And what if my fate was linked with the sadness of bloody moments,
> That curdled in darkness, like the pus of open abscesses.]

Here, the poet contrasts the fertile Volga River to his losses. While once he was soothed to sleep, his darkness is now filled with a sorrow that no lullaby can ameliorate:

> Iz vos-zhe, oyb s'hot in Afrike fremder fartoplt mayn leydn in tsveyen,
> Fargresert di atsves in hartsn, der elnt farshvign gevorn...
> Ikh veys dokh: di teg vi fartstaytn, zey kumen un geyn, fargeyen,
> Un s'klaybn zikh shtile mes-lesn un bindn tsunoyf zikh in yorn... (13–16)

> [So what if in the strangeness of Africa my suffering has doubled,
> The sadness in my heart is increased, the loneliness is silenced...
> I know: as in times past, the days come and go, and pass on,
> And the silent days and nights collect and bind the years together...]

Believing that nothing he does will make any difference during the endless days and nights, he expresses his despair in an almost biblical tone. The feeling of separation from his family and home multiplies in the strangeness of his new environment where he has no one with whom to share his struggles. Though he weeps for the lost songs of the farmers, there is no one to hear. Instead, he searches for greater meaning:

> Iz vemenen art es, a shtayger, az emetser veynt a fartserter,
> Az emetser benkt in der finster nokh lider fun Volger 'batrakes'?
> Iz vemenen art es, a shtayger, az hele fartrikenen verter,
> Un s'rinen tseveytogte reges, vi ayeter fun ofene makes? (17–20)

> [So who cares at all, for instance, if someone weeps brokenly,
> If someone is filled with longing in the dark for the songs of the Volga farm
>   labourers?
> And who cares at all, for instance, how harsh a place it is, if clear words dry out,
> And painful moments ooze like pus from open abscesses?]

Thus, 'chronic homelessness'[41] floods the poet. 'Un ikh vel nokh voglen a mider oyf shtoybike vegn on keynem, | Un efsher nokh Afrikes elnt oyf topltn elnt tsebaytn' [And I will still roam on wearily, alone along dusty roads, | And still perhaps exchange Africa's desolation for twice the loneliness] (23–24).

Immigrants may always regard themselves to be the 'other'. In 'what may be perceived as a hostile world in relation to the geographies of ethnicity',[42] someone who never feels at home is never 'chez nous [...], neither here [...] nor there'.[43] There is also the sense that 'I belong where I am not'.[44] Fram shifted from one world to another, and, like the thousands of 'Jews who had left homes and countries where they had put down roots over generations in Jewish environments governed by Jewish concepts and characters, came to South Africa and found an alien country, an alien language, an alien culture'.[45]

Fram's poem 'In tsveyen' offers a further example of how 'diaspora is an important site of a modern Jewish aesthetic',[46]

> Fun rusisher[47] rakhves tsu Afrikes umet...
> Fun vayse midboryes un glimike shneyen —
> Tsu zunike vaytn fun eybikn zumer,
> O, filt men zikh elnt in tsveyen! (1–4)

> [From Russian expansiveness to Africa's sadness...
> From white deserts and gleaming snow —
> To sunny distances of everlasting summer,
> Oh, one feels the loneliness doubly!][48]

The poet sets out the emotional implications of the settler's sense of hybridity, through the opposition of the white deserts of snow and the endless summers. The image of 'elnt-farblonzhete shifn' [lonely and lost ships], used in line 12, emphasizes the physical distance of separation and the psychological state of being far away from home. The part-rhyme of 'umet' and 'zumer' in lines 1 and 3, and the repetitive 'u'-sound in 'fun', 'tsu', and 'rusisher' sound ominous, and the 'O' in line 4 endorses the traveller's uncertainty.

Binding together the impact of physical and emotional separation intensifies the atmosphere moving towards the fifth stanza:

> O, Afrikes umet mit Ruslands georemt,
> Der umet fun shvaygn in blutike veyen —
> In shikere nekht fun farshikertn dorem,
> Do filt men zikh elnt in tsveyen. (17–20)

> [Oh, Africa's sadness made poorer with Russia's,
> The loneliness of keeping quiet in bleeding pain —
> In drunken nights of the intoxicated south,
> Here we feel the loneliness twice over...]

Despite the welcoming and intoxicating climate, the immigrants cannot come to terms with the extreme differences between the soft, flat landscape, pale skies, and gleaming snow of his homeland, and the hot plains of Africa. This response is emphasized by the adjectives 'blutike' [bloody], 'shikere' [drunk], and 'farshikertn' [drunken] in line 19.

Similarly, 'Nokh vos zol ikh forn?', written soon after Fram arrived in South Africa, also expresses his sense of unsettlement and dislocation:

> Nokh vos zol ikh forn, un vu zol ikh forn,
> Az s'zaynen farkirtst mayne vegn gevorn,
> Az s'zaynen gevorn farshnitn di vaytn,
> Un kh'veys nisht oyf vos kh'vel mayn elnt tsebaytn. (1–4)

> [Why should I leave and where shall I go,
> When my options are few,
> And when places have been limited?
> I don't know what I'll get in place of my loneliness.]

Although part of an immigrant community of other *landslayt*, countrymen, with similar outlook and memories, the narrator feels alone and lost. Wrestling with the hope of moving again, 's'vet nokh a shprits ton mit freyd a baginen' [there'll still be a spray of joy at dawn] (5), he foresees that he would simply meet with the same obstacles once more, 'Un efsher vet merer un shtarker nokh vey ton | In fremde merkhokim un leydike breytn?' [And perhaps it'll hurt more and ever more strongly | In distant places and empty spaces?] (7–8). No matter the location, there would always be difficulties for one who does not belong. These are some of the outcomes of 'rootlessness, nomadism and dispersal',[49] when moving away from the familiar way of life often becomes unbearable:

> Ikh veys, ikh vel keyn zakh nisht kenen farmaydn,
> Un umetum vartn di zelbike leydn.

> Ikh veys es, avade, nishto vos tsu gloybn,
> Un vandern vider mit trukene shtoybn. (9–12)
>
> [I know, there is nothing I'll be able to prevent,
> And everywhere there awaits the same suffering.
> I know this for sure, there's nothing to believe in,
> But to carry on wandering with the dry dust.]

Without support and comfort, hope and friendship, he wanders the 'tunkele vegn' [dark roads] (13), where there is 'Nishto vu tsu geyn un bay vemen tsu fregn' [Nowhere to go and no one to ask] (14), and 'nishto vos tsu gleybn' [nothing to believe in] (11). Here, the poet grapples with emotional challenges, and the meaning of life continues to elude him in 'Ikh hob gemeynt' [I Thought] (1930).[50]

> Ikh hob gemeynt, az do vel ikh gefinen shoyn mayn ru,
> Az do veln derfrayen mikh di teg,
> Az s'vet mikh mer nisht onlokn der veg
> Tsu vogln vayter, ergets andershvu. (25–28)
>
> [I thought I would find peace here,
> That here the days would be free,
> That the path would no longer entice me
> To move again, to another place.][51]

Written shortly after his arrival in South Africa, his 'umruikayt', his restlessness, pain, and disillusionment lingered on: 'Iz ober fun dos-nay mir vandern bashert, | Un zukhn nokh a treyst in ergets andersvu' [But destined all anew is wandering for me, | To seek another comfort somewhere else] (31–32). Through these ephemeral musings, together with the concrete images of cushion and shirt in the contemporaneous poems 'Mayn mame hot mir tsugeshikt a kishn' and 'Mayn opfor', the poet threads his continued connection to his old home.

Similarly, in 'Efsher',[52] the 'place that expelled him'[53] becomes the space of reflection and self-reflection. The separation arouses ceaseless anguish, when 'Shver iz di rege fun tsesheydung' [Heavy is the moment of parting] (1):

> Vet di benkshaft shtendik rinen? —
> Veln oyf fremdn breg
> Oyfgeyn freylekhere teg? (5–7)
>
> [Will the longing always ooze? —
> Here on foreign shores
> Will happier days arise?]

Once more, the poet recognizes the depth of the wound; echoing the image of open abscesses in 'Iz vos?'. Aching for his lost past while hoping for better times, he comments on how

> Do hob ikh ober tsebaytn
> Naye heym oyf fremde vaytn,
> Vider fun dos nay gedarft. (9–11)
>
> [Here I had to exchange
> My new home for foreign distances,
> Yet again had to start anew.]

So Fram still considered himself the outsider, highlighting this with the specific descriptions of particular places and people he knew. Having left behind 'Dayn balibtn barg un tol' [Your beloved mountain and valley] (55), 'Dayn boym, dayn groz, dayn vald un feld' [Your tree, your grass, your forest and field] (62), and also 'Dayn altn shokhn lebn dir' [Your old neighbour beside you] (60), he aligns himself with those in similar circumstances. The use of the second person pronoun also connects his fate to that of his people — 'heymloz vi a hunt' [homeless like a dog] (53). As the last traces of his heritage are erased, he finds himself withering on strange soil, 'nisht dernert' [unsustained] (71), unable to share in age-old community rituals, the 'simkhes[54] groyse un in shive'[55] [great celebrations and mourning] (87). The outcome is as he predicted at the start of the poem: 'Veyst: — nishto sheyn keyn tsurik... | Hinter zikh farbrent di brikn [You know: — there is no going back... | I burned the bridges behind me] (18–19).

Once more, like the cushion in 'Mayn mame hot mir tsugeshikt a kishn', the concrete presence of the poet's suitcase as well as his other belongings become metaphorical containers for his losses, but the straps that bind them together can no longer hold fast:

> Yener shverer, temper veytog —
> Letster grus fun letstn shneytog,
> Tshemodanes, kishns, rimens —
> Alts fun lange rayzes simens —
> Plonterst zikh in pek un shtrik. (13–17)
>
> [That heavy, blunt pain —
> The last farewell after the last snow-day,
> Suitcases, cushions, straps —
> All signs of long journeys —
> Entangled in parcels and string.]

As the *shabes khale*, the plaited Sabbath loaf, provides earthly sustenance and spiritual upliftment, the poem ends with an affirmation: 'Tsu bentshn, vi gebentshtn broyt | Biz shtiln onkum funem toyt [To bless, like blessed bread | Until the quiet coming of death] (97–98).

Fram's 'abiding emotional concern',[56] his longing for home and his consequent feelings of 'aynzamkayt'[57] [loneliness] played out in poems written long after he had left Lithuania. Highlighting the immigrant conflict between moving forward and looking back, Fram represents Isaac Bashevis Singer's 'Yiddish-speaking Jew, [with] his fear of physical and spiritual effacement, and his desperate effort to sustain the values and languages of his history'.[58] Constructed through nostalgic longing for his birthplace, his poems evolved through the stages of loss, displacement, adjustment, adaptation, and acculturation, his memories and imaginings providing a limitless source of subject matter for him.

Notes to Chapter 2

1. Cesarani, Kushner, and Shain, 'Introduction', p. 2.
2. Nancy Foner, 'Migration, Location and Memory: Jewish History through a Comparative Lens',

in *Place and Displacement in Jewish History and Memory*, ed. by Cesarani, Kushner, and Shain, pp. 131–40 (p. 131).

3. *Lider*, p. 14.

4. *Lider*, p. 18.

5. *Lider*, pp. 16–17.

6. *Lider*, p. 7; may also be translated as 'Divided'.

7. *Lider*, p. 24.

8. Sherman, 'Introduction', p. 14.

9. *Efsher* was published in pamphlet form in 1947. Several excerpts appeared later in *Dorem Afrike*.

10. Omer-Sherman, p. 111.

11. Ibid., p. 270.

12. In Omer-Sherman, p. 7.

13. Genesis 12. 1–17.

14. Dovid Katz, *Words on Fire: The Unfinished Story of Yiddish* (New York: Basic Books, 2004), p. 170.

15. Richard Gottheil and Théodore Reinach, 'Diaspora', *Jewish Encyclopedia* < http://www.jewishencyclopedia.com/articles/5169-diaspora> [accessed 4 December 2020]: The term 'diaspora', from the Greek meaning 'scattering', originally referred to groups of Jews who migrated to particular regions and created communities there. The Jewish diaspora now indicates groups living anywhere outside Israel, and is also used more broadly in cultural studies.

16. Passover meal commemorating the Exodus from Egypt.

17. Jennifer Langer, 'Introduction', in *If Salt has Memory*, ed. by Jennifer Langer (Nottingham: Five Leaves, 2008), pp. 9–23 (p. 9).

18. Sidra DeKoven Ezrahi, *Booking Passage: Exile and Homecoming in the Modern Jewish Imagination* (Berkeley: University of California Press, 2000), p. 240.

19. Peter Read in M. Langfield, 'Lost Worlds: Reflections on Home and Belonging in Jewish Holocaust Survivor Testimonies', in *Place and Displacement in Jewish History and Memory*, ed. by Cesarini, Kushner, and Shain, pp. 29–42 (p. 30).

20. Paolo Bartoloni, *On the Cultures of Exile, Translation and Writing* (West Lafayette: Purdue University Press, 2008), p. 103.

21. Cesarani, Kushner, and Shain, 'Introduction', p. 11.

22. Read in Langfield, p. 30.

23. The original term for this Christian concept is '*Der Ewige Jude*, literally the eternal Jew, but understood as the wandering Jew' (R. Edelmann, 'Ahasuerus, the Wandering Jew: Origin and Background', in *The Wandering Jew: Essays in the Interpretation of a Christian Legend*, ed. by G. Hasan-Rokem and A. Dundes (Bloomington: Indiana University Press, 1986), pp. 1–10 (p. 10)).

24. Omer-Sherman, p. 268.

25. Ibid., p. 111.

26. Justin Daniel Cammy, 'Vogler, Elkhonen', *YIVO Encyclopedia of Jews in Eastern Europe* (2 November 2010) <https://yivoencyclopedia.org/article.aspx/Vogler_Elkhonen> [accessed 3 July 2020].

27. *The Penguin Book of Modern Yiddish Verse*, ed. by Howe, Wisse, and Schmeruk, pp. 388–404.

28. Novershtern, 'Kulbak, Moyshe'.

29. Krutikov, 'Raysn: The Belarusian Frontier of Yiddish Modernism'.

30. Ravitch, 'A por khaverishe araynfir-verter', n. p.; 'Dovid Fram un zayn lider', p. 59.

31. Omer-Sherman, p. 269.

32. Ezrahi, *Booking Passage*, p. 238.

33. Discussions of Yiddish terminology relating to the indigenous peoples in context follow in Chapters 3 and 4.

34. A neologism specific to South African Yiddish.

35. Eric Rosenthal, *Encyclopaedia of Southern Africa*, 4th edn (London: Warne, 1967), p. 178.

36. Davis, p. 46.

37. Bartoloni, p. 101.

38. Edelmann, p. 10.

39. This line refers to Fram's first experience of exile.

40. According to Joseph Sherman, Fram returned to Lithuania in 1921: 'Singing with the Silence, p. 41.
41. Shreiber, p. 274.
42. Bartoloni, p. 100.
43. Andre Aciman, 'From the Other Bank', in *If Salt has Memory*, ed. by J. Langer, pp. 24–41 (p. 39).
44. Anne Landsman, *The Devil's Chimney* (Johannesburg: Ball, 1997), p. ix.
45. Hyman Polski, *In Afrike* [In Africa] (Johannesburg: Pacific Press, 1952), p. v.
46. Ezrahi, *Booking Passage*, p. 228.
47. Lithuania was part of the Russian Empire at the time, so Fram refers to both Lithuania and Russia as home.
48. Amelia Levy translated the poem as 'Divided': 'From the spaciousness of Russia | To Africa's lonely plains | From far-off desert places, and snows | Of gleaming white, | To the sun-swept distances where endless summer reigns! | How deep the self-division in my solitary plight.', in L. Goodman, 'David Fram: A Study in Growth', p. 29.
49. Barbara Kirshenblatt-Gimblett and Jonathan Karp, *The Art of Being Jewish in Modern Times* (Philadelphia: University of Pennsylvania Press, 2008), p. 7.
50. *Lider*, pp. 12–13.
51. For alternative translations, see Sherman, 'What Balm for the Heart...?', p. 10; Z. Levy, 'A Premier Yiddish Poet in South Africa', p. 33.
52. 'Efsher' (extract), *Dorem Afrike* (August 1949), 21.
53. Aciman, p. 30.
54. The term refers to celebrations such as bar mitzvahs and weddings.
55. The seven days of ritually prescribed mourning after the passing of a loved one.
56. Sherman, 'What Balm for the Heart...?', p. 7.
57. Zygielbaum, 'Dovid Fram's yuvil', p. 3.
58. In Omer-Sherman, p. 1.

CHAPTER 3

Looking Inward, Looking Out:
From the Outside, Looking in

As Fram made contact with different groups in South Africa, his poems incorporate his reactions to these interactions. 'Fun tate-mames yidishe' [From Jewish Parents] (1929)[1] and 'Ikh bin a Yid' [I am a Jew] (1938)[2] emphasize the effects of the poet's displacement and his continuing commitment to his Jewish identity in the foreign environment. Several poems construct 'the Self and the Other [...] in terms of reciprocal elements [...] ramifications and encroachments, interconnections and border-crossings'.[3] 'Tsu di shvartse' [To the Black Man] (1929)[4] and 'Matatulu' [Matatulu] (1953)[5] position their protagonists between a traditional and an urban way of life. Doing so evokes parallels with the circumstances of the Yiddish-speaking immigrant outsider and the indigenous Other.

In 'Fun tate-mames yidishe', Fram reflects on the cultural influence of the mother and father and also forbears in general. Linking past, present and also future, the poem is dedicated to 'Di kinderlekh fun der ershter yidisher folksshul in Yohanesburg, geheylikt', that is, to the children who attended of the first Yiddish Folkshul [Yiddish folk school] in Johannesburg. For many immigrants like Fram, 'Yiddishkayt was a Yiddish-based, non-observant Jewishness — the treasure of European Jewish life [and] a product of the Diaspora.'[6] Whereas Yiddish was a language of the Jewish people, Yiddishkayt refers to aspects of Jewish culture, which in the religious sense means 'Jewish learning, observance, *mitsves*, *kashres*, *shul*, but in the worldly sense it means secular Jewish nationalism'.[7] As part of an extensive body of nostalgic literature that can be found in many cultures, the poem focuses on the specific details of a particular immigrant group's attitude to dislocation. Written after Fram left his birthplace, 'Fun tate-mames yidishe' emphasizes the value of Yiddish in perpetuating Jewish heritage, and ensuring its survival. Endorsing this continuity, the poet uses a traditional folk ballad form of four verses of four lines, with regular rhyme and metre, and the rhythm and rhyme of a typical circle dance.

The first quatrain describes the poet's delight watching the children doing traditional dances and hearing them sing in Yiddish. Fram expresses his regret that their parents had become alienated from Yiddishkayt, and were ashamed of or embarrassed by Yiddish. Although such linguistic assimilation was natural,[8] the 'fayer heyliker' [holy fire] (4) still continues to burn in the next generation:

> Ir hot in Yidish poshetn tsezungn ayer freyd,
> Zikh gleybike, tsefridene in karahod gedreyt,
> Un s'hot geklungn kishefdik dos kindishe gezang,
> Nokh vos ikh hob an elnter gebenkt vi ir fun lang... (5–8)

> [You sang out your joy in simple Yiddish,
> And faithfully in contentment twirled the circle dance,
> And the childlike singing rang out enchantingly,
> For which I had forlornly longed for ages...]

Through their enactment of the old, familiar songs and dances, the children embrace their Jewish values:

> Ikh hob gebenkt an elnter, un dokh hob ikh gevust,
> Az s'tsaplt zikh a heylikayt bay yedern in brust:
> — Dos Yidish, vos es zaftikt zikh oyf lipelekh bakheynt —
> Fun vos me hot aykh, kinderlekh, fun kindvayz on antveynt. (9–12)

> [I have longed forlornly, and yet have I known,
> That a holiness quivers in each and every breast:
> — That Yiddish, so smooth on charming little lips —
> From which they weaned you, children, away in infancy.]

He is overjoyed to watch the children perpetuate their heritage, 'Un s'hot a fayer heyliker in hartsn zikh tsebrent' [And a holy flame flared up in their hearts] (4), an image which is repeated in line 10, quoted above. Coming from a religious background, Fram uses language from that context in this secular poem, and phrases such as 'fayer heyliker' and 'gleybike heylikayt' deepen the 'yomtovdiker' [celebratory] atmosphere. Without being dogmatic about holiness, sanctity, or religious belief, the poem projects an alternative value system.

The children's innocent enjoyment of their Jewish heritage expresses his own attachment to Yiddishkayt, 'Nokh vos ikh hob an elnter gebenkt vi ir fun lang' [For which I had forlornly longed for ages] (8); emerging 'oyf lipelekh bakheynt' [on charming little lips] (11). Even though their parents had deprived them of it, fortunately there were others who had affirmed it, 'Piyonern hobn oysgeleygt far aykh a heln veg' [Pioneers set out a bright path for you] (13).

As the poet shares the children's pleasure, 'Dan hot mayn simkhe oyfgebroyzt mit ayerer tsu glaykh' [Then did my joy well up with yours together] (15). As they rejoice, and keep the warmth of the language and traditions alive, the poet celebrates with them, 'Az voyl iz mir, kinderlekh, tzu freyen zikh mit aykh!' [How happy I am, children, to rejoice along with you!] (16).

'Ikh bin a Yid' [I am a Jew] also confirms Fram's traditional outlook and his ongoing commitment to his culture. Even when those around him were discarding tradition, Fram highlighted his connection to it:

> Ikh bin a Yid, a Yid fun khumesh un tanekh.
> Es rint in mir dos alte blut fun Yosefn un Moshe'n.
> Es rint in mir an eydelkayt fun mayn sprakh,
> Un nokh a melekh yidishn mayn zeyde hot geheysn. (1–4)

> [I am a Jew, a Jew of Chumash and Tanakh
> And in me flows the old blood of Joseph and Moses.

> There flows in me the honour of my language,
> And another king of Yiddish was my grandfather.]

The stanza links the poet's Jewish literary lineage to the holy Hebrew books, to his biblical forefathers, Joseph and Moses, and also personally to his revered Yiddish *zeyde*, his grandfather. While the specific mention of the *khumesh*[9] and *tanekh*[10] (1) implies Fram's knowledge of these tracts, he was not necessarily observant. The poem affirms the value of Jewish traditions in both religious and secular contexts, recognizing the suffering that can go with maintaining them.

> Durkh doyres hunderter hob ikh mayn veg geshpant,
> Getuvelt zikh in blut, in kedushe un in tume.
> Ikh hob geveynt fartsert oyf khavers fun mayn land,
> Un hob geveytokt eynzam far mayn ume. (5–8)

> [Through hundreds of generations my journey was a struggle,
> Soaked in blood, in holiness and in shame.
> I cried brokenly for friends of my land,
> And ached for my people alone.]

In 1941, Itsik Fefer (1900–1952) also published a poem entitled 'Ikh bin a Yid',[11] in which he too affirms his core beliefs using 'Ikh' [I]. Fefer also asserts the significance of Jewish identity and heritage, and regards them as sources of sustenance as well as sorrow:

> Der vayn fun doyresdikn doyer
> Hot men geshtarkt in vanderung,
> Di beyze shverd fun payn un troyer
> Hot nit farnikhtet mayn farmeg. (1–4)

> [The wine of enduring generations
> Strengthened me on my wanderer's way.
> The evil sword of pain and lamentations,
> Nothing that I hold dear could slay.][12]

Like Fram's, Fefer's poem resounds with the might of his forebears, 'Es shtalt mayn rum durkh tsayt un yorn | Ikh bin a Yid!' [My horn sounded this message back: | 'I am a Jew!'] (15–16),[13] and Samson in 'zey flegn shtikn mir di oygn — | Ikh bin a Yid' [And as they pierced my eyes, I said: | 'I am a Jew!'] (23–24), and Moses in 'Di fertsik yor fun uralt-lebn | vos kh'hob gekrenkt in midber-zamd' [My forty years of wandering | In the wilderness] (26–27). Spurred on by the wisdom of Solomon, Isaiah, and Rabbi Akiva and Bar Kochba's strength, Fefer perpetuates these communal bonds:

> Mayn folk, mayn gloybn un mayn bliyen,
> [...]
> Fun unter shverd hob ikh geshriyen:
> Ikh bin a Yid! (4; 7–8)

> [My people, my faith, and my head unbowed.
> [...]
> Under the sword I cried aloud:
> 'I am a Jew!']

Fefer's use of anaphora reinforces the emphatic sound and forceful rhythm, to match the strength of his credo.

Fram's directness and clarity of expression may have been influenced by Fefer's 'proste reyd' [simple speech] as opposed to the expressionism of avant-garde poetry.[14] Their traditional and biblical content as well as their use of literary devices suggest similar literary influences. Dovid Hofshteyn, whose poetry influenced Fram,[15] was the mentor of *Vidervuks* [New Growth], the group of young Yiddish literati in Kiev. Fefer also belonged to this group, and his poetry was popular among Yiddish readers both in the Soviet Union, with western Yiddish left-wingers,[16] and appealed to the masses, too.

Fram, however, focuses on the passing down of the Jewish cultural heritage: 'Un dokh durkh groyer tog, durkh vogendike teg — | Shabeses hobn zikh far undz in likht getsundn' [And still through grey days, through every weekday — | Sabbaths lit the candles within us] (11–12). On the other hand, a Romantic spirit of continuous revolution runs through Fefer's poetry.[17] Fefer's energetic commitment to Jewishness extends to include national pride, Soviet patriotism, and hatred of the enemy:

> Un zi mit has tsunoyfgefort;
> Di shvung fun makabeyer heldn
> In mordes-blut in maynem zend,
> Fun ale shayters fleg in meldn:
> Ikh bin a Yid. (44–47)

> [Till my hatred stirred,
> And I felt the blood of the Maccabees,
> Whom the tyrants slew —
> I cried from all the gallows-trees:
> 'I am a Jew!']

Through the repeated battle cry for every vicissitude and triumph, Fefer supports his political position in addition to his commitment to being Jewish. He read 'Ikh bin a Yid!' aloud when he was in America in 1943 for the Jewish Anti-Fascist Committee's fundraising drive against Nazi Germany. An avowed Communist who supported Stalin wholeheartedly, he amalgamated revolutionary romanticism with the propaganda of the workers' movement, 'Ikh bin a zun fun di Sovetn, | Ikh bin a Yid!' [And I am a son of this Soviet land | 'I am a Jew!'] (70–71), and endorsed this objective by declaring 'Ikh bin a Yid vos hot getrunkn | Fun Stalinishn kos fun glik' [I am a Jew who has drunk up | Happiness from Stalin's cup] (80–81), and also 'Vel ikh unter di royte fonen' [Under the red flag I shall live] (106).

In contrast, Fram's heroes embody peace and light. Through their sombre commitment to observance and ritual, he is hopeful that the God of the Jewish people will see their travail,

> Shabeses zoyvere mit khesed un mit gnod —
> Zey flegn undzer tser mit heylikeyt bakhanen.
> O, Got derbarmiker! Du 'Adoyni Ekhad'!
> Vi gut es iz far dir in undzer brokh tsu veynen... (13–16)

[Pure Sabbaths with devotion and with grace
Would charm our heartache with holiness.
Oh God! You 'the One God!
How good is it for you to weep for our suffering...]

This deep attachment to inherited rituals ignites the flame of Judaism and also highlights the suffering of the Jewish people:

Vu trern brenen nokh in tsiter fun levone...
In tsiter fun di nekht, ven undzer blut umzist
Geforbn hot di erd, di shteyner oyf di gasn.
Mit vos ober bin ikh mer zindik farn krist,
Vos hot mit blindik groyl nit oyfgehert tsu hasn. (20–24)

[Where tears still burn in the quivering of the moon...
In the shaking of the nights when our useless blood
Poured over the earth, the stones on the streets.
Why am I more sinning than Christians,
Who with blind terror did not stop hating.]

Where Fram's poem evoked soul-searching, Fefer was driven by his fiery political stance and hatred towards multiple enemies:

Kh'vel mayn vayngertner farplantsn
Un fun mayn goyrl zayn der shmid,
Kh'vel nokh oyf hitlers keyver tanstn!
Ikh bin a Yid! (104–11)

[On this soil I will thrive,
Whatever the enemy may do,
The liberty of the world we shall save.
I shall dance on Hitler's grave.
'I am a Jew!']

At the end of each stanza, Fefer emphasizes his determination to triumph in the brief, repeated line with its exclamation mark. However, Fram is not driven by revenge:

Neyn, gliklekh bin ikh, got, vos s'hot mayn reyne hant
Nokh keynem, keynem nit gekoylet un geshundn... (27–28)

[No, happy am I God, who has not with my pure hands
Not anyone, anyone slaughtered or destroyed...]

Content that he has not shed the blood of his enemies, Fram preserves his heritage:

Neyn, gliklekher far zey — kh'bin gliklekher a sakh,
Vayl keynem hob ikh nit gelestert un gepaynikt,
Ikh bin a Yid — a Yid fun khumesh un tanekh,
Un shtarbn ken ikh shtil in frumen, zisn ta'anug. (29–32)

[No, happier than them — I am much happier,
While I have given no one suffering or pain,
I am a Jew — a Jew of Chumash and Tanakh,
And I can die quietly, in observant, sweet pleasure.]

Rather than retribution, Jewish learning provides the solace Fram seeks. In 1971, confirming Fram's link to an Eastern European literary tradition, 'Ikh bin a Yid' was reprinted in honour of 'Yehoash-yor'[18], the year of Yehoash, who has been described as 'der groyster dikhter un tanekh–iberzetser in Yidish' [the greatest Yiddish poet and translator of Tanakh].[19]

Encouraged by fellow-writer Rachmiel Feldman, who believed immigrants should immerse themselves in the life and values of their new home, Fram also looked outwards to others by placing Black men at the centre of his narrative poems. In 'Tsu di shvartse', the poet turns his focus towards those around him, responding to local stimuli.[20] The poet addresses the other directly, 'Hot keyn moyre un antloyft nisht fun mir, shvartse' [Don't be afraid or run away from me, Black man][21] (1–2) and 'S'klemt a vey oykh vi bay aykh bay mir in hartsn' [There is a choking in my heart as there is in yours] (3). Here, Fram converses with the marginalized and the voiceless man. He empathizes with the futility of the man's wanderings, hunger, and loneliness. Setting up a dialogue between them, by asking questions he becomes a witness to the circumstances of another.

He notices in particular the man's physical difference and sculpted strength, 'Ayer brust azoy geshmidt, vi fun tshugon?' [Your breast was smelted so, like cast iron?] (12). Hoping to befriend him, the poet recognizes the other's understandable hesitation, 'Nisht dershrekt zikh far dem bleykh fun mayn gezikht'. [Do not be afraid of the paleness of my face] (2). Despite these differences, they are nevertheless alike because they both bleed when stabbed or cut: 'Un ven emetser zol ayer layb tseshnaydn | Oykh fun shvartser hoyt a rizl ton fun blut!' [And when someone cuts your body | Also from black skin red blood will trickle!] (19–20). Fram also perceives that they have a similar moral outlook: 'Un oykh ir farshteyt, vos shlekht iz un vos gut' [And you too understand, what bad is and what good] (18).

When Fram wrote the poem, immigrants used the term 'shvartse' conversationally and ubiquitously as a descriptor or differentiator. Depending on context, it may also have been pejorative. The term 'shvartse' also occurs in 'Oyf transvaler erd' [On Transvaal Earth]. Although people of colour refer to themselves as Black, nowadays the Yiddish term is never acceptable. However, in the context of the poem, the form of Fram's title may be a dedication: he was empathetic to Black people's desperate plight. Further, in writing about the Other, Fram was also writing about himself, interweaving his own experiences, which mirror his own difficulties. When he first arrived in Africa, he was a *smous* [itinerant peddlar]; because he too was poor, he understood the man's struggle.

Imagining what it is like to be someone else is the core of our humanity. It is the essence of compassion, and the beginning of morality. It is hard to be cruel once you permit yourself to enter into the mind of the victim.[22]

Depicting 'the unjust racial social structure, reminiscent of [the] situation in Eastern Europe',[23] the poet recognizes their kinship, 'Ikh farshtey aykh, un ikh trog mit aykh tsuzamen | Ayer freyd un ayer shvaygendike peyn' [I understand you and I carry with me like you | Your happiness and silent pain] (5–6). In 'identifying with the Blacks as an oppressed people',[24] the protagonist represents 'humanity persevering through overwhelming hardships'.[25] The poet also goes further, 'Un ir trogt in zikh vi mir di zelbe laydn | Un ikh vart azoy vi ir oyf ayer likht' [And you carry like me the same suffering | And I too am waiting for His light] (3–4); the motif of 'likht' appears in the last stanza with one significant alteration: as 'undzer likht' (36), becomes 'ayer likht', 'our light' becomes 'your light', they both hope for relief.

As a narrative example of this outlook, Fram's epic 'Matatulu' places the heroic Black man centre stage. At the outset, Matatulu is described as a 'mentsh' (1), literally 'a man', but, more significantly here, the Yiddish word is an epithet connoting human decency. His physical stature is emphasized: 'Zayn kerper naketer iz glantsik, fet un shveys | Bashmirt mit reynem oyl fun shmekedike flantsn' [His naked body shone with fat and sweat | Smeared with pure oil from aromatic plants] (10–11), and also his sense of well-being: 'Ho, gezunter, yunger, shtarker Matatulu!' [Ho, healthy, young and strong Matatulu!] (109).

Matatulu is hardworking with 'dem koakh funem oks, di flinkayt fun zhiraf' [the strength of an ox, the agility of a giraffe] (17), and the power of 'der odler, di pantere' [the eagle and the panther] (45). These comparisons underscore his animality, innocence, and freedom. As Matatulu relishes the warmth of the sun, 'vi gut, vi varem s'iz di groyse zun' [how good, how warm is the great sun] (9), content with his situation, 'Zayn ponim iz bagosn mit a breytn shmeykhl' [His face is filled with a broad smile] (20). Living there,

> Er bedarf do gornisht inem bush; keyn shikh, keyn kleyd,
> Zayn beged iz di fel fun a shakal.
> Zayn hoyz — on dort der erdisher rondavel. (23–25)
>
> [In the bush, he needs nothing more, neither shoes or clothes;
> He covers himself with the skin of a jackal.
> His house is a mud rondavel.][26]

Befitting the tradition of his people, he is also an assured hunter, 'Ven er yogt nokh mit "assegai" un blankn shpiz | A tsiterdikn hirsh, vos falt farblutikt in di derner' [When he chases with his assegai[27] and shiny spear | A quivering deer falls bloody to the ground] (52–53). And then:

> Ho, s'iz groys di freyd — a shprung, a tsi, a ris,
> Er heybt di khaye oyf bagaystert far di herner
> Un shlept zi inem kral arayn dan vi a gvar. (53–55)
>
> [How great is the joy — a spring, a twist, a turn,
> He grabs the animal by its horns
> And drags it to his kraal,[28] like a strong man.]

Because Yiddish is 'in dialogue with other languages and cultures [...], dialogue across the boundaries of individual and group identity [is part] of its tradition'.[29] By including local Zulu hunting and marriage customs, the Yiddish poem becomes representative of a crossover between cultures. Additionally, the inclusion of terms such as *lobola*, *assegai*, and kraal exemplifies how Yiddish may function as a 'fusion language'.[30] In reverse, by introducing the Black man as a 'gvar' (55), Fram connects

Matatulu to his grandfather, also described as 'a gvar, a farbroynter fun zun' [a strong man browned by the sun] ('Baym zeydn', 17). Further, Matatulu 'hot zikh oysgerut in bush-feld vi der boym' [rested in the Bushveld like the tree] (71), and the poet's grandfather too was most at home in 'pukhiker velder' [downy woods] ('Baym zeydn', 17). This fluidity allows Yiddish to play 'a major role in the concept of Jewish literature as both a local and a transnational phenomenon',³¹ where in-between, transitional communities either protect or abandon their original culture. By adapting to the new society, their 'affinities and alliances [may] cross national boundaries.'³²

All goes well for 'der shtarker Matatulu' [the powerful Matatulu] (57), until he longs for a wife; 'Ayede khayele in dzhungl, veys er, hot zayn por, | Es hot di shlang afile zikh gefunen do a vayb' [Every animal in the jungle, he knows, has his partner. | Even the snake has found himself a wife.] (79–80). In order to fulfil this need, Matatulu is required to pay his future father-in-law *lobola* [a mutually agreed-on bride price], in this case fourteen oxen. To do so, 'Er loyft bagaysterter tzu yener groyser shtot | Fun vos er hot azoy fil vunder shoyn gehert' [He runs enthusiastically to the big city | Where he heard there were many wondrous things] (100–01). He then decides 'nisht lebn merer punkt vi der volf fun royb' [to live like a wolf from prey no longer] (106). Abandoning his jackal skins, he instead 'trogt shoyn hoyzn mit a hemd, mit zokn, | Un vestlekh hot er azoy fil, un shvere unbakveme shikh' [wears trousers with a shirt, with socks, | And he also had many vests, and heavy, uncomfortable shoes] (117–18). His altered clothing and manner signal what he has lost.

> In shtot hot Matatulu, mit der tsayt, gebitn zikh ingantsn
> Der bush, di vayte stepes oysgeleygte zunike un fraye,
> Dort vet er shoyn far di levones merer zayne tents nisht tantsn. (110–12)
>
> [In the city, in time, Matatulu changed completely,
> [Away from] the bush, the wild plains, spread out in sunny freedom,
> There where he will never again dance under the moon.]

When he lived in the wild like the eagle and panther, ox and giraffe, Matatulu was the epitome of nobility; as such, the depiction may be related to the stereotype of the 'noble savage'. Once in the city, he became regarded as a mere 'khaye', a lowly 'animal' (1, 12, 114, 216), a 'hunt', a 'dog' (116) because of the way his white boss treats him. 'Zayn modne arbet vaybershe gefalt im azoy shver' [He has to do womanly work which he finds very hard] (121). Matatulu's white employers 'veysn zey den nisht, az s'iz zayn yikhes groys' [remain unaware of his great honour] (133) amongst his own people, where he 'kon zey zikher keynem nisht farshteyn' [cannot understand anyone] (137). So he loses his identity and sense of himself: 'Er ken aleyn zikh poshet nit derkenen ver er iz' [He himself does not know who he is] (122), and instead 'dremelt ayn farbenkter nokh zayn kral' [dreams with longing of his kraal] (155), and 'tulyet zikh atsind tsu zikh aleyn fun shrek vi a faryogte khaye' [comforts himself alone in fear like a pursued animal] (113). Where the animal imagery once showed Matatulu's power and self-sufficiency in his familiar environment, it now indicates his fall from grace as an outsider.

The bloody death of the deer earlier in the poem and the image of 'di zun zikh ayngetunkt in blut' [the sun itself had become dipped in blood] (187) portend what is follow. Where Matatulu used to be the hunter, he becomes the hunted, the white man's prey. While 'Matatulu shtelt zikh op nokh oyf a vayle in "lokeyshn"' [Matatulu spends time in the location][33] (193), the police patrol for offenders. Matatulu hears a voice in the dark, 'Vu flistu, tayvl eyner? ... shtey, dayn "speshl"'[Where are you going, you devil? ... wait, your 'special'][34] (209). When he makes a run for it, 'Men nemt im vi a vilde khaye iber ale gasn yogn' [They chase him through the streets as if he were a wild animal] (216). Whereas he used to hunt deer for his beloved near his kraal, now instead,

> In finsternish a fayerdiker shos...
> S'iz Matatulu oyf der erd glaykh vi a leyb gefaln
> Un bislekhvayz es gist zikh oys fun im zayn blutiker fardros... (218–20)

> [In the darkness a shot rings out.
> Matatulu's body falls to the ground
> And slowly his bloody sorrow pours out...]

Once healthy and youthful, all that remains of Matatulu's strength is 'Der letster tsapl mit zayn toyter fus' [The one last tap with his dead foot] (224); having lost his innocence, the only way out for him is death.

Thus, place provides a crucible for the friction between and melding of 'social and cultural meanings that reflect histories and backgrounds, including a worldview shaped by the experience of ethnicity [and] race'.[35] As the 'concept of the transnational [...] in history and literary study [...] aims to give voice to marginal groups *within nations*',[36] Fram's poems endorse his rich ethnic background, while also engaging with that of his new environment. In addition, Yiddish is always 'in dialogue with other languages and cultures' and 'dialogue across the boundaries of individual and group identity'[37] is part 'of its tradition'.[38] In reflecting the binaries of the poet's Jewish and South African identities, the integration of these texts far from the epicentre of Yiddish provides a useful prism to illuminate a cross-cultural dynamic. Where conflict continues to flare up around issues of race and colour among members of multicultural and multilingual migrant communities, the poems instead envisage dialogue between them.

Notes to Chapter 3

1. *Lider*, p. 77; *Antologye*, ed. by Rozhansky, p. 293.
2. *A shvalb oyfn dakh*, p. 69; *Di yidishe post*, 20 May 1938, n. p.; *Dorem Afrike* (July–August 1971), 23.
3. Starck-Adler, 'Multilingualism and Multiculturalism in South African Yiddish', p. 157.
4. *Lider*, pp. 19–21.
5. *A shvalb oyfn dakh*, pp. 89–92; *Dorem Afrike* (December 1953), 17–19.
6. Irena Klepfisz in Shreiber, 'The End of Exile', p. 277.
7. Cedric Ginsberg, Email to the author, 23 September 2011.
8. Starck-Adler, p. 162.
9. Pentateuch, the Bible.
10. Canonical Hebrew texts.
11. Itzik Fefer, 'Ikh bin a Yid' [I am a Jew], in *A shpigl oyf a shteyn* [A Mirror on a Stone]: *An*

Anthology of Poetry and Prose by Twelve Soviet Yiddish Writers, ed. by Khone Shmeruk (Jerusalem: The Magnes Press, 1987), pp. 694–97.

12. Itzik Fefer, 'I Am a Jew', in *An Anthology of Modern Yiddish Literature,* ed. and trans. by Joseph Leftwich (The Hague: Mouton, 1974), pp. 321–24.

13. While Fefer does not use inverted commas to indicate speech, Leftwich's translation does.

14. Gennady Estraikh, 'Fefer, Itsik', *YIVO Encyclopedia of Jews in Eastern Europe* (6 August 2010) <https://yivoencyclopedia.org/article.aspx/Fefer_Itsik> [accessed 3 July 2020].

15. See Chapter 1.

16. Estraikh, 'Fefer, Itsik'.

17. Ibid.

18. *Dorem Afrike* (1971), 23.

19. Ibid.

20. Sherman, 'David Fram Centenary Tribute', p. 4.

21. Zulu, Xhosa, or Sesotho.

22. Ian McEwan, 'Only Love and then Oblivion: Love Was All They Had to Set against their Murderers', *The Guardian*, 15. September 2001 <https://www.theguardian.com/world/2001/sep/15/september11.politicsphilosophyandsociety2 > [accessed 7 December 2020].

23. Starck-Adler, 'Multilingualism and Multiculturalism in South African Yiddish', p. 168.

24. Davis, p. 46.

25. Ibid.

26. Traditional hut with mud walls and thatched roof (Afrikaans).

27. Traditional Zulu hunting weapon.

28. Traditional hut with mud walls and thatched roof.

29. Wirth-Nesher, 'Tradition, the Individual Talent, and Yiddish', p. 3.

30. Levy and Schachter in Wirth-Nesher, 'Tradition, the Individual Talent, and Yiddish', p. 7.

31. Ibid.

32. Levy and Schachter in Wirth-Nesher, 'Tradition, the Individual Talent, and Yiddish', p. 7.

33. Official and separate Black informal settlements, here probably either Alexandra or Soweto townships.

34. A 'special paper', i.e. a 'pass' (*dompas*), the identity document that every Black person was required by law to carry at all times during the apartheid regime, which allowed them to move around.

35. M. Langfield, 'Lost Worlds', in *Place and Displacement* ed. by Cesarini, Kushner, and Shain, pp. 29–42 (p. 32).

36. Levy and Schachter in Wirth-Nesher, 'Tradition, the Individual Talent, and Yiddish', p. 7.

37. Wirth-Nesher, 'Tradition, the Individual Talent, and Yiddish', p. 8.

38. Ibid.

CHAPTER 4

A Panorama of Portraits

Many of Fram's poems resonate with empathy. Looking back and looking forward, he describes his familiars in a Lithuanian setting, and also the strangers he encountered. Later, in South Africa, the lyric and epic forms of 'Baym zeydn' [At Grandfather's] (1925–26)[1] and 'Reb Yoshe un zayn gortn' [Reb Yoshe and his Garden] (1927),[2] are reminiscent of Kulbak's 'Raysn' [Byelorussia],[3] Chaim Nachman Bialik's poem 'Mayn gortn' [My Garden], and Shaul Tchernichowsky's idylls.[4] Transporting the Eastern European tradition to South Africa, 'In a zunikn tog' [On a Sunny Day] (1930)[5] is nevertheless set in Lite. The influence of the men Fram admired then finds a parallel with the protagonists of 'Matatulu' [Matalulu], discussed in Chapter 3, and 'Matumba' [Matumba] (1983).[6] *Efsher* [Perhaps] paints a picture of the unequal power dynamic after the discovery of gold on the Witwatersrand[7] in the 1880s. In 'Vert den gringer derfun' [Where Lies the Comfort?] (1929),[8] Fram also noted the cruel impact of discrimination.[9]

Katherine Hite refers to empathy as a 'reaching for [...] someone both familiar and unfamiliar',[10] where literature may offer a 'special kind of conduit for sympathetic feelings',[11] and several of Fram's poems evoke compassion for the Other. They emphasize Fram's 'liberal inclinations' and 'his strong belief in human equality and brotherhood',[12] where his humanism led to his identification with the Black people poetically and politically.[13] 'Fun shop tsu shop' [From Shop to Shop][14] and 'Tsu di shvartse' [To the Black Man], discussed in Chapter 3, mirror their daily struggles, 'an expressive act that lays the groundwork for recognition'.[15] In contrast, 'Burn' [Farmers and/or Afrikaners][16] describes the lives of local whites, the Boers. As Yiddish-speaking immigrants interacted with others, they 'negotiated enormous moral and cultural shifts and modified [...] their ethics',[17] which Fram exposes in 'Dimantn' [Diamonds].[18] In these poems, Fram exposes racial and political discrimination and their repercussions on social behaviour.[19]

With the backdrop of forest and field, Fram's verse monologue 'Baym zeydn' conjures his boyhood visits to the family farm. Witnessing the day-to-day life there, he highlights his close relationship with his grandfather, 'a gvar, a farbroynter fun zun un pukhiker velder' [a strong man browned by the sun and downy woods] (17). He admires his 'pleytstes tsevaksene, breyte un hoykh | Farbroynte vi bronzene harbstn mit gilderne shtralen bazunte' [well-developed shoulders, broad and tall | Browned like bronzed autumns with gold sunny rays] (23–24). Rooted in the soil, enjoying a symbiotic relationship with nature, like Reb[20] Yoshe and Reb Itshe in two other poems, the old man seems in touch and in tune with the land, 'Es hobn geshmekt zayne kleyder in reykhes fun tsaytike felder' [Whose clothes were steeped with the aroma of ripe fields] (18), reliant on and mirroring its seasons and rhythms. Fram's Romantic 'tendency to hero-worship'[21] of 'Baym zeydn' echoes Kulbak's epic cycle 'Raysn'. Set near Vilna, it also describes the simplicity of the lives of his forebears who were farmers too. In depicting an intimate connection with nature,[22] the poems share an idealized atmosphere: 'O, der zeyde fun Kubelnik iz a yid a posheter, | A poyer mit a pelts un mit a hak un mit a ferd...'[23] [Ah, my grandpa in Kubelnik is a simple sort of fellow; | A farmer with a horse and with an ass and with a sheepskin...] (1–2).[24] Here, Kulbak, like Fram, focuses on the heroic figure of his *zeyde*, and also 'Yidn proste, yidn vi di shtiker erd' [As common as the clay are all] (4), who 'Un dem gantsn tog gehorevet vi khlopes' [Toil the live long day like ordinary peasants] (6). Their exhaustion afterwards is clear:

> Der zeyde, o, der zeyde kletert koym aroyfet oyfn oyvn,
> Er iz der altitshker baym tish antshlofn shoyn gevorn,
> Nor di fis — zey veysn, firn zey aleyn im op tsum oyvn...
> Dem zeydns gute fis, vos dinen im kama yorn... ('Raysn', 9–12)

> [Grandpa — ah, my grandpa ... he can hardly climb the oven
> Half asleep at supper, his poor old eyes kept closing;
> And yet, his feet have somehow found their own way to the oven;
> My grandpa's loyal feet, which served him for so many years.]

The accretion of visual detail brings the farmer to life, 'Er hot in di velder di shvartse getogt un genekhtikt tsuzamen' [He spent days and nights together in the woods] (21), where he harvested 'bulbes' [potatoes] (20) and 'burikes royte, gezunte' [healthy red beets] (22). The tone is affectionate and respectful as Kulbak observes the older man going about his daily activities.

As a boy, Fram learnt the skills of planting and picking directly from one who was 'bound to the earth, to life [...] like the soil of a garden which prefers potatoes to roses',[25] as well as the religious rituals as he watched his grandfather's commitment to morning prayers,

> Tut oyset pamelekh der zeyde fun kop zayne tfiln
> Un geyt unz tsu vekn: — di bulbes iz tsayt shoyn tsu grobn.
> Nor mir viln keyner dem shlof aza zisn tseraysn. ('Baym zaydn', 35–37)

> [Slowly he took off his *tfiln*[26] from his head
> And went to wake us — the potatoes were ready for picking,
> But none of us wants to tear ourselves away from our sleep.]

Cognizant too of how the other man contains his temper and keeps his own counsel, the poet observes how, even when annoyed, he continues working:

> Un beyz iz gevezn der zeyde un tomid fun shvaygn gehaltn,
> Gebrodzshet tsevishn di yodles in mokh dem tseshoybertn, kaltn,
> Biz zun flegt oyf shpitsn fun beymer a royte zikh zetsn farleshn. (23–27)

[And when he became angry, my grandfather diligently kept silent,
Plodded between the firs through the dishevelled, cold moss,
Until the red sun disappeared behind the peaks of the trees.]

However, there were times when his patience wore thin and he reprimanded the children: 'Nor plutsim a brum tut der zeyde: "vos shteytstu di hent in di bokes? | S'i shpetike nakht dokh gevorn, shoyn tsayt dokh dos ferdl tsu shpanen"' [But suddenly grandfather growls: 'Why are you standing with your hands on your belly? | It's already late at night, it's time to harness the horse'] (80–81).

These stanzas display a 'sensitivity and openness to responses',[27] as Fram realizes that his taciturn forebear, though solid as pine trees, is not always a paragon. He also takes time to relax and view the outcome of his labours,

Lozt langzam, pamelekh baym zayt funem vogn zikh sprayzn,
Un s'knoylt zikh gedikht fun zayn pipke a roykh a farnepelter, groyer,
In shtilen baginen farflokhn in zilberne krayzn.
Tsufridn fartsiter dem roykh in di lungn mit etlekhe tsien. (42–45)

[Very slowly he would stride beside the wagon,
And a grey foggy smoke would thread thickly from his pipe,
In silver circles in the quiet dawn.
The smoke thrills in his lungs with each satisfied draw.]

As the old man makes his weary way home, the smoke from his pipe mingles with the dawn light, his 'hent hobn zayne geshvartst zikh' [his hands blackened] (20) after work; only then 'hot zikh geaylet shoyn der zeyde in khate di vetshere esen' — did 'my zeyde [hurry] to his home to eat dinner' (28). Here, Fram pictures someone comfortable within himself, settled in his environment, and dedicated to his work, even though his labour is tiring and hard. At the end of the day, a warm hearth awaits him; there his neighbours gather to chat and celebrate together:

Un do, in dem kleynem, faroykhertn shtibl mit blotike, erdike diln,
Do flegn shadkhonim fun gegent farforn, di mumes shidukhim do reydn.
Do kumn klezmorim oyf mazel tovs, simkhes, oyf khasenes freylikhe shpiln.
Un ale — me shpirt zikh gemitlekh un heymish baym altn yishuvnik,
                                                    dem zeydn. (182–85)

[And here, in the small, smoky room with muddy, earthen walls,
The matchmakers journeyed from afar, spoke about the engagements.
They offered their good wishes and played musical instruments at celebrations
                                                    and weddings.
And all — felt cozy and happy at the old village Jew's, my grandfather.]

This hardworking farmer, in tune with the land and his surroundings then became Fram's poetic prototype. Reb Itshe, in 'In a zunikn tog', is similar in both stature and his connection to nature: 'Un ot, in aza min baginen gezesn aleyn iz reb Itshe | In hoyf oyf a kupe mit kletser, gevaremt zikh unter di shtraln' [And here in the faint dawn Reb Itshe sits alone | In the yard on a heap of wood, warming himself in the sun's rays] (45–46). In this way, Reb Itshe savours the smell of the 'frishe' [fresh] (47) dawn, the 's'bliyen dos frukhtbeymer' [blooming of the fruit trees] (51) and the 'bletelekh roze' [the 'rose petals'] (53) that sway in the breeze.

Similarly, the central character in Fram's 'Reb Yoshe un zayn gortn'[28] is a forest Jew who knows every berry and mushroom by name. This poem emphasizes the synergistic relationship between the man and the land, alternating between them: 'Si Yoshe alts a hant, fun altsding vil er visn: | A burikl, a mer, an ugerke mit pupn' [So Yoshe wants to know it all, as if filling his hand: | A little beetroot, a carrot, a cucumber with pips] (13–14). With characteristic nostalgia, the poet describes the forest Jew who, season by season, planted and tended his crops of radishes, cucumbers, beetroots, and 'aportn', Lithuanian apples, until the time came to gather them, and to crush delicious juice from the berries,

> Dan yedn shtiln herbst klaybt Yoshe zikh tsuzamen
> Di yagdes in a flash un tsukert ayn mit bronfn.
> A zeltener getrank, vos shmekt in toyzent tamen. (41–43)

> [Every quiet autumn Yoshe gathers
> The berries in a bottle with sugar and liquor.
> A special drink that tastes of a thousand flavours.]

Once he has picked his crops and savoured the fruits of his labours, Reb Yoshe is content:

> Dan kvelt er on fun freyd, vos shpart fun ale zaytn
> Fun hartsn un fun dr'erd, fun kelmishn un tsvaygn.
> Un s'trogt zikh aza glik arum in tife vaytn;
> Un altsding horkht zikh tsu tsum shabesdike shvaygn. (125–28)

> [Then he beams with happiness, which flows from every side
> From heart and from earth, from tree stumps and branches.
> And such joy fills the entire expanse;
> And everything takes heed of the Sabbath-like quiet.]

This description draws attention to the close relationship between the man and his natural environment. Joy courses through his 'hartsn' [heart] (126) and from the 'erd' [earth] (126), as the sap flows through the trees, with the aura of 'shabesdike shvaygn' [Sabbath-like quiet] (128).

Confirming how 'empathy is more readily induced from those who seem like us',[29] the poem focuses attention on someone who is at peace with his environment that the poet knows so well. As he enjoys the designated day of rest, the description is reminiscent of 'Ikh benk' [I long],[30] with its 'association with [...] people, families, communities and the intangible values they share'.[31] The poet recognizes the arduous life and 'poyerisher pratse' [peasant toil] (4), the 'shvere farmaterter vokh' [exhausting weekday gloom] (8) in the 'groyer, farshvigener velt' [grey silent world] (16). He also understands their fatigue.

In Fram's lyric 'Fun shop tsu shop', on the other hand, the central character's dislocation and alienation reflects his own. Set in the Transvaal,[32] the Black man leaves the rural area where he was born to earn a living in the city. The poet's 'emotional response comes with respect [rather than] objectification'.[33] Having once been a *trayer*,[34] earning a living in any way he could, Fram understood the struggle. Hence, instead of distancing himself, empathy is his 'affective component of understanding'.[35]

Azoy a gantsn tog — fun shop tsu shop —
Iz er arumgegangen betlendik a dzhob[36] —
A shtikl arbet zol men im vu gebn. (1–3)

[A whole day like this, from shop to shop
He went round begging for a job —
Hoping someone would give him a bit of work somewhere.]

Although unable to speak the stranger's language, the poet nevertheless perceives the parallels between them. However, he 'resists full identification with, and the appropriation of, the experience of the other'.[37] Instead, he points out the protagonist's physical strength in his purposeful attempt to make a life for himself against the odds: 'Er iz geven yung un kreftik vi an ayzn | Un dafke hot zikh im gevolt nokh lebn' [He was young and strong as iron | And yes, he still wanted to live] (4–5). As the labourer trudges on, his difficulties weigh him down, and no one takes pity on him: ' "Vork, ay vont tu vork … may bas, ay vont a dzhob" … | Nor keyner ruft zikh oyf zayn betenish nit op — ' ['Work, I want to work, my boss, I want a job' … | But no one responds to his begging —] (15–16). Here, the poet's compassion evokes the other's hopeless plight; but though he identifies with him, 'the experience of the other is not [his] own':[38]

Derlangt men mer nit shtil a shokl mitn kop:
Neyn, nito keyn arbet do, farshteyst? — Neyn! …
Un vider veys er vayter shoyn nit vu tsu geyn. (17–19)

[They give him nothing more than a shake of the head:
No, there is no work here, understand? — No! …
And once again he does not know where to turn.]

Unlike the poet, the shop owners from whom the Black man seeks employment have no sympathy for him:

Er hot azoy fil gute, vayse mentshn shoyn gezen
Un keyner hot zikh iber im a hungerikn nit derbarmt
Mashmoes, keyner darf nit hobn do zayn pratse un zayn shveys. (21–23)

[He has already seen many good, white people
And no one yet has taken pity on him in his hunger,
Presumably, no one here needs his labour and his sweat.]

Plagued by the memory of his last meal, the man's hunger overtakes every other need: 's'triknt im di shpayekhts azh fun hunger in zayn moyl' [when hunger still dries the saliva in his mouth] (30), and his hopelessness is embedded in the trudging rhythm of the lines,

Iz kayklt er zikh iber shtot a gantsn tog,
Punkt vi a shvarster knoyl
Un benkt farkhalisht nokh a bisl proste 'mili-pap'[39] —
Di tsayt gedenkt er shoyn nit ven er hot dos gliklikher gehat. (31–35)

[And he rolls around the city the whole day
Like a black ball
And starving longs for a bit of simple mielie pap —
He does not remember the last time when he had some.]

While Fram would have hankered after the traditional 'burekes' [beetroot] (22) and 'bulbes' [potatoes] (20), the Black man craves his porridge. His mouth waters as he imagines how he would

> Shepn shporevdik mit alemen fun heysn blekh
> Dos aynkaykln in zayne shvartse hent s'zol vern shvarts vi pekh
> Un nokhdem leygn dos mit groys hanoe in zayn moyl. (37–39)

> [Scoop up carefully from a hot tin with everyone
> Rolling it in his black hands so it becomes as black as pitch
> And then putting it in his mouth with great pleasure.]

As he rolls the *mili-pap* from one hand to the other to cool it, ash and charcoal coat his hands. The use of the vernacular for porridge indicates the poet's hyper-awareness, which draws him closer to the other, whilst still maintaining his separateness. This 'desirable empathy involves not full identification but what might be termed empathic unsettlement',[40] enabling visibility in the face of diversity, in preference to discriminating 'on the basis of overrating and glorification, or contempt and inferiority'.[41] Thus, while the poet observes 'merging patterns and correlations',[42] he recognizes that the 'other's loss is not identical to [his] own'.[43] Written by a Yiddish-speaking white immigrant and steeped in the language and customs of the local inhabitants, 'Fun shop tsu shop' and 'Tsu di shvartse' are unique for their time.

Like Fram's 'Baym zeydn', 'Reb Yoshe un zayn gortn', and 'In a zunikn tog', the long poem 'Matumba' idealizes the ordinary man. Fram transfers the emphasis from himself, the uprooted male, to people such as Matatulu and Matumba; in an alien and hostile environment, they too have lost their identities.

As Dominic LaCapra describes 'a kind of virtual experience through which one puts oneself in the other's position',[44] the narrative of Matumba's downfall, which illustrates how the urban environment can destroy the uprooted and despised outsider, may be related to the poet's own unsettlement as well as those of his Yiddish readers.[45] Like many Jewish immigrants, who had settled in remote towns and villages and only later moved to cities, Fram could identify with the rural village life of the Blacks.

Fram's affinity for the suffering hero echoes an abiding theme of the Romantic poets. Reminiscent of a folk song, 'Matumba' is written in quatrains, each a complete unit that moves the plot towards its climax. 'Grant[ing] a special value to outcast figures'[46] who bond with the land in a mutually beneficial relationship, they also romanticize the peace of country life. The poem describes Matumba's former life, his migration to the city, his sense of alienation as the Black underdog, and his interaction with his white employer.

In the Bushveld, Matumba lives peacefully with his family and livestock,

> Matumba iz gekumen fun vaytn kral,
> [...]
> Ergets-vu in a vinkl fun Transvaal,
> Iz gebliben zayn royte, erdishe khate. (1, 2–4)

[Matumba came from a distant kraal⁴⁷
[...]
Somewhere in a corner of the Transvaal,
His red, simple home remained.]

He also had 'dray vayber | Tsu pashn in kral zayne ki' [three wives | To look after his cattle in their kraal] (5–6). These descriptions reveal aspects of kraal life, the shared customs and sense of community that were left behind. Consequently, like Fram's community, the uprooting of indigenous Black people led to their sense of alienation.

When Matumba leaves home to work for white employers in the city, losing his home, his family, and a traditional way of life lived close to the soil, he falls victim to the white man's pass laws.⁴⁸ In the cultural clash between the traditional customs of lobola⁴⁹ and polygamy as opposed to the Europeans' monogamy, tensions between and misunderstandings about these contribute to Matumba's personal calamity.

The description also embodies the poet's 'affective response';⁵⁰ and his admiration for his grandfather carries over to the stranger's circumstances. The use of the term 'khate' [home] in 'Matumba' (1), referring to Matumba's mud hut, creates a congenial link to the old man's wooden farmhouse in 'Baym zeydn' (28). Both the poet's *zeyde* and the tribal chief Matumba were content with their idyllic way of life:

> Er iz gevezn tsufridn mit dem vos er hot shoyn gehat,
> Er hot gevust, az er hot zayne vayber shtark holt
> Un shlofn hot er gekont mit zey tsu zat. (22–24)

> [He was happy with what he already had,
> He knew that he loved his wives greatly
> And he could sleep with them to his fill.]

However, as is tribal custom, there is also Matumba's obligation to pay lobola of twelve oxen for his favourite wife Sesula, who was 'Vi a zeltener ferd in stadole' [Like a rare horse in the herd] (32).

In line with his Romantic perceptions, Fram perceives Matumba's existence as blissful, like his grandfather's. However, Matumba is 'tseraysn' [torn] (36) away when he must go to earn money for taxes, which 'ober dray yor gehat nisht batsolt' [he had not paid for three years] (39). He leaves the security of his enclave, 'Ale dray vayber ... bay zikh aheym. | Oy, hot er zikh biter zey dan gezegnt [All three wives ... behind at his home | Oy, how bitterly he bade them farewell] (45–46). Matumba, like Fram's *zeyde*, was used to the settled existence, and city life comes as a shock to him. However, the poem is not the platform for the poet's political opinions. Instead, his sympathy emerges as Matumba's life unravels.

His working conditions are demeaning; as a result his loss of status, he also loses his strength, 'Itst ligt er azoy vi a kretsiker hunt | Un klaybt brekelekh fun tish bay dem vaysn' [Now he lies like a scratching dog | And collects scraps from the table of the whites] (67–68). Sapped and belittled, 'Iz Matumba gevorn farshrumpn fun tsar, | Er hot zikh ingantsn gebitn' [Matumba shrank with grief, | He became completely changed] (81–82). He longs for 'zayn khate' [his home] (52), a yearning with which Fram would have identified, as was indicated in the poem 'Ikh benk'.

Matumba also wants 'Zayn "assegai" '[51] which 'hot er sheyn lang nit gesharft' [He hadn't sharpened his assegai in so long] (55), identifying him as a warrior among his own people. The protector of his clan, 'in hartsn gebrent hot a fayer' [in [Matumba's] heart there burned a fire] (56) when he becomes anxious that some ill may befall Sesula because he is not there to take care of her. Fram relates to Matumba's difficulties, having been similarly dislocated, obliged to spend endless days in the city, ground down by economic pressures.

While Matumba does the chores, dusting the house, and polishing the floors on his hands and knees, he watches his employer performing her intimate ablutions,

> Zi — ire hor flegt zi kemen,
> Halb-naket un rayznt azoy vi a leyb —
> Zi flegt zikh far im gornisht shemen. (90–92)

> [She would comb her hair,
> Half-naked and alluring like a lion,
> She was not embarrassed in front of him.]

Straightening her still-warm bed, Matumba sees her putting on her clothes, one tantalizing item at a time,

> Un tsaytvays flegt zi in shtayfn korset
> Farshnurevn hart ire brustn,
> Dan flegt er arayngeyn farbetn dos bet,
> Nokh varm fun tayve un glustn. (93–96)

> [And sometimes she would lace her breasts tightly
> in a stiff corset,
> Then he would go in and straighten the bed,
> Still warm with lust and glowing.]

The woman's seductive behaviour in his proximity as he works offers a foil to the earlier vignette in which the chieftain danced freely with his half-unclothed wives.

In a state of confusion at the sight of the white woman's state of undress, Matumba is overwhelmed with longing for Sesula, his true love.

> Un eynmol in friling hot er bay ir tir
> Gevart vi a khaye farborgn,
> Er hot zikh meshuge gevorfn oyf ir
> Un hot zi shir-shir nisht dervorgn. (101–04)

> [And once in spring by her door
> He waited like an animal concealed,
> He madly threw himself at her
> And he almost choked her.]

Unable to control himself, Matumba rapes and strangles his employer, 'Tsvey kerpers tsemisht' [Two bodies intertwined] (109), one Black and one White. Found guilty of murder, Matumba goes to the gallows alone, far from his beloved, 'Fartsitert, gefaln, Matumba iz toyt, | Oh, Sesula, Sesula' [Struck with fear, fallen, Matumba is dead, | Oh Sesula, Sesula] (119–20). Away from his familiar territory, in an alien environment, the warrior and patriarch is nothing more than a servant who loses his sense of worth and dignity — and ultimately his life. Matumba's migration and the consequent erasure of his language and culture correspond to the poet's own losses 'predicated on racist and antisemitic ideology',[52] both in Russia and then in South Africa.

Fram names his protagonists, Reb Yoshe, Reb Itshe, Matatulu, and Matumba, as well as Matumba's favourite wife, Sesula. Particularizing the Blacks by naming them was innovative, yet the white woman in 'Matumba' remains nameless and undeveloped. Thus, the poems offer 'a rare display of a Black man's subject position in any writing of this time, not only in Yiddish'.[53] The poet's concern is with the suffering incurred through differences of race, religion, or skin colour in 'dos land fun gold un zunshayn, fun vays un shvarts' [this land of gold and sunshine, of White and Black].[54]

As Fram adapted physically to his environment, his writing absorbed multicultural and multilingual possibilities. Local speech and Yiddish became interwoven, and the poems incorporate indigenous descriptors, which include 'lobola', 'assegai', 'fis-bend' [wire ankle rings], 'pikanin' [small child], 'mili-pap' and 'kraal', and the site-specific terms 'location' and 'pass', thus expanding Yiddish literary language.

The poem 'Burn' encapsulates the lifestyle of the white Afrikaner farmers in the platteland [countryside], whose language and culture differentiated them from the British white South African farmers:

> Mit halbn tog — gekumen iz a fule shtub mit gest;
> Di burn in garniters oysgeputst
> Mit breyte hit un hengendike grobe hent. (1–3)

> [At midday there was a full room of guests;
> Farmers dressed up in their best outfits,
> With broad hats and huge hands.]

In this way, the farmers enjoy a day of leisure, listening to music, talking, and relaxing as they

> Gezupt di kave fun der flakher shal,
> Zikh tsugehert geshmak tsum gramafon
> Un emese hanoe do gehat. (47–49)

> [Sipped coffee from the saucer,
> Listened with pleasure to the gramophone
> And had great enjoyment.]

Like Reb Yoshe and Reb Itshe, the eponymous farmer is also satisfied after a day in the field, surveying and harvesting his crops, and he 'Derlangt a lek dem shpits mit naser tsung | Un take zikh bagavert bay derbay' [Licked the tip [of the cigar] with a wet tongue | And really enjoyed it] (57–58). Later, in a smoke-filled room, with his neighbours keeping him company, 'Di paypn hot men oysgebitn' [The pipes were exchanged] (62). This communal leisure time is again reminiscent of the vignette in 'Baym zeydn' when the grandfather takes time out to smoke his 'pipke' [pipe] (43).

Sitting separately from their farmer-husbands, the corpulent wives are lethargic in their Sunday best,

> Di vayber zaynen do gezesn mat
> Mit kerpers ongegosene mit schmaltz,
> Mit fete geyders un mit fule brist,
> Azoy, az shver gevezn iz tsu geben zikh a rir. (3–6)

> [The wives sat there listlessly
> Bodies covered in fat,
> With fat arms and full breasts
> And it was difficult to move themselves.]

For the women as much as for their menfolk, this is the contentment that comes after the labour of the week. They relax and enjoy themselves 'Azoy hot men in eynem zikh farbrakht | Gemitlekh in der yomtovdike ru' [That is how they all passed the time | Companionably in celebratory rest] (67–68).

However, in this comfort zone, the 'burn' stridently act out the racial divide with their labourers, describing how 'Di kafers vet men oyshisn vi hint' [The kaffirs we will shoot like dogs] (43). Originally applied to Black inhabitants of Southern Africa, the term 'kaffir' also signified a non-believer.[55] Like 'shvartse', it was used in everyday speech and by many immigrant writers. After 1948, it became part of apartheid's demeaning and discriminatory verbal pantheon. Legally proscribed since 2000, anyone found guilty of such hate speech in any language faces a fine and even incarceration.

In 'Vert den gringer derfun', the poet freely expresses himself in Yiddish to alert his fellow Jewish immigrants to racial divisions and inequities around them:

> Un du kukst arum mit fardrus, un du zest,
> Vi me git, un me nemt, un me taylt, un me mest,
> Vi es tsitern hent — fule hoyfns mit gold! ...
> Nor dem, vos es kumt, iz tsu karg zayn getsolt... (16–20)

> [And wherever you glance you are filled with remorse,
> Men give and men take and still more accrue,
> And hands with abundance are swollen and coarse
> But meagre the measure to those that it's due.][56]

Disturbed by the chasm between the opportunities offered to whites and those withheld from Blacks,[57] Fram wrote,

> Un fun shefe un gob, fun tsekvolner erd
> Iz nisht alemen glaykh tsu banisn bashert,
> Un der, vos farzeyt un vos shaft un vos boyt,
> Iz bagrenetst in zun un ba'avelt in broyt. (21–24)

> [And from bounty and plenty, from gift swollen earth,
> Equal pleasure is not predetermined for all;
> And the being who scatters and labours and builds,
> Is confined in the sun, and is injured in bread.][58]

Although he reacted to these social and political conditions, the poet preferred personal engagement: 'Er vet nit shraybn kayn revolutsiyonere himnen' [He would not write any revolutionary hymns].[59]

> Iz den gringer derfun, az es tsaytikt di troyb
> Un es gildert a shtral vu-nisht-vu oyf a shoyb?
> Az oyf shoybn a sakh iz fargoshn di zun
> Vert den gringer derfun? (25–28)

> [What balm for the heart if an earlier spring
> Ripens vines or illumined some window panes
> If to many a window pane no sunbeams cling?
> What balm for the heart?][60]

In a similar vein, *Efsher* enlarges on the fate of the Black workers, and how their daily challenges impact on their lives,

> Opgerisn fun vayber,
> Fun der heym zikh opgefremdt —
> Aynzam, umetik, farklemt,
> Punkt vi blunder, shvartse verem
> In di erdishe gederem —
> Grobn zey zikh do, di kafers — (341–46)

> [Torn from their wives,
> Estranged from their home —
> Lonely, sad, grieving,
> Like blind, black worms
> In the bowels of the earth —
> There they dig, the kaffirs —]

In contrast with this darkness, the poem also reflects the majesty of the 'afrikaner goldene medine,' [African golden land][61] where 'Groyse himlen, zun un likht, | Knoylt zey zikh do gedikht' [The great heavens, sun and light | Are thickly knotted together] (348–49).[62] However, neither the golden warmth of the sun nor the earth's buried wealth will ever belong to the diggers:

> Zukhn gold far di magnatn,
> Farn gliklekhn un zatn
> Un zey benkn nokh zayn kral
> Ober do di shvere tisus
> Mitn shtoyb fun heysn gold —
> Karge, skripendike penes. (350–55)

> [Searching for gold for the magnates,
> For the happy and sated,
> They simply long for their home
> But here the heavy phthisis
> In the dust of hot gold —
> Only stingy, scraping pennies.]

After their arduous labour, the only outcomes for the workers are loneliness, illness, endless poverty, and death, 'Biz shtiln onkum funem toyt...' [Until the quiet coming of death...] (98).[63]

Later, in the verse monologue 'Dimantn', the poet explains the industry from a different vantage point. The narrative draws on his personal experiences as a diamond dealer,[64] and pinpoints the ubiquitous corruption, greed, and envy in the trade. The translation used here is the poet's own, but it does not coincide exactly with his Yiddish original.[65] Referring to himself as 'your dad' [dayn tate] (187), the poet opens his hand to show his daughter his 'brilyantn' [brilliants], to convince her of their value, 'Du zest zey, mayn kind oto-do' [You see them, my child, do you see] (1–2).

Once again, the immigrant-outsider Fram empathizes with the exploited Black labourers. However, although this situation weighs on his conscience, others 'hobn keynmol nisht bamerkt vi gelitn | Arum hobn mentshn fun hunger geshvoln' [never noticed the suffering | Of men who were swollen from hunger] (155–56). Whereas Matatulu, Matumba, his grandfather, Reb Yoshe, and Reb Itshe epitomize what it requires to be a 'mentsh' [decent man], the dealers and magnates are the opposite. Here, the narrator includes himself as he reflects on how his own ethics have deteriorated:

> Zey zaynen far mir in a finsterer sho
> Bashafn geven durkh hent umbavuste
> Durkh leydike teg un durkh oventn puste. (2–4)

> [They were collected for me in a dark hour,
> Mined by unknown hands,
> Through empty days and hollow nights.]

Thus, contrary to their bright beauty, the diamonds also bring bitterness and disillusionment, they 'frirn | In eygenem fayer' [freeze | in their own fire] (20–21). While they seemed to offer hope for a better life,

> Vos zukhn un benkn, un filn, un lekhtstn
> Neshomes farfulte mit veytog un krekhtstn,
> Vos veynen in velt vi der elnter vint.
> Neshomes fun mentshn, vos lebn vi hint... (27–30)

> [For those who seek,
> filled with longing and pain,
> and who cry out in the world like the lonely wind,
> living like dogs...]

— they soon lose their shimmer in the soulless enterprise. Those who have been corrupted by and are in thrall of the diamonds also live in darkness.

The narrator further describes how, 'Brilyantn — far dir kh'hob, mayn kind, zey gezukht' [Diamonds — for you, my child, I sought them] (30), hoping that 'Du vest vi ale zey tsiterik libn' [You would love their shimmering light as everyone else does] (34). Hence, he tries to persuade her that he did it for her benefit.

> Ikh hob nor in dimantn finster gegloybt,
> Far zey hob ikh shtil vi a betler geknit
> Un oftmol afile dem tayvl geloybt.

> [I believed in the power of the diamonds,
> For them I kneeled quietly like a beggar
> And often even praised the devil.] (36–38)

Obsessed with them, he constantly touches them,

> [...] gevisht un sortirt
> In tsimer bay shverer, farshlosener tir,
> Mit finger fartstitert [...] (48–50)

> [[...] washed and sorted
> In a room behind heavy closed doors
> With shaking fingers [...]]]

He holds them 'gevarmt in buzem' [warm to my breast] (47). His intense involvement seems to have become a substitute for his relationship with her: 'Mayn lebn fun zey hob ikh bloyz nor getrakht, | Ikh hob fun di shteyner gekholemt baynakht' [I cannot think of a life without them, | I dreamt about them at night] (52–54). In his fantasies, they light up the world around him, 'Un itst zeyer glants, zeyer kalter' [And here their gleam, their purity] (8) and 'Der glants fun brilyantn, di fayerlekhe grine, | Di fayerlekh royte, di gele, di bloye' [The gleam of diamonds, the fiery green, | The fiery red, the yellow, the blue] (14–15). He reiterates their magnificence, aware that he, like everyone else, does not see how dangerous their shimmering may be:

> Far zey hot er hel vi a shtern geblitst,
> Un azh fun der zun hot er heyser gebrent
> In zeyere karge, farfroyrene hent. (102–04)

> [And for them they shine more brightly than stars,
> As if to hold the sun that burned so hot
> in their greedy, frozen hands.]

The precious stones too are like ice, 'Mit kaltkayt fun toyter, fargliverte kelt' [With coldness of death, glazed cold] (11), and 'Dan zestu di dimantn kalt, vi zey friren | In eygenem fayer' [You see, the cold diamonds how they freeze | In their own fire] (20–21). The poet has been changed by the stones, becoming like them: 'Flegt shtendik mayn harts vern harter un harter' [My heart has hardened] (63), and 'Biz ikh hob derfilt durkh tsendlinger yorn, | Az ikh bin gevorn ingantsn farshteynert' [with the passing of the years | Has become like stone] (68–70). Instead of personal relationships, 'Di dimantn hob ikh nor kalte geklibn | Un durkh zeyer fayer farfrorn gevorn' [I chose diamonds even though they are cold | And I have become frozen in their fire] (91–92).

Hence, in order to succeed in this underworld, where people cheat to get the best deal, and are involved in crimes such as illegal diamond buying, the poet becomes their accomplice: 'In zeyere simkhes hob ikh zikh bateylikt, | Geven a farmitler fun ganeyve un mordn' [I attend their festivities and take part in their thefts and murders] (174–75).[66] He also finds himself surrounded by 'vayber fun tunkele zate haremen' [women from dark harems] (166), 'dames fun raykhe salonen' [women from rich salons] (168), as well as 'hurn in nakht oysgelasn' [naked whores of the night] (169). These women are not dissimilar to the diamonds, 'Zey hobn gekoyft un farkoyft di brilyantn, | Gehandlt, geshvindelt, geyogt' [As stones are sold and resold, they are | Handled, swindled, chased] (142–43). Their impurity also demeaned him, 'Gekukt zey farsklaft vi a hunt in di oygn' [all look [him] in the eyes as if [he] were a dog] (173). Because the diamonds had become 'heylik' [holy] (73) to him, he has been left 'elnt in velt kh'bin farblibn aleyn nor' [alone in the world] (70) with his 'oytsres' [treasure] (72).

Even the natural world mirrors his downfall: 'Der vint oyf farlozene, elnte pleynen | Far mir flegt keseyder dan veynen un veynen' [The elements too echo my pain, | and the wind too cries and cries] (79–81). He knows he leads a spiritually barren life within a degenerate and exploitative society,[67] and tries to communicate these sentiments to his daughter,

> Ikh hob vi a mentsh nisht gekont merer lakhen,
> Ikh hob nisht gekont merer gloybn un libn
> Di ale gefiln kh'hob lang sheyn farlorn. (88–90)

> [I could not laugh like everyone else,
> I could no longer believe or love.
> I have lost all feeling.]

By earning a living in a reprehensible way, the poet discarded his real diamond, his relationship with her.

Unlike him, 'Du vest mit di dimantn mayne zikh shemen' [You are ashamed to have my diamonds] (191). The girl's 'Neshome fartrakhte un yunge' [Young and thoughtful soul] (26) and high moral values contrast with his own weaknesses. While he longs for her love, the young girl's response is unequivocal, 'Un haynt, ven far dir kh'hob gebrakht mayn farmegn, | Hostu im tseshmisn in harbstikn regn' [Today, when I brought you the diamonds, | You threw them into the autumn rain] (171–72). The result is that 'Atsind inem harbst bin ikh umetik eyner | Geblibn aleyn mit di tayere steyner' [Now in autumn I am lonely and empty | Remaining alone with the valuable stones] (179–80). Once 'klor' [clear] and pure, now they are 'farsholtene', accursed. His greed for their beauty has destroyed his humanity, but she retains her value: 'Bist raykher avade, mayn kind, fun dayn tatn, | Fun yene farsholtene, klore karatn... [You are nevertheless richer, my child, than your father, | From those accursed, clear stones] (200–05). In a letter to his sisters, Nechele and Rivke, Fram confirms these difficulties, and his failures to sell 'parcels' of stones.[68] Soon after, he also expresses anger and sadness at his resulting degradation in the struggle to make ends meet.[69]

In the 1950s, Fram enjoyed a more settled lifestyle on a farm. In 'Volkns iber Hekpoort' [Clouds over Hekpoort][70] he intended to put all Africa in a poem. Only two of the five sections, describing the bush and wildlife, entitled 'In Afrike' (1978–85), were completed.[71] The unpublished pages in Fram's archives dwell on the devastating effects of drought on crops and creatures, and also evoke the lives of Whites and Blacks. By way of contrast, Fram's 'Revrend Vilyam Skot' [Reverend William Scott],[72] is 'a sensitive tribute to those whites who were struggling courageously to advance the social and political development of the Black majority in South Africa'.[73]

As conflicts caused by intolerance persist, Fram illustrates the effects of socio-political inequities in South Africa, where Jews saw an altered reflection of their previous status in Europe.[74] Even when the Jewish immigrants acquired English and/or Afrikaans, they remained a separate minority, a community distinct from the British,[75] and from the Afrikaners. Highlighting the challenges faced by minority languages and cultures, Fram compared the struggle for the linguistic and cultural survival of Yiddish with that of Afrikaans: 'We are surrounded by a greater and stronger culture against which we fight.'[76]

This chapter suggests that Fram's early encounters continued to influence him. Driven by empathy for the Other with 'a sensibility attuned to the[ir] pain',[77] his new horizons brought him heartache as well as pleasure, 'And out of the fullness of joy | Africa was on the verge of tears'.[78]

Notes to Chapter 4

1. *Lider*, pp. 147–209; *Literarishe bleter* (1925–26).
2. *Lider*, pp. 91–99.
3. Published in *Di tsukunft* [The Future] (1922), n. p.
4. Niger, p. 617. L. Goodman, 'David Fram: A Study in Growth', p. 28.
5. *Lider*, pp. 123–32.
6. *A shvalb oyfn dakh*, p. 85–88; *Dorem Afrike* (December 1953), 16–18.
7. Goodman, 'David Fram: A Study in Growth', p. 30; Niger, p. 617.
8. Lider, pp. 5–6; Amelia Levy, trans. in Goodman, 'David Fram: A Study in Growth', p. 28.
9. Zalman Levy, 'A Premier Yiddish Poet in South Africa', p. 33.
10. Katherine Hite, 'Empathic Unsettlement and the Outsider within Argentine Space of Memory', *Memory Studies*, 8.1 (2015), 38–48 (p. 39).
11. Ibid.
12. Davis, p. 48.
13. Ibid.
14. *Dorem Afrike* (July–September 1984).
15. Hannah Pollin-Galay, *Ecologies of Witnessing: Language, Place and Holocaust Testimony* (New Haven: Yale University Press, 2018), p. 26.
16. *Lider*, pp. 210–49; (extract), *Dorem Afrike* (May–June 1971), 13.
17. Rosenblatt, p. 56.
18. *A shvalb oyfn dakh*, pp. 60–64; (extract), *Dorem Afrike* (1953), 17–18. Fram whittled down the original from 200 to 135 lines. Numerous versions are located in the *David Fram Papers*, Folder 11, pp. 407–11.
19. Starck-Adler, 'South African Yiddish Literature and the Problem of Apartheid', p. 10.
20. Traditional respectful Yiddish form of male address.
21. *The Oxford Companion to English Literature*, ed. by Birch.
22. Novershtern.
23. Kulbak, 'Raysn', p. 389.
24. Ibid., p. 388.
25. Zaramb, p. 27.
26. Phylacteries.
27. LaCapra, p. 105.
28. 'The publication of this poem in the New York journal *Oyfkum* (1927) brought Fram into the international arena of Yiddish poetry', Sherman, 'What Balm for the Heart...?, p. 7.
29. Hite, p. 42.
30. *Lider*, pp. 89–90.
31. Langfield, p. 40.
32. Present-day Gauteng.
33. LaCapra, p. 40.

34. The term 'trayer' was used by the Yiddish immigrants to describe someone who tried to earn a living in any way he could (Feldman, 'David Fram at Fifty', n. p.).
35. Ibid. p. 102.
36. English names are transliterated in Yiddish in keeping with Fram's usage in the poems.
37. LaCapra, p. 103.
38. Ibid., p. 40.
39. Traditional maize meal porridge.
40. LaCapra, p. 102.
41. Ibid.
42. Shmuel Rozhanzky, trans. in Starck-Adler, 'Multilingualism and Multiculturalism in South African Yiddish', p. 158.
43. Ibid., p. 79.
44. LaCapra, p. 102.
45. Rosenblatt, p. 80.
46. *The Concise Oxford Companion to English Literature*, ed. by Drabble, Stringer, and Hahn.
47. Traditional, round mud hut with pointed straw roof.
48. 'Pass' (*dompas*). The legal identity document that every Black person was required to carry to be able to move around (cf. Chapter 3).
49. Among Zulu, Xhosa, and Ndebele tribes it is customary for the bridegroom to pay lobola to the bride's family before marriage.
50. LaCapra, p. 105.
51. Traditional hunting weapon.
52. Starck-Adler, 'South African Yiddish Literature and the Problem of Apartheid', p. 9.
53. Rosenblatt, p. 81.
54. Levy, 'Dovid Fram's arayntrit in der yidish-dikhtung un zayn shpeterdike gang', p. 38.
55. Rosenthal, p. 278.
56. Amelia Levy, trans., quoted in L. Goodman, p. 30; also quoted in Sherman, 'What Balm for the Heart', p. 8.
57. Sherman, 'David Fram Centenary Tribute', p. 2.
58. Sherman, trans., quoted in Levy, 'A Premier Yiddish Poet', p. 33.
59. Niger, p. 618.
60. Amelia Levy, trans., in L. Goodman, p. 30; also in Sherman, 'What Balm for the Heart', p. 8.
61. Sherman, 'Introduction', p. 1.
62. 'Efsher' (extract), in Zygielbaum, 'Dovid Fram's yuvil', p. 4.
63. 'Efsher' (extract), *Dorem Afrike* (August 1949), p. 21.
64. Sherman, 'Singing with the Silence', pp. 39–44.
65. *David Fram Papers*, Folder 11, pp. 407–12,
66. The translations, line numbering, and verse breaks in Fram's Yiddish poem do not coincide with his own English version. The translations in the discussion are mine.
67. L. Goodman, p. 30.
68. *David Fram Papers*, Folder 3, 207–08 (26 August 1949).
69. Ibid., pp. 209–10, letter to Rachmiel (Richard) Feldman (29 August 1949).
70. Sherman, 'What Balm for the Heart...?', p. 7.
71. Three excerpts were published: 'Afrike', *Dorem Afrike* (November–December 1978), 4; 'In Afrike' [In Africa], *Dorem Afrike* (July–September 1983), 36; 'In Afrike', *Dorem Afrike* (January–March 1985), 7.
72. *Dorem Afrike* (December 1955), 2–3; (January 1956), 10–11; (March 1956), 4–6; (May 1956), 23–25; (June 1956), 23–25; (July 1956), 3–5.
73. Sherman, 'Singing with the Silence, p. 43.
74. Sherman, 'Serving the Natives', pp. 505–21.
75. Rosenblatt, p. 59.
76. Correspondence with Afrikaans journalist and poet Ignatius Mocke in 1948, in Sherman, 'What Balm for the Heart...?, p. 9.
77. L. Hunt, *Inventing Human Rights: A History* (Norton: New York, 2008), p. 39.

78. Sherman, trans., in 'David Fram Centenary Tribute', p. 10, and in 'What Balm for the Heart...?, p. 8; from Fram's, 'Araynfir, "In Afrike"', *Dorem Afrike* (July–September 1983), p. 37. Fram's Yiddish version is unavailable.

PART III

Holocaust Memory and Representation

'Listening to a witness makes you a witness.'
ELIE WIESEL[1]

Although the havoc of the Holocaust resulted in the tragic destruction of the families, communities, and homelands of the Jews of Eastern Europe between June 1941 and December 1944, Yiddish remains central to many aspects of Jewish identity:

> [t]he field of post-war Yiddish studies has predictably been marked by erasure and loss [...] often motivated by preservation, articulated in an elegiac mode. How can it be otherwise when the object of that scholarship is a language that was nearly annihilated?[2]

David Fram was not present in Europe at the time, and thus he was neither witness to the Holocaust nor a survivor in the conventional sense. However, by continuing to use Yiddish as a living language, amalgamating past and present, he created his responses far from its locus, when 'the preservation of [his] language and culture [became] an ethical imperative'.[3] Because numerous other local writers also felt it to be 'the most sacred and crushing of obligations',[4] those years brought a 'banayen fun Yidish' [renewal of Yiddish][5] in South Africa. Publications include Dovid Wolpe's *A volkn un a veg* [A Cloud and a Way] (1978) about his imprisonment in Dachau, and Michael Ben-Moshe's two poetry collections, *Opris, Lider* [Sharp Incline, Poems] (1952) and *In likht fun ovent* [In the Light of Evening] (1971). While Sarah Aisen's[6] *Meydl lider* [Girlhood Poems] appeared before the Holocaust, in 1937, her *Geklibene lider un poemes* [Selected Lyrics and Poems] (1965) and *Shirim nivharim upoemot* [Selected Poetry] (1973) included memories of *di alte heym* [the old home] and depictions of the golden land, South Africa. Prose publications include J. M. Sherman's *In land fun gold un zunshayn* [In the Land of Gold and Sunshine] (1956). The first South African full-length novel in Yiddish, it addressed the isolation of Jewish immigrants who 'never really adjusted to life in the harsh environment of Africa [and] looked back with nostalgia to the world they left behind in Eastern Europe'.[7]

In Hyman Ehrlich's memoir of his hometown, *Dankere* [Gostini] (1956), he recalls his shtetl childhood in Russia. Nehemiah Levinsky's collection of short stories, *Der regns hot farshpetikt* [The Rains Came Late] (1959) describes the interplay between the immigrant Jews and indigenous Afrikaners. *Kalman Bulan* (1968–71), a trilogy by Mendl Tabatznik, focuses on the disruption caused by migration, and the resulting acculturation and assimilation. Joseph Sherman translated numerous Yiddish short stories in the collection *From a Land Far Off: A Selection of South African Yiddish Stories* (1987),[8] affirming the value of the language of the victims.

Such endeavours challenge Theodor Adorno's 1949 interdict against Holocaust representation and aestheticization and exploitation, insisting that 'to write poetry after Auschwitz is barbaric'.[9] Under circumstances as dire as the Holocaust, poetry's lyrical beauty would be 'an obscene contradiction',[10] doing 'an injustice to the victims'.[11] Further, he stated that to 'try and paraphrase atrocities is to diminish the experience',[12] and that any attempt to orient testimony using poetic norms, or to condense incomprehensible suffering into a few melodious lines, 'make[s] an unthinkable fate appear to have some meaning; it is transfigured, something of its horror is removed'.[13]

Referring to its 'ineffability', Elie Wiesel also contended that because 'the Holocaust transcends history, it defies comprehension'.[14] Lawrence Langer suggests further that any such representation may 'violate the inner incoherence of the event, casting it into a mold too pleasing or too formal'.[15] Berel Lang concurs with Claude Lanzmann that creative works trivialize or undermine tragedy, questioning the morality of creating any art that seeks to talk about atrocities, and the ability of language to 'express the inexpressible'.[16] Lang also adds that 'rhetoric [...] imperil[s] the humanity of its subjects'.[17] In such instances, '[s]peechlessness alone could reflect integrity, [because] to seek to portray reality with inadequate words would betray reality and the voiceless dead at its core.'[18] Simon Srebrnik, the lone survivor of Chelmo, endorsed this: 'No one can describe it. No one can recreate what happened here.'[19]

Thus, in striving to 'give form to chaos',[20] and in order to 'portray or comprehend an event that is generally regarded as unimaginable',[21] Fram's aesthetic work runs counter to proscriptions by Adorno, Wiesel, and Lanzmann that only those who had endured the Holocaust, such as Abraham Sutzkever, were entitled to represent it.

Further, while documents and archives are the accepted modes of recording history, these often prove inadequate in the face of trauma, and philosophers such as Friedrich Nietzsche 'question [their] usefulness'.[22] As what 'really happened'[23] is not made up of one linear version or one set of circumstances, straightforward facts alone are unable to provide access to real history, let alone fully acknowledge its physical and emotional horror; 'history as a discipline is inadequate for understanding'.[24] And even as documents assert their faithfulness to the facts, they may be 'pervaded by error, partiality, myth',[25] and may prove inaccurate and unreliable in telling 'what [was] experienced and witnessed'.[26] As 'questions of representation cannot be expunged from the attempt to understand the Nazi genocide [...] certain acts of representation do more than give us "the facts"';[27] what is also called for, is alternative language forms to 'witness [...] the crisis within history which precisely cannot be articulated'.[28]

Adorno later relaxed his argument, which together with those of Wiesel and Lanzmann had shaped so much scholarship, and Aharon Appelfeld, survivor-witness and writer, affirms the necessity to 'transmit the dreadful experience' of the Holocaust 'from the category of history to the category of art'.[29] Hence, in the light of reassessment, Brett Ashley Kaplan moves away from the 'insistence on the absolute impossibility of Holocaust representation towards recognizing how attempts to represent it, even if flawed, can encourage complex forms of memory work'.[30] Where a 'horrific subject [...] resulted in [something that] might be called "aesthetically beautiful"',[31] an ethical and respectful approach should be adopted to avoid trivializing or betraying the victims. As a consequence, rather than terrorizing the viewer or contributing to an ethical rupture, the '"illicit" aesthetic pleasure of unwanted beauty'[32] may in fact transform the trauma of Holocaust memory positively and 'can enhance Holocaust remembrance',[33] and by deepening the engagement with suffering[34] may 'deepen [the] search for Holocaust understanding'.[35]

Within a variety of aesthetic representations, '[p]oetry [...] inhabits an uncertain space somewhere between the specificity of history and the generality of philosophy'[36] to create a personal Holocaust narrative. Rather than deploying the factual depositions of historical documents, its multi-levels, metaphor, and multilayering reflect the 'chaotic nature of life and experience'.[37] Making no claim to be historically factual, 'literary texts are essential, if not to restore the record through speculation, then to mark the spaces, gaps and aporias that cannot be filled.'[38]

After thirteen years of poetic silence, galvanized by the disastrous news from Europe, Fram wrote *Efsher* [Perhaps], an autobiographical poem that questions all accepted values,[39] its 2500 lines written with abandon and defiance.[40] Simultaneously, his *kine* [lamentation], *Dos letste kapitl* [The Last Chapter], intertwines the predictable daily life of the peasant folk in the tradition of 'Baym zeydn' [At Grandfather's] with scenes of merciless, bloody destruction of the once-vibrant Jewish Lithuania.

Seventy-five years after the end of the war, we are in a different space than when Wiesel and Adorno put forward their arguments against Holocaust representation. As Hitler and then Stalin destroyed Eastern European Jewry and its Yiddish base, we are the last generation who have been able to hear this language spoken by survivors in the flesh. With the ever-present risks of distortion and denial of what happened, acts of recording have become all the more urgent.

Recognizing that art should not exploit or sensationalize violence, nor give comfort by softening the actuality of what occurred by offering palliative or optimistic outcomes, or false hope, the following chapters focus on Fram's Yiddish oeuvre together with the poems of ghetto-survivor Abraham Sutzkever and paintings by Marc Chagall, suggesting instead that 'unwanted beauty'[41] may 'ward off forgetting',[42] and may also make an essential 'contribution to Holocaust memory'.[43]

Notes

1. In Ariel Burger, *Witness: Lessons from Elie Wiesel's Classroom* (New York: Mariner Books, 2018), p. 1.
2. Wirth-Nesher, 'Tradition, the Individual Talent, and Yiddish', p. 8.
3. Hana Wirth-Nesher, 'Modern Yiddish Literary Studies: A Shifting Landscape', *Poetics Today*, 35.3 (2014), 211–24 (p. 213).
4. Aaron, p. 6.
5. Wolpe 'Yidishe literatur in Dorem Afrike', p. 21.
6. Also Sore Ayzen or Ayzn, or Sarah Eisen.
7. Sherman, 'South African Literature in Yiddish and Hebrew', p. 7.
8. In his introduction, Sherman credits Fram as being instrumental in encouraging the project, and for introducing him to Woolf Levick, who contributed to the translations.
9. Adorno, p. 392.
10. Ibid.
11. Ibid., p. 313.
12. Ibid., p. 362.
13. Ibid.
14. In Gary Weissman, 'Questioning Key Texts: A Pedagogical Approach to Teaching Elie Wiesel's *Night*', in *Teaching the Representation of the Holocaust*, ed. by Marianne Hirsch and Irene Kacandes (New York: Modern Language Association of America, 2004), pp. 324–37, (p. 325).
15. L. Langer, *Admitting the Holocaust*, p. 555.
16. Berel Lang, 'Introduction', in *Writing and the Holocaust*, ed. by Berel Lang (New York: Holmes and Meir, 1988), pp. 1–16 (p. 7).
17. Ibid.
18. Hilda Schiff, 'Introduction', in *Holocaust Poetry*, ed. by Hilda Schiff (New York: St Martin's Press, 1995), pp. xiii–xxiv (p. xxi).
19. In Claude Lanszmann, *Shoah: An Oral History of the Holocaust* (New York: Pantheon, 1985), p. 5.
20. Valencia, p. 265.
21. Stephen C. Feinstein, 'Mediums of Memory: Artistic Responses of the Second Generation', in *Breaking Crystal: Writing and Memory after* Auschwitz, ed. by Efraim Sicher (Urbana: University of Illinois Press, 1998), pp. 201–51 (p. 201).
22. Geoffrey Hartman, 'Introduction', in *Holocaust Remembrance: The Shapes of Memory*, ed. by Geoffrey Hartmann (London: Blackwell, 1994), pp. 1–23 (p. 3).
23. Nancy J. Peterson, *Against Amnesia: Contemporary Women Writers and the Crises of Historical Memory* (Pennsylvania: University of Pennsylvania Press, 2001), p. 7.
24. Shoshana Felman and Dori Laub in Peterson, p. 7.
25. Nietzsche in Hartman, p. 3.
26. Irving Howe, 'Writing and the Holocaust', in *Writing and the Holocaust*, ed. by Lang, pp. 174–99 (p. 182).
27. Michael Rothberg, *Traumatic Realism: The Demands of Holocaust Representation* (Minneapolis: University of Minnesota Press, 2000), p. 234.
28. Peterson, p. 7.
29. Amy Hungerford, 'Teaching Fiction, Teaching the Holocaust', in *Teaching the Representation of the Holocaust*, ed. by Marianne Hirsch and Irene Kacandes (New York: Modern Language Association of America, 2004), pp. 180–91 (p. 180).
30. Brett-Ashley Kaplan, *Unwanted Beauty: Aesthetic Pleasure in Holocaust Representation* (Urbana: University of Illinois Press, 2007), p. 6.
31. Ibid., p. 210.
32. Ibid., p. 3.
33. Ibid., p. 2.
34. Ibid., p. 1.
35. Ibid., p. 20.
36. Andrew Bennett, *The Author* (London: Routledge, 2005), p. 125.

37. Ibid., p. ix.
38. Ibid.
39. Wolpe, 'Dray periodn in shafn fun Dovid Fram', p. 17.
40. Feldman, n. p.
41. Kaplan, *Unwanted Beauty*, p. 2.
42. Marianne Hirsch, cover note for Kaplan, *Unwanted Beauty*.
43. Kaplan, *Unwanted Beauty*, p. 2.

CHAPTER 5

Holocaust Poetry of
Memory and Postmemory:
David Fram, Sarah Aisen,
Leah Benson-Rink, and Hayah Fedler

'Ikh fil, ikh trog oyf zikh tsurik di gele late'

[I feel I wear the yellow star once again][1]

Because Fram left Panevezys when he did, he escaped the Holocaust. What he lost was his family and community; what he took with him, besides his bundle of personal possessions, was his *mameloshn* [mother tongue]; what he built was a rich body of Yiddish poetry far from its original locus. His oeuvre offers useful insights into the understanding of a particular Jewish survivor experience. Where singularity implies the universal, Fram's personal narrative of loss also affords a fine-grained understanding of historical processes in a specific time and place as reflections of cultural memory and postmemory of the *khurbn* [Holocaust]. Going beyond the singular work of a singular author as object of inquiry, this chapter also discusses three other Lithuanian South African poets.

Fram's choice of Yiddish as the vehicle in which he could express himself most profoundly affirms its continued relevance while at the same time memorializing the lives of its speakers. Until the Nazis occupied Lithuania and annihilated 95% of its Yiddish-speaking community between June 1941 and December 1944, Yiddish was a fully lived language with its own rich history and literature. After the depredations of Hitler and Stalin, one third of the Jewish people had perished, and the destruction of Yiddish culture was almost total. Nevertheless, it remains central to many aspects of Jewish identity, history, and culture, with the weight of maintaining its memory shifting to subsequent generations. Many writers like Fram felt it to be 'the most sacred and crushing of obligations'[2] to save the language, providing a poetic record of an otherwise lost past, and preserving its memory.

This chapter discusses Fram's poems 'Dos letste kapitl' [The Last Chapter], 'An entfer der velt' [An Answer to the World] (1971), 'Lesterung' [Blasphemy] (1969), and 'Undzere kedoyshim' [Our Martyrs] (1969). His contemporaries, Sarah Aisen (1910–1980), Leah Benson-Rink (1892–1974), and Hayah Fedler (d. 1953), also left

Eastern Europe before the genocide. Aisen's 'Leb ikh nokh' [I Live Still] in *Geklibene lider un poemes* [Selected Songs and Poems] (1965), Fedler's 'Mayn heym' [My Home] in *Bleter-fal* [Falling Leaves] (1953), and Benson-Rink's 'Mayn kholem' [My Dream] in *Oysgetunkt in trern* [Dipped in Tears] (1954) also confirm their determination to retain the *mameloshn*.

Although they were not survivors in the conventional sense, and their poems are not about death camps, the widespread nature of the Lithuanian killing fields caused them to suffer losses in Panevezys, Zagare,[3] and Telsiai[4] respectively. Subjective, self-reflexive, introspective, and emotional, their poems incorporate deep-rooted memories of *der heym* [home], and their Jewish culture, and also nuanced representations of the Holocaust.

According to Marianne Hirsch,

> Postmemory's connection to the past is not mediated by recall, but by imaginative investment, projection and creation [...]. It is to be shaped, however indirectly, by traumatic events that still defy narrative reconstruction and exceed comprehension. These events happened in the past, but their effects continue into the present.[5]

Hence, written at a remove from the arena of destruction, their poems become evocations of postmemory.

Postmemory may also refer to 'a kind of collective, cultural memory that reflects the after-effects and after images of the multinational landscape of the Holocaust'.[6] This expanded definition articulates its reach across generations and its effects on creative expression, which 'move[s] beyond the more immediate experience of survivors towards a reflection on the traumatic events of the Nazi genocide no matter in or through which landscapes they are remembered, referenced, discussed'.[7]

The poems grapple with the tragic reality of a lost people in a shattered world. Recording the impact of the *khurbn*, they uncover and reveal the depth of the poets' personal wounds caused by the loss of family and friends. Through the use of metaphor, comparisons, description, repetition, and rhyme, they strive to express the unspeakable. In providing a valuable aesthetic space for recording history and offering testimony, where 'meaning is gained from observation and experience',[8] they function as both literature and memorial.

Fram's 'An entfer der velt'[9] directly describes what happened in the killing fields of Lithuania; its long lines, slow rhythm, and lack of stanza breaks offer no relief, as if to convey the heavy weight of mourning,

> Ikh fil, ikh trog oyf zikh tsurik di gele late.
> Fun vaytn knoylt zikh nokh fun kalkh-oyvn der roykh,
> Vu s'hot zayn letstn Sh'ma Yisroel[10] oysgelebt mayn tate,
> Vu s'hot mayn mame oysgehoykht ir letstn hoykh. (1–4)

> [I feel I wear the yellow star once again.
> In the distance there still billows the smoke from the limekiln,
> Where my father lived out his last *Sh'ma Yisroel*,
> Where my mother breathed her last breath of air.]

The central image, the infamous yellow star, is an all-too-familiar referent, as the poet imagines himself to be one of the victims, pinning the patch to his own breast. In this way, he aligns himself with them so closely that their experiences become his own. The notion of postmemory suggests a process of 're-remembering',[11] when a 'secondary [...] relationship with times and places [...] never experienced or seen'[12] may become 'vivid enough so that it feels as if they are in fact remembered'.[13] Thus, when Fram writes the poem as though he had been there and also marked for death, the poems manifest multiple levels of recuperation.

The poet's father breathes his last, his prayer merging with the billowing smoke from the chimney above the ovens. The horror intensifies with the image of the chimney with its rank cloud, and its personal impact on the poet: these are not anonymous victims, but parents and members of his community: 'Vu brider zaynen tsu dem toyt farlitene gegangen, | Vu oyfhelekh geshtelt hobn in vakl zeyer shtiln trot' [Where brothers went to their deaths with resignation, | Where infants trod their quiet shaky steps] ('An entfer der velt', 5–6). Well-aware of what awaits them, they walk wearily onward: 'Ven laykhtste shtrof gevezn iz: — 'farbren im, | Dos iz der psak — dem henkers shvartser kol' [When the lightest penalty was: 'burn him', | That is the judgment — the hangman's black voice] (11–12). Emphasizing the all-inclusiveness of the devastation, the poet enumerates the destroyed cities and victims. The enormity of the mass deaths that took place in the shtetlekh, perpetrated by the Lithuanian death squads, is juxtaposed with the stark death machines in the camps:

> Azoy zaynen gegangn Yidn tsu dem shayter —
> Fun Varshe un Pariz, fun Kovne un fun Bon.
> Milyonen hobn zikh getsoygn vayter, vayter
> Tsum shvartsn eshafot ... oy, gantse zeks milyon! (17–20)
>
> [Thus did the Jews go to the pyre —
> From Warsaw and Paris, from Kaunas and from Bonn.
> Millions were drawn further, further
> To black execution scaffolds ... oh, a whole six million!]

The haunting rhythm and the tone of disbelief and anguish augment the impact of the visual images as the perpetrators show no mercy: 'Hot men keseyder unz gehargt un gevorgn — | Vos greser s'iz der mord — alts freylekher iz zey' [They constantly killed and choked us? — | The greater the killing — the happier they are] (13–14).

The poet also despairingly notes the world's indifference and lack of intervention, 'Oyf dem — di gantse velt gekukt hot un geshvign, | Geshtanen glaykhgiltik mit aropgelozte hent', [On this — the whole world looked on and kept silent, | Stood by indifferent, with hands hanging at their sides] (21–22). That the great powers did nothing to intervene is recorded historical fact. Placing this circumstance beside the poet's emotional despair at the tragic outcome, the reader recognizes the vast and also personal implications of the inaction: 'Un meysim kupes-vayz hot men gelozn lign, | Un nokhanand gebrent, geshokhtn un gebrent...' [And they left the dead lying in piles | Burning continuously, slaughtered and burnt...] (23–24).

By creating a record of who was there, 'Dos letske kapitl' also bears witness for the men and women, grandmothers and grandfathers, brides and grooms and the children who were unable to do so for themselves,

> Oy vey iz mir, Lite — ot zaynen, ot lign —
> Azoy fil harugim: — mayn khaver, mayn bester,
> Mayn shokhn, mayn korev, mayn eynstike shvester... (72–74)

> [Oh woe is me, Lithuania — here they are, here lie —
> So many slaughtered: — my friend, my best friend,
> My neighbour, my relative, my only sister...]

In this sorrowful reflection, the poem provides an example of how 'the past remains a part of our everyday lives',[14] suggesting both a 'landscape of living memory' and a 'landscape of loss'.[15]

Like Fram, Aisen was born in Panevezys.[16] Her collection *Geklibene lider un poemes* includes the cycle *Tsu mayn folk* [To my people], in which the elegy 'Leb ikh nokh' is filled with yearning for what she lost.

> Leb ikh nokh
> un du binst toyt
> Di royte blumen zaynen royt
> Un boymer zindn zikh in gold
> Un kh'hob nokh alts dikh yingl holt. (1–5)

> [I live still
> But you are dead
> The red flowers are still red
> And the trees shine in their gold
> And still I love that young boy.]

The poem is modest and contained, with an underlying sensuality and emotional intensity. Focusing on the personal relationship, the flower image and the lively colours provide a distressing contrast to her heartache. She dresses up to visit her beloved as if he were alive, but they are mourning clothes to pay her respects, 'Tu ikh zikh on mayn nayen rok | Un shvartsn shlayer oyfn kop' [I put on my new dress | And black veil on my head] (6–7). When the evening bells clang, 'Es vart dayn shtume troyerike tir' [I wait at your quiet sad door] (10), where even the hedge seems grey. She has to walk a long way to be with her 'lost boy' (11), but no matter how long she waits she will never see him again. The final line, 'Leb ikh nokh, un du binst toyt' [I still live but you are dead] (12), repeats the first two lines of the poem, enclosing it in melancholy. The lyrical tone and attention to detail heighten the contrast with the past's happier times.

Fram's 'Lesterung'[17] also memorializes the dead. In it, the poet decries the way his Jewish compatriots were doomed, contending with his own country's aggression and the world's inaction. He also expresses anger, accusing and blaming God for what transpired: 'Hostu aleyn zey gor gefirt tsu shekhtn in Treblinke' [You yourself took them to be slaughtered in Treblinka] (70). Calling God to account in this manner is a common Jewish trope: Abraham did at the time of the destruction of Sodom and Gomorrah; Moses spoke up on behalf of the Israelites when God planned to destroy them for having worshipped the golden calf; Habakkuk, one of the Hebrew prophets, openly questioned God's workings and the inexplicability of suffering, 'O Lord, how long shall I cry, and thou wilt not hear! I cry out to thee of violence, and thou wilt not save!'[18] Further, Rabbi Levi Yitschak of Berdichev[19] in his 'Kaddish',[20] also known as the 'Din Toyre mit Got' [Lawsuit with God], questions Him on behalf of His people, demanding the reason for their punishment. In 'Lesterung', in similar fashion, Fram accuses Him directly: 'Derfar hostu di gaz-oyvns farfult mit mayne brider, | Un hostu dem gzar aroysgelozt — dayn stade tsu farbrenen? [Therefore, you loaded the gas ovens with my brothers | And pronounced your decree — to burn your flock?] (77–78).

The description of the Jewish community as His 'stade' [flock] (78), both records a pastoral way of life and echoes the psalms of the shepherd, David, for example in Psalm 23: 'The Lord is my Shepherd, I shall not want.' The peacefulness contrasts with the hellfire of the extermination camps. As a result, the poet suffers a crisis of belief and abandons all rituals. He no longer binds the leather thongs of his *tfiln*[21] around his arm and head every morning, and his *talis*[22] bag lies forgotten (35–36). Nevertheless, he also feels shame on having chosen to abandon observance when the victims were forced to do so (42–44).

Leah Benson-Rink's 'Mayn kholem'[23] recalls, like a dream, the contented life she enjoyed in Telsiai with her family before the Holocaust:

> Gehot hob ikh a tatn mit a mamen,
> Hobn zay gliklikh gelebt tsuzamen
> Mit shvester tsvey tayere un sheyne
> Un a brider a gerotene — nor eynem.   (1–4)

> [I used to have a father and mother,
> We lived happily together
> With two beautiful sisters
> And one exceptional brother.]

Then they were all taken away to their deaths, together with other families; her brother Motl was murdered in the death camp Ponar, outside Vilna.

> Un ale zaynen zey dort umgekumen
> Durkh di merder, in a tog fun zumer:
> Tate-mame, shvester un der bruder
> Der guter, grosser un barimter. (5–8)

> [And all of them perished
> By the murderers on a day of summer:
> My parents, my sisters and my brother
> The good, the strong and the renowned.]

Overcome by sorrow, Benson-Rink uses metaphorical language in order to express her pain, 'An angry/cruel wind [that] beat at my door' [Hot a vint a bayzer oyfgepralt mayn tir] (12). Her people are lost to her forever, and she cannot ever forget any of them, 'Hob ikh keynem nit gekont fargesn' (9). She cries out at lives so tragically cut short in a personal poem filled with tears. Like Fram's, Rink's poem becomes a metonymy for the millions of lost lives.

In 'Undzere kedoyshim',[24] Fram develops his themes of loss and memorialization by incorporating the Jewish mourning ritual of rending a garment as the central image and framing device. He addresses those who perished directly:

> Nokh aykh, ir brider mayne, hob ikh haynt gerisen kriye —
> Dem sharf fun heysn meser bizn leyb mit veytik ayngeshnitn
> Es shteyt nokh far di oygn mayne yene shvartse tliye
> Oyf velkher ir hot ayer toyt oyf kedushe eybiker tsebisn. (1–4)

> [For you, my brothers, I rend my garment today —
> The sharpness of the burning knife cutting through to the body with pain,
> Those black gallows still remain before my eyes
> On which your death was wrenched in eternal martyrdom.]

In tearing his shirt to mourn the dead, the poet also binds himself to those whom he refers to as 'brider' [brothers] (1), thus evoking the blood tie. Wounding himself as the blade cuts through the cloth, the act is also a poignant reminder of how his sister had lovingly sewn the garment for him ('Mayn opfor'). He feels his own physical pain as well as theirs; even when his loved ones have been wrenched away, the bond with them remains.

While the adjective 'heysn' [burning] may infer the burning of the victims at Auschwitz, extending the parameters of the poem, the reference to the 'shvartse tliye' [black gallows] (3) is metonymical, encompassing not only death by hanging, but also the other ways in which the Jewish people have been destroyed. The victims' fate seems all the more unjust to him, given their piety,

> Ikh ze aykh nokh, ir kedoyshim heldishe, ir geyt tsu der akeyde
> Mit festn trot, derhoybene fun shrek, baloykhtn mit a shmeykhl
> Azoy vi s'volt farbay a frume, shtralendike eyde
> Fun yedn gleybike tsu Gots gebenshtn heykhl. (5–9)

> [I still see you heroic martyrs, you walk towards the sacrifice
> With steadfast step, elevated in terror, illuminated with a smile
> As if were passing by, a pious radiant congregation
> Of faithful Jews towards God's holy temple.]

Unjustly, death comes while they make their way to prayer, the 'frume, shtralendike eyde' [pious radiant congregation] (7) are lit up with belief and faith, 'baloykhtn mit a shmeykhl' [illuminated with a smile] (6). His 'brothers' become 'kedoyshim' [martyrs] as they go to their 'kedushe' [martyrdom] (4), in 'heldishe' [heroic] (5) fashion.

> Ikh ze aykh nokh, giboyrim Yidishe, gehangene fun sheker
> Fun sine un fun has, un khayishe retsikhes
> In blutikn geklang fun shrayendike gleker
> Ven s'filt der talyen oys zayn merderishe shlikhes. (10–13)

> [I see you still, heroic Jews, strung up because of lies,
> In malice and hatred, and savage murder,
> In bloody peals of screaming bells,
> When the hangman fulfils his murderous task.]

The terror is heightened by the bells' death knell as the killers foment hatred to justify their deeds. The victims, who are murdered simply because they were Jewish, seem to the poet to be 'mutike derleyzer' [courageous redeemers] (14), who reach a state of sanctity after their deaths: 'Azoy min shtil un reyn, on tsorn, on gebeyzer, | Vi Got volt aykh gekusht mit getlekher neshike' [So quiet and clean, without wrath, without anger, | As if God would have kissed you with a holy kiss] (15–16).

The reward for their martyrdom is eternal life, 'Vi Got volt aykh geshikt tsu lebn vayter eybik' [As if God would have sent you to live again forever] (17); as the victims are freed from earthly travail, the poet describes how 'Geleytert ze ikh aykh, vi durkh a loyterer yeriye' [Clear and pure I see you as through a transparent curtain] (18). Within his feelings of kinship towards them, he takes pride in the way they carry themselves: 'Mispalel zayn mayn folk far aykh vet frum un gleybik | Un undzer greste shtolts — iz itster ayer tliye' [Praying my people for you, observant and believing | And our greatest pride — now is your gallows] (19–20).

During the concluding hour of Yom Kippur service, members of observant congregations have their last opportunity to ask forgiveness before the doors of heaven are closed. The poet hopes that the world will also do so after failing to save the victims:

> To rut in ayer shlof, ir yidishe giboyrim,
> Di kedushe hilt aykh ayn azoy vi tsu ne'ile.
> Farovelt vet di velt far aykh faln koyrim
> Un betln farn toyt vet zi bay aykh mekhile. (21–24)

> [So rest in your sleep, you Jewish heroes,
> Sanctity envelops you as if it were Ne'ila.[25]
> Bereaved the world will still prostrate themselves before you
> And beg forgiveness of you for this death.]

This stanza relates to how the world stood by and watched the 'akeyde' [sacrifice], analogous to the biblical binding of Isaac; a similar connection is made in 'An entfer der velt' (5, 28). Although this time there is no ram in the thicket to stay the execution, the ritual of tearing the fabric continues to bind the community together.

> Un ir bay undzer folk farblaybn vet ir heylik!
> Oy vey, lemai bin ikh nisht eyner fun der eyde!
> Mit velkher kh'volt gevolt zikh teyln ayer kheylik
> In shtoltz tsuzamen geyn mit aykh tsu der akeyde. (25–29)

> [And you will remain holy among our people!
> Oh, woe, that I am not one of that congregation!
> With whom I would have wanted to share your destiny
> And proudly walk together with you to the sacrifice.]

These concluding lines affirm the poet's kinship to those who perished, his people, his congregation, close community, martyrs and heroes, regretful that he was not with them. Since his own family perished while he survived in far-off Africa, he also infers his feelings of guilt.

Fram's poignant references to ritual and customs indicate his knowledge of Jewish observance. However, in this poem, the performance of religious rituals is also ironic: for those who were gassed and incinerated there were no graves and no Kaddish[26] was intoned. While the poet appears accepting of God's will in 'Undzere kedoyshim', his struggle is apparent in the poems 'An entfer der velt' and 'Lesterung', in which he rails against Him and subsequently abandons his own observance and faith. By providing evidence of the lives of the dead, Fram's poems provide a memorial.

Hayah Fedler's poems may also be usefully placed in the context of Marianne Hirsch's arena of postmemory. Recollecting the intimacy and comfort of family in her birthplace Zagare, she describes its destruction during the Holocaust.[27] 'Mayn heym'[28] [My Home] imagines the dark town where everyone is asleep:

> In der nakht gans oft,
> Ven alts arum shloft,
> Un di shtilkayt arum
> Azoy soydesdik shtum —
> Zet alts zikh azoy klor
> Nit vi in kholem, — nor in var... (1–6)

> [Often in the night,
> When everyone is sleeping
> And the silence around,
> So mysteriously quiet —
> I see everything clearly,
> Not in a dream, only in reality...]

However, these opening lines do not state the sinister reality that all those she loves have perished. Despite Adorno's proscription of such representation, the poet attempts to reconstruct what had occurred in the shaping of the poem.

Then, gaining courage, the poet becomes more specific: 'Zhager! Vi tayer iz mir dayn nomen, | Tsushtert, farvisht hot Hitler-Homen' [Zagare! How precious is your name | Wiped out, obliterated by Hitler-Haman][29] (31–32). The desperation of the words matches the enormity of her loss, as she uses dialogue and everyday speech to address her birthplace directly: 'Ober itst — mayne shvester, brider, tate, mamen | In groysn masn-keyver — ir ligt tsuzamen' [But now, — my sister, brothers, father, mother | You lie together in a huge mass grave] (37–38).

Overcome with remorse, she cannot forget how she left her family to perish when 'Khotsh der goyrel hot mir fun dir fartribn' [exile took me away from you] (39). Unable to take flowers to their graves, all she can do is light a candle on their *yortseyt*, in the hope that 'Eybik laykhtn ayer heyliker ner-tomid' [May your holy light burn eternally] (44). Fedler, like Fram, describes what happened to her hometown, obliterating the way of life as she remembered it. In evoking memories of place and the fate of her silenced people, the verses become a reliquary of longing and serve as testimony for all that was lost, 'In hartsn zikhroynes' [Precious memories in my heart remain] (36).

While asserting the survivors' need to 'bear witness not only to the Nazi destruction but to the world the Nazis sought to destroy',[30] their poems also affirm what Jack Kugelmass and Jonathan Boyarin describe as 'the desire to pass along something of the Eastern European heritage to coming generations'.[31]

The impact of Fram's loss is heartbreaking when one extrapolates his tenderness towards his family described in an earlier poem 'Mayn opfor' [My Departure],[32] which describes their mutual anguish when he immigrated to South Africa:

> Un kh'hob in nakht in harbstiker farlozn zey aleyn,
> Tseshnitn hot mayn shtume harts a trukn-sharfer vey,
> Un s'hot a vildn shpar geton mit trern a geveyn
> Farshtikt in triber elntkayt an elntn geshrey. (13–16)

> [And in the autumn night I left them on their own,
> My quiet, severed heart is full of pressing, sharp pain,
> And many lonely tears we moan,
> Pierced with dismal loneliness we cry in vain.]

Fram's as well as Fedler's poems record the 'traces of an existence',[33] epitomizing how historical forces shape individual lives.

As Sidra DeKoven Ezrahi states, Jews have 'preserve[d] for nearly two millennia a community of rememberers'.[34] Fram preserves the memory of Lithuania before, during, and after the *khurbn*. His poems affirm Elie Wiesel's assertion that the telling of their stories gives those who did not survive 'the voice that was denied them'.[35] Thus, in the situation where 'the plaintiff himself is divested of the means to state his own case',[36] Fram gives voice to 'a yomer fun kreyen vos pikn di beyner' [a lamentation of crows that picked the bones' (47) described in 'Dos letste kapitl'.[37] Because '[i]t had to be said or sung somehow',[38] the poems throw some light on the personal impact of the Shoah. However, his hope is that 'Di retshlekh fun a folk, der iberblayb fun plite | Vet opvaksen tsurik un lindern dem brokh…' [The remnant of a people, the remaining refugees | Will grow back and alleviate the disaster…] ('An entfer der velt', 53–54). Thus, the poet transforms 'the history of a culture, distilling [...] the complex anguish of the event into a few perfectly finished lines or pages';[39] the poems connect to a destroyed past, going some way to resist the historical amnesia of the Lithuanian Holocaust.

After the apocalypse, 'S'iz erd gevorn faykht, bafrukhpert fun di toyen, | Vos ayngezapt hot zat do yeder boynt un kveyt' [Earth became moist, fertilized by the dew, | Which each tree and blossom absorbed] (35–36), and so 'An entfer der velt' closes in the spirit of hope. In a 'still small voice', like the voice of God that Elijah heard,[40] the remnant of a people ensures the future survival of the whole, 'Der faygnboym in ru vet vaksn bay dayn tir' [The fig tree begins to blossom by your doorway] (50). Perpetuating the memory of the victims, '…himlen iber unz gekukt hobn derfreyte | Mit shabesdiker ru oyf pratse fun der vokh…' [...heavens above us look down gladdened | With sabbath-like rest after the toil of the week...] (55–56).

Recording the bloodbath that erased Lithuania's Jews, Fram's poems offer independent testimony. While historical documents date the offensives and tally the dead, poetry's images represent what may otherwise be unrepresentable. By expressing the otherwise inexpressible, and, in speaking the unspeakable, they may provide the reader some way to access the unthinkable. As Fedler writes in 'Mayn heym':

O! Vu zaynen ale iden geblibn?
S'trogt mikh mayn dimyen in park ariber
Dort vu kedoyshim farshotn in griber
Elnt keyn metseyver fun keynem farshribn.
ver zol kumen a trer dortn lozn — (20–25)

[O! Where are all the Jews?
I go around in the park in my imagination,
There the holy martyrs were shot in their graves
With no gravestones inscribed for them,
Who will come there and shed a tear —]

Emblematic of resistance to the erasure and amnesia of a language with the annihilation of its speakers, these poems connect with their lost past.

Fram's poems counter Walter Benjamin's fear that '[e]very image of the past that is not recognized by the present as one of its own concerns threatens to disappear irretrievably'.[41] The metaphors evoke the wounds, and the metaphors survive: 'art is what we go back to when everything is over'.[42] Poets such as Aisen, Benson-Rink, Fedler, and Fram translated memory into metaphor to commemorate a lost community: 'Bletelekh griner, in nekht, nor zey klogn | Un tsvaygn zikh shoklendik — kadish dort zogn' [During the night the green leaves moan | And the swaying branches say Kaddish] ('Mayn heym', 29–30).

By offering lines of continuity these poets record a landscape of memory and a personal response to history. In so doing, they enable the imaginative reconstruction of events and a reassembling of the shards of the Shoah, concerning specific individuals, particular incidents, and the lost culture of a once vibrant Jewish community. Although they never returned to Lithuania, they memorialize the personal and greater catastrophe from far away.

Notes to Chapter 5

1. David Fram, 'An entfer der velt' [An Answer to the World], *Dorem Afrike* (July–August 1971), 50 (line 1).
2. Aaron, p. 6.
3. Yiddish: Zhager.
4. Yiddish: Telz.
5. Hirsch, *The Generation of Postmemory*, p. 107.
6. Ibid.
7. Ibid.
8. Pollin-Galay, *Ecologies of Witnessing*, p. 2.
9. *Dorem Afrike* (July–August 1971), 50.
10. 'Hear, Oh Israel ...': the first words of the prayer recited morning and evening, and at the time of death (Deut. 6. 4–9; Num. 15. 37–41). The *Sh'ma* prayer also has a long tradition within Jewish martyrology.
11. Marianne Hirsch and Leo Spitzer, *Ghosts of Home: The Afterlife of Czernowitz in Jewish Memory* (Berkeley: University of California Press, 2010), p. 9.
12. Ibid.
13. Ibid.
14. Laura Levitt, *American Jewish Loss after the Holocaust* (New York: New York University Press, 2007), p. 43.

15. Ibid.
16. Aisen completed her studies at a *gimnazye* [high school], and, even more unusual for a woman of the time, she went on to the Kaunas Hebrew Teachers Seminary and to university. In the interwar period, she was a member of the *Mir aleyn* [Myself Alone] literary group. She wrote sensitive lyrics in both Hebrew and Yiddish, and her first collection, *Meydl lider* [Girlhood Poems] (1937), was published in Kaunas. Her poems cover many themes; her most memorable are simple statements of a woman's grief, women's life cycles, personal vignettes, and elegies to her birthplace. Like Fram, she published poems in *Shlyakhn* [Paths], and the Johannesburg monthly journal *Foroys* [Onward]. They were also the only two South Africans to be included in Joseph Leftwich's *The Golden Peacock: An Anthology of Yiddish Poetry* (Robert Anscome: London, 1939), p. 779.
17. *A shvalb oyfn dakh*, pp. 127–29; (extract), *Dorem Afrike* (May–June 1969), 3.
18. Habakkuk 1. 2.
19. A renowned Hasidic Rabbi (1740–1810).
20. A famous song-prayer, his plea has been set to music. See Burton (Berel) Leiser, 'Der Berditchever Rov', *Mendele: Yiddish literature and language*, 07.136 (20 January 1998) <http://www.columbia.edu/~jap2220/Arkhiv/vol07%20(1997–8)/vol07136.txt> [accessed 22 December 20].
21. Phylacteries. The *shel rosh* is bound around the head, the *shel yad* around the hand and arm every morning.
22. Prayer shawl.
23. *Oysgetunkt in trern*, p. 84.
24. *Dorem Afrike* (March–April 1969), 17.
25. Final prayers on the Day of Atonement, Yom Kippur.
26. Mourner's prayer; also uttered on the *yortsayt*, the anniversary of the day of death.
27. Fedler was born in Zhager. Her first collection of poetry was published in South Africa in 1951. *Bleter-fal* appeared posthumously in 1954.
28. *Bleter-fal*, p. 54.
29. Both Hitler and the biblical Haman intended to annihilate the entire Jewish people.
30. Kugelmass and Boyarin, 'Introduction', p. 5.
31. Ibid. p. 14.
32. *Lider*, p. 14.
33. Annette Wieviorka, 'On Testimony', in *Holocaust Remembrance*, ed. by Hartman, p. 25.
34. Ezrahi, *Booking Passage*, p. 26.
35. In Richard Kearney, *On Stories* (London: Routledge, 2002), p. 48.
36. Jean-Francois Lyotard, *The Differend: Phases in Dispute* (Manchester: Manchester University Press, 1988), p. 8.
37. (extract), *Dorem Afrike* (January–March 1984), 12.
38. Marie Syrkin quoted by Omer-Sherman, *Diaspora and Zionism in Jewish American Literature*, p. 83.
39. Susan Gubar, *Poetry after Auschwitz: Remembering What One Never Knew* (Bloomington: Indiana University Press, 2003), p. 558.
40. *The Holy Scriptures* (Jerusalem: Koren Publishers, 1989), 1 Kings 19. 11–13.
41. Peterson, *Against Amnesia*, p. 160.
42. David Albahari, in J. Langer, 'Introduction', p. 13.

CHAPTER 6

The Place of Witness:
Holocaust Representation in
David Fram and Abraham Sutzkever

'Yidn, shraybt un farshraybt' [Jews, write and record]
SIMON DUBNOW,[1] Riga Ghetto, December 1941

Affirming the significance of Yiddish and its continuity, this chapter contrasts a selection of David Fram's Holocaust poems with several by Abraham Sutzkever, a witness-participant in the Vilna Ghetto, Lithuania, who also gave evidence at the Nuremberg Trials. The discussion focuses on how their environments and experiences influenced their poetic outcomes, noting commonalities and differences. This comparative methodology[2] encourages cross-fertilization,[3] through which the study hopes to 'broaden [the] archive of memory',[4] so that '[Holocaust] meanings [may] evolve from the encounter'.[5]

   As their poems contend with the impact of historical events, both Fram and Sutzkever wrestle with aspects of belief and prayer, envisaging action or retaliation instead of silence and submission, striving to 'portray or comprehend an event that is generally regarded as unimaginable'.[6] While art should not exploit or sensationalize violence, or provide comfort by softening the actuality by offering palliative outcomes or false hope, the 'unwanted beauty'[7] of their poems may 'ward off forgetting';[8] thus, art may 'enhance Holocaust remembrance'.[9] In addition, where these poems become 'valuable for providing evidence',[10] they may also be regarded as a form of testimony, for '[a]lthough its lessons are not comforting, the Holocaust did more than just "happen"; it emerged, it persisted, it persists.'[11]

   Fram's *Dos letste kapitl* [The Last Chapter] (1947) evokes the beauty of the Lithuanian landscape and Jewish life, expresses his sorrow after these were destroyed, and reaches for hope in the future. Writing with urgency in 1945, when the truth became evident, Fram completed the poem in Johannesburg. On the other hand, Sutzkever gives evidence of the struggles of daily life through single personal incidents that illuminate his state of mind. Confined in the Ghetto, present while the decimation was happening around him, Sutzkever's 'Ikh lig in an oren' [I am Lying in a Coffin] (30 August 1941) focuses on his survival; 'Der tsirk' [The Circus] (June–July 1941),[12] describes his reaction to a life-threatening incident;

'Tsum kind' [To my Child] (18 January 1943) encompasses his soul-searching after the murder of his baby, while 'A vogn shikh' [A Wagonload of Shoes] (31 December 1942) memorializes his murdered mother. 'Glust zikh mir tsu ton a tfile — veyst ikh nit tsu vemen' [I Feel Like Saying a Prayer — But to Whom?] (17 January 1942) reveals his inner conflict. After that, in 'Di blayene platn fun roms drukeray' [The Lead Plates of the Rom Printing Press] (12 September 1943), he proposes fighting back against the enemy. These poetic testimonies were also impacted by '[p]ersonality, educational background, family life, economic status, political and religious leaning'.[13]

While some may regard poetry and testimony to be incompatible, because only the latter may represent actual historical occurrences, poetry may also become testimony when it works through the '"ill-understood" but devastating effects of traumatic events'.[14] While '[p]oetry [is] less likely to be historically precise'[15] than documentation, it can also encompass 'ethics, theology, relations, politics, and human meaning'.[16] Although both Sutzkever and Fram were born in the Russian Empire, by the time World War II began, Fram was in South Africa and Sutzkever was in Vilna. In that 'the Holocaust does not become one totalizing signifier containing the same meaning for everyone',[17] the poets' different environments impacted their angles of vision and viewpoints, it may be useful to also interpret testimony through the lens of place.[18]

Fram's 'Dos letste kapitl'[19] provides lyrical descriptions of memories of his homeland, with which Sutzkever would have identified, having come from a similar background. Fram's poem opens at a time when the country embraced her Jewish children, 'Azoy vi a mame' [like a mother] (7), and when the local inhabitants and the Jewish newcomers lived together in amity: 'Do lebn besholem vet er mit di Goyim, | Zey veln im ale derkenen' [Here he could live in harmony with the Gentiles, | They would all acknowledge him] (12–13). This amiable relationship is emphasized in a further description:

> Un s'vinken derhoybn tsu im horizontn
> Mit heymisher ru, balebatish mit verde —
> Tsu im, tsu dem Yid oyf litvishe erdn. (16–18)

> [And horizons winked at him politely
> With homely calm, respectable and worthy —
> To him, to the Jew on Lithuanian soil.]

Having set the broader scene, the poet then homes in on members of his close family in particular: 'A Yid iz gekumen amol in der Lite, | Der Yid iz gevezn mayn zeyde, mayn tate' [Once a Jew arrived in Lithuania, | That Jew was my grandfather, my father] (39–40). Initially, their neighbours overlooked their Jewishness and his community celebrated their age-old customs and traditions freely:

> Der Yid hot farflantst dort a lebn in Yidish:
> Shabosim, yon-toyvim, havdoles un kidesh!
> Barmitsves un khasenes, zilberne menoyres
> Un bekhers, un koyses far simkhes un brisn —
> Geburtn fun naye, fun yidishe doyres — (20–24)

[The Jew implanted there a life in Yiddish:
Sabbaths, festivals, *havdolah* and *kiddush*!
Bar mitzvahs and weddings, silver candelabra
And chalices and goblets for celebrations and circumcisions —
For the birth of new, Jewish generations —]

Thus, the immigrants put down roots and settled in, feeling comfortable enough to enjoy their festivities to the full:

Un zmires tsezungn bay vareme tishn
Mit tishtekher klore oyf shabes farshpreyte,
Mit likht in di laykhter un khales gegreyte. (25–27)

[And Sabbath songs sung at warm tables
With clean cloths spread out for Sabbath,
And candles in the candlesticks and brides ready prepared.]

The inclusion of details of the Jewish way of life emphasizes its deep significance to them: unfortunately, because of their differences, their neighbours targeted them during World War II. Although 'Es hot zey dos gloybn geshtarkt un gemutikt' [Belief strengthened them and gave them courage] (33), their Jewish observances and prayers could not save them: 'Zey zaynen shoyn dortn atsind nishto mer' [Now they are there no longer] (45).

In the place of Sabbath songs 'Dort trogt zikh arum itst a leydiker yomer' [There spills out an empty lament] (46) that offers no solace:

Un s'feln dort ale, ale — nishto iz shoyn keyner
Bloyz meysim, harugim un kupes mit beyner,
Afile on kadish, on treyst, on baveyner... (48–50)

[And now there, all, all are missing — there is no one left
Except the murdered, the dead and piles of bones,
Without even a Kaddish, without comfort, without mourners...]

Where idealized descriptions of the old ways of the *yeshuvniks* [countrymen], the forest Jews, and innkeepers[20] give 'an added poignancy',[21] contrasting with scenes of 'grotesque brutality',[22] in which the streets of his hometown in Lithuania later ran with Jewish blood:

Di hent dayne zaynen mit blut haynt bagosn,
Dos blut vest shoyn keynmol fun zey nit farvashn,
Es hot zikh in dir dayn bizoyen farloshn
Un s'zaynen farfoylt itst mit mord dayne gasn. (58–62)

[Your hands today are drenched with blood,
That blood you will never be able to wash away,
You have lost your shame,
And your streets are now rotten with murder.]

Similarly, before its destruction, Vilna, like Panevezys had a strong sense of community. It was the centre of Yiddish scholarship, literary, and linguistic studies. As the home to the Strashun Library, YIVO [The Yiddish Scientific Institute],[23] and *Yung Vilne*, the association of modernist leftist writers, poets, and artists, there was a strong sense of Litvak cultural identification.[24] This spirit fired up cultural resistance when the Germans invaded Lithuania in June 1941 and set up ghettos to confine the Jewish community.[25] On Hitler's order, Alfred Rosenberg and his cohort forced Sutzkever, Shmerke Kaczerginski, and other YIVO staff members to sort valuable documentation of Jewish life and culture. Intended for shipment to Germany, this was to be displayed after Hitler had fulfilled his intention to annihilate 'not only bodies but also the human environment in which [...] communication could take place'.[26]

In order to try and counter this nihilism, all Vilna Ghetto inhabitants were urged to write letters, memoirs, poems, and diaries as Sutzkever and Kaczerginski also spearheaded the underground organization, the Paper Brigade. Frantically documenting what was happening, they hoped to create archives that would outlast them to serve as evidence in any medium so as to prevent their disappearance from 'world memory'.[27] They then smuggled valuable historical and literary Judaic material, and records of their suffering and communal tragedy out of the Ghetto, in the hope that these artefacts would be recovered after the war was over,[28] to tell the world the truth from their own point of view. This pressing need to testify was born in the awareness of the huge and radical scale of destruction and elimination of the Jews of Eastern Europe, and they did what they could to counteract it. They understood all too well that without documentation, the history of their tragic fate would be lost.

Thus, Sutzkever wrote poetry to communicate with others, to record the daily lives of the inhabitants of the Ghetto, to explore his own reactions, and to buoy up his spirits. Though he wrote from and of personal experience, he intended the poems to be read. Transmission was critical; without it, their existence and experiences were ephemeral; they would have evaporated like breath: '[w]ritings [...] were a protest against death, and a refusal of it, through the creation of memories that would outlive them.'[29]

After escaping a round-up, Sutzkever composed 'Ikh lig in an oren',[30] as an immediate response:

> Ikh lig in an oren,
> vi in hiltserne kleyder,
> ikh lig,
> zol zayn, s'iz a shifl
> oyf shturmishe kvalyes,
> zol zayn, s'iz a vig. (1–6)
>
> [I am lying in a coffin
> as I would lie
> in stiff wooden clothing.
> This could be a small boat
> on dangerous waves,
> this could be a cradle.]

Still and silent, waiting for danger to pass, the poet's mind soars free. By transforming the coffin into a place of safety like Noah's Ark, or the *Oren Kodesh*, the Holy Ark, or into a little basket, like the one in which the infant Moses was saved from Pharaoh, Sutzkever finds comfort. 'An introspective poet, though his subject matter comes from outside himself',[31] his imaginings offer the possibility of life, and perhaps even divine intervention.

The short, intense lines create the narrow shape of a coffin on the page; they are also practical, enabling easier recall afterwards should he survive. Although the poem infers a single incident, the poet used his secret hideout repeatedly over the space of two years when numerous round-ups took place. Written in the first person, 'the authenticity of experience conveyed is important [...], whether the reader interprets the poetic "I" as reporting the poet's actual experience or [not].'[32] Even had the episode not happened, or not as described, the poem would still contain his emotional truth. Despite the desperate physical constriction in a suffocating space, it also contains hope. Rendered physically helpless, Sutzkever creates dynamic metaphors, a conjuring act that gives him a sense of agency.

From there, the poet imagines himself calling out to one he loves, 'ruf ikh dir, shvester' [I call you, sister] (10), convincing himself that she can hear him 'un du herst mayn rufn | in vayt' [and far away | you can hear me calling you] (11–12). He also remembers

> dayn shvartsapl
> dayn otem
> dayn likht. (16–18)

> [your eyes
> your breath
> your light.]

Even though she is long dead, these signs of her life remain within him.

By never mentioning the enemy by name, this act of erasing the Nazis' existence is one of resistance.[33] This choice gives him strength and lifts his spirits,

> Un itst in an oren,
> vi in hiltserne kleyder,
> zingt alst nokh mayn vort. (22–24)

> [And in a coffin now
> as in stiff wooden clothing
> my speech still moves into song.]

Enclosed in the dark, the poet realizes that life is 'Haynt do, morgn dort' [Here today, gone tomorrow] (20–21), and lines 22 and 23 echo lines 1 and 2 like a death knell. Nevertheless, by giving voice to his sense of dread, his song gives him the spirit to survive. These 'individual anecdotes, images and objects serve as "points of memory"[34] opening small windows on the past'.[35] Despite and because of the traumatic events, the poet created an object of beauty, a potent act, so that 'the redemptive detail, the play of words, images and sounds [...] will secure life by transforming it into art'.[36]

In Sutzkever's poem 'Der tsirk' [The Circus],[37] he captures what he perceived as a 'deeply humiliating, personal experience',[38] which he also briefly described in his 1946 witness statement: 'In the first days of August 1941, a German seized me in Dokumenskaia Street as I was going to visit my mother. He said, "Come with me, you will act in the circus" '[39] Following the mocking and frightening order, the poet becomes the 'der lets', the clown, providing public entertainment at gunpoint: 'Un ikh vos bin geven der lets in shendelekhn spektakl | hob nit gehat keyn mutvil tsu aroysshtameln a klole' [And I who was a clown in that disgraceful spectacle | Had no courage to stammer a curse] (77–78).[40]

In this episode, he and his fellow captives, a blind old Rabbi, a young boy, and an old peasant woman, become marionettes in a bitter display. Taunted by their captors,[41] Sutzkever considers himself to be ridiculous. Unable to utter a single word to defend himself let alone anyone else and fearing for his life, he is overwhelmed by feelings of humiliation: 'un nit tsu mol dem koakh zikh a varf tsu ton in toyt, | vi mayne brider in der tsayt fun adryan dem roymer' [No strength to throw myself into the death, | As did my brothers in the time of Hadrian the Roman] (79–80). Although he wishes he could ally himself with 'mayne brider' [my brothers], he simply accedes to the soldier's orders:

> Nor merer nokh: ikh hob geknit a naketer far dem
> Un mit trern vi mit shvartse pokn
> Gebetn genod. (85–87)
>
> [Worse: I knelt naked before him,
> And with tears like black pox,
> I begged for mercy.]

Naked and defenceless, Sutzkever breaks down in front of his fellow Jews and the enemy. Harshly condemning his reaction, he likens his tears to a malignant disease. Because he perceives his passivity as cowardice, he becomes angry 'against all the beautiful words he once used, and above all against himself for not dying the death of a martyr'.[42]

Again, only one form of resistance seemed open to him, and so, to deprive the Germans perpetrators of their power, he refused to name them, thus consigning them to 'verbal annihilation'.[43] Focusing on 'intense moments of subjective experience',[44] the poet also confronts his own reactions to the 'catastrophic moment'.[45] Overcome with despair and self-blame at his reaction to the round-up, he only allowed publication of 'Der tsirk' thirty-eight years later.[46] As Shoshana Felman suggests, 'poetry [may be] an exemplary instance of testimony [...] work[ing] through the effects of suffering that are not yet fully understood.'[47]

Afterwards, in his testimony, he was able to name perpetrators and certain street names to locate the *Aktion*, which had provided the subject matter for his poem:

> On 17 July 1941, I witnessed a large pogrom in Vilna on Novgorod Street. The inciters of this pogrom were the forenamed Schweichenberg [sic] and Martin Weiss,[48] a certain Herring, and Schonhaber, a German Gestapo chief. They surrounded this district with Sonderkommandos, drove all the men into the street, told them to take off their belts and to put their hands on their heads.
> (Nuremberg Trial Proceedings)

In contrast, in the poem 'Der tsirk', he struggled to make existential sense of the episode, 'Zog mir, brider, mayner, zog, zog | Vos iz er, vos batayt er, undzer hintisher gerongl?' [Tell me good brother | What is it and what does it mean, this dog fight we're in] (1–2), his inner conflict ignited by a high-risk, personal incident. By using the first person in 'Zog mir' [Tell me] when referring to his own battles, he draws us into his existential crisis.

In 'Tsum kind',[49] invoking his new-born child, Sutzkever asks how a father can be consoled for his murder during the greatest slaughter ever experienced,[50]

> Tsi fun hunger
> tsi fun groyser libshaft
> nor an eydes iz derbay dayn mame. (1–3)

> [Whether out of hunger
> or my great love for you
> only your mother can bear witness to it.]

Further, although the only person with whom he can truly share his anguish is his wife, he tries to share it with us through the poem. However, as the child's death 'weighed on his conscience'[51] and on his spirit, requiring the most radical act to regain wholeness,[52] it seems to him that nothing less than devouring the child would suffice.

> Ikh hob gevolt dikh aynshlingn, mayn kind,
> baym filn vi dayn gofl kilt zikh op
> in mayne finger. (4–6)

> [I wanted to devour you, my child,
> when I felt your little body cooling down
> between my fingers.]

By likening the loss to the most ordinary of activities, the waiting for a glass of tea to cool, he also evokes his former taste for life:

> glaykh ir volt in zey gedrikt
> a vorme gloz tey,
> filndik dem ibergang tsu kaltkayt. (7–9)

> [as if I'd clasped them
> round a glass of warm tea
> and felt its slow transition into coldness.]

This quiet poem sets up a private and heartbreaking dialogue between father and son. In his search for the correct words, he hopes to uncover meaning when life has become utterly meaningless:

> Far vos hostu fartunklet dem bashaf,
> mit dem vos du host tsugemakht di oygn
> un gelost mikh betlerdik in droysn. (23–25)

> [Why have you darkened all Creation
> by closing your eyes
> and leaving me outside, a beggar.]

Rather than railing at the universe or God, here the addressee is the lost child who never had the chance to experience even a small measure of joy: 'Dikh hot nit derfreyt keyn vig, | vos yeder ir bavegung' [No cradle has delighted you, | with its every rocking movement] (28–29). The only possible natural equivalent to his fate is the destruction of the sun itself: 'Es meg di zun tsebreklen zikh vi gloz — | Vayl keyn mol hostu nit gezen ir shayn' [Let the sun smash itself like glass | since you have never seen its light] (30–31). The reader then catches a glimpse of the cause of death, the inhuman acts of deception and betrayal:

> A tropn sam hot oysgebrent dayn gloybn.
> Du host gemeynt:
> S'iz varm-zise milkh. (32–34)
>
> [A drop of poison has burnt out your trust.
> You thought:
> it's warm sweet milk.]

However, the poet does not cry out against the human enemy, and makes 'no mention of the Germans who poisoned the baby and only the gentlest allusion to the actual murder.'[53] Again, as the only way of asserting himself against the perpetrators, '[t]he Germans are subjected to almost total linguistic extinction.'[54] Not mentioning them renders them invisible; thus, he 'annihilates the foe by denying his existence'.[55]

In his reconstruction in the courtroom afterwards, Sutzkever could incorporate the facts as well as names of the German perpetrators and their leader, Muhrer, the expert on the Jewish question.[56]

> At the end of December 1941 Muhrer came to the hospital in Street Number 6 and said that an order had come from Berlin to the effect that Jewish women should not bear children and that if the Germans found out that a Jewish woman had given birth, the child would be exterminated [...]. [I]n the ghetto my wife gave birth to a child, a boy. I was not there at that time, having escaped from one of these so-called 'actions.' When I came to the ghetto later, I found that my wife had had a baby in a ghetto hospital. [...] In the evening when the Germans had left, I went to the hospital and found my wife in tears. I saw that my baby was dead. He was still warm.

The Vilna poet's personal experiences rendered him unique, as a 'direct victim of Nazi atrocities, an articulate activist, and an authority by virtue of both sense and conscience'.[57]

Aching because of his personal tragedy, Sutzkever grapples with his inability to save his child. In 'Glust zikh mir tsu ton a tfile — veyst ikh nit tsu vemen'[58] he again wrestles with perplexing and unanswerable questions. However, he has no idea to whom to address his appeals: 'Der, vos hot amol gehert mikh, vet zi nit farnemen' [He who once used to comfort me, won't hear it now] (2). Implying that he did pray in the past, he cannot shake off the habit: 'Halt zi mikh in klemen' [The prayer holds me like a vise] (4).

He turns to the heavens for the right words, even while believing that they will remain unheard,

> Nor a tfile zogn muz ikh, emets gor a nonter
> paynikt zikh im mayn neshome un di tfile mont er, —
> vel ikh on a zinen
> plaplen biz baginen. (9–12)

> [Yet I must say a prayer. Someone very near,
> within me, tortured, demands the prayer.
> Senseless, I begin to babble
> until dawn.]

The poet's musings make no sense, even to himself. There is no mention of God, but a greater presence is inferred.

Sutzkever wrote 'A vogn shikh'[59] [A Wagonload of Shoes] after the Germans murdered his mother in 1943.[60] Whereas his eyewitness testimony afterwards provides factual evidence, this poetic representation extends our understanding of his state of mind and emotions.

> Di reder yogn, yogn,
> vos brengn zey mit zikh?
> zey brengn mir a vogn
> mit staplendike shikh. (1–4)

> [The wheels are chasing, chasing,
> What do they bring with them?
> They bring me a wagon
> With shaking shoes.][61]

The ghoulish 'gift' of empty shoes, sent back to the Ghetto in a cart by the murderers, becomes a synecdoche for those who once wore them. Here, the intense rhythm and pounding repetition emulate the sound of the wheels and the beating of the poet's heart. The short lines with their repeated words, 'yogn, yogn' [chasing, chasing], and the exact, emphatic rhyme scheme, 'yogn' / 'vogn' and 'zikh' / 'shikh' effectively convey the desperation of the cart's tumultuous journey.

For the poet, the horrific episode is personal. He is heartbroken when he sees the shoes that his mother kept for special occasions, discarded in the same cruel way as she and the other victims had been.

> Kindershikh un skrabes
> kh'derken mayn mames shikh!
> zi flegt zey bloyz oyf shabes
> aroyftsiyen oyf zikh. (25–28)

> [Through children's shoes and threadbare boots
> I recognize my mother's pair!
> She would only wear them on shabes
> She kept them for best.]

Sutzkever, however, makes no mention of the Lithuanian auxiliary group 'the *Ypatingas burys*, [whose members] functioned under the authority of Martin Weiss, roam[ing] the streets of Vilna in search of young male Jews, who after being found, were never seen again.'[62] Only later did the community realize that the victims 'had been taken to the Paneriai[63] forest outside the city and killed'.[64] To substantiate the truth of crimes against humanity, Sutzkever 'read and submitted to the court a document he had found after the liberation in the office building of German district commissar Franz Murer that specified the Germans' reuse of the clothing of Jews they had executed at Ponary'.[65] By individualizing his baby son and his mother he memorializes them; they also represent the murdered millions.

Life in the Vilna Ghetto consisted of day-to-day challenges and obstacles, food shortages and starvation, illness and disease, the need to stay hidden and unobserved because of the constant threat of *Aktionen*, and desperate attempts to avoid deportation and death. The dilemma of whether to try to escape the Ghetto, and whether to join the partisans in the forest, was ever present. By the autumn of 1943, informed that the Ghetto would be liquidated, the Fareynikte Partizaner Organizatsie [United Partisans' Organization], which included Sutzkever, called for an armed revolt.

Creating a courageous portrait of an imagined resistance through forceful self-defence and fighting back, 'Di blayene platn fun roms drukeray' [The Lead Plates of the Rom Printing Press][66] offers a contrast to the subdued victim of 'Der tsirk', the despair of the father in 'Tsum kind', and the futility of prayer in 'Glust zikh mir tsu ton a tfile': 'durkh nakht zikh getsoygn, tsu nemen di platn, | di blayene platn fun roms drukeray' [We made for the press plates, to seize | The lead plates at the Rom printing works] (3–4). Shaped by 'imaginative investment, projection and creation [...] however indirectly, [of] traumatic events',[67] the poet urges the would-be victims to break into the Rom Printing Press, the oldest and most famous Jewish printing house in Eastern Europe.

While Sutzkever often used his poetry to 'speak to himself'[68] as an 'affirmation of the solitary consciousness',[69] his strategy in this poem involves 'political activism endorsing partisan resistance as a way to recreate the Jewish word, to testify through action'.[70] By transfiguring words into weapons instead, he hopes those usually focused on the Talmud will take up arms to regain their freedom. Because their supplies are minimal, they must recast metal Hebrew type into lethal bullets, and also transform themselves into resistance fighters: 'mir, troymer, bedarfn itst vern soldatn | un shmeltsn oyf koyln dem gayst funem blay' [We were dreamers, we had to be soldiers, | And melt down, for our bullets, the spirit of the lead] (5–6). At the time of a life-or-death crisis, the melting down of the lead letters represents a symbolic shift from traditional Jewish culture based on books and learning, to include armed self-defence. When circumstances demand, words may become lethal:

> Dos blay hot geloykhtn baym oysgisn koyln,
> makhsheyves — tsegangn an ot nokh an ot.
> a soyre fun bavl, a soyre fun poyln,
> gezotn, gefleytst in der zelbiker mos.
> di yidishe gvure, in verter farhoyln,
> muz oyfraysn itster di velt mit a shos! (13–18)
>
> [Letter by melting letter the lead,
> Liquefied bullets, gleamed with thoughts:

> A verse from Babylon, a verse from Poland,
> Seething, flowing into the one mold.
> Now must Jewish grit, long concealed in words,
> Detonate the world in a shot!]

Whereas in 'Der tsirk', unable to stand up for himself, he berated himself for his inadequate and cowardly response to his fellow-sufferers, in this poem he envisages victory for those standing up to their oppressors.

Drawing a parallel between the Jewish Ghetto fighters and the defenders of biblical Jerusalem, and the Maccabees — a trope also used by Fram and Fefer, who drew inspiration from Moses, Joshua, Samson, and Bar Kochba — Sutzkever's poem highlights their 'heldishe yidishe hent' [heroic Jewish hands] (20), and qualities of strength and 'gevure' [grit]. Looked to for leadership, Sutzkever also became a symbol and representative of resistance.[71] At that stage, the Jews were still debating rebellion before the Ghetto was destroyed.[72] Although the poem was written in 1944, when he had already left to join the partisans,[73] he backdated it to 12 September 1943 to endorse this role, so that '[h]is voice called out to [...] those refugees who were still "thinking Vilna", holding onto the pre-war community as a social anchor'.[74] After the *khurbn*, 'Di blayene platn fun roms drukeray' appeared in a collection together with numerous other poems that 'incorporated historical chronicles and messages of Jewish resistance into the neo-romantic poetics he had developed before the war'.[75]

In the case of Fram's community, it was the neighbours who had once welcomed them, who ganged up with the Nazis, and in *Dos letste kapitl* the poet cries out, 'Mayn Lite, mayn heymland' [My Lithuania, my homeland] (51), directly accusing his country and countrymen of the heinous murder of his people:

> Du host zey dervorgn,
> Mit dayne farblutikte negl atsinder,
> Du host zey dershtikt — dayne eygene kinder! (53–55)

> [You strangled them,
> Now with your bloody fingers,
> You choked them — your own children!]

His incredulity is emphasized through the graphic language: 'dershokhtn' [slaughtered] (52), 'dervorgn' [strangled] (53) and 'dershtikt' [choked] (55) — there is no mercy for anyone. The depredation of the Holocaust is in horrifying contrast with the previous abundance; instead, the pastures have become killing fields and the mother has turned murderess. The streets run red, and the perpetrators' hands are covered in gore, but there is neither guilt nor remorse.

With no one to avenge the victims, he feels driven to take up arms against the perpetrators himself:

> Nor ven kh'volt itst kenen a meser a sharf ton,
> A sharf ton a meser azoy vi a britve,
> Volt ikh dayne merder, mayn yidishe Litve,
> Di gorgls tseshnitn mit heyser nekome. (76–79)

> [But if I could now sharpen a knife,
> Sharpen a knife like a razor,
> I would cut the throats of your murderers,
> My Jewish Lithuania, in burning revenge.]

Thus Fram, like Sutzkever, also imagines retribution, even though it is too late to save the victims. As the innocents went to the *akeyde* [sacrifice] like Isaac (85), but without the possibility of being saved, the poet envisages violent acts: 'Nekome far alte farpaynikte zeydes, | Far gantse fartilikte yidishe eydes' [Revenge for old tortured grandfathers | For entire annihilated Jewish communities] (83–84). Having earlier evoked the 'Jewish paradigms of living'[76] he valued, he now seeks to relieve his anguish at what had occurred when the Germans forced the Jews of Panevezys were forced into a ghetto in June 1941. There, they suffered abuse, degradation, starvation, and torture at the hands of the *Einsatzgruppen* and their local Lithuanian collaborators. Most of them were murdered in the nearby forests of Pajuostės Miškas, Kaiserlingas, and Žalioji Giria.[77]

> Un demolt vet efsher azoy dokh nit vey ton,
> Un s'veln nit shtikn azoy mikh di trern,
> Un efsher, efsher mayn veytok vet laykhter dan vern... (91–93)

> [And then maybe it would not hurt so much,
> And maybe my tears would not choke me,
> And perhaps, perhaps my pain would then become lighter...]

Fram's poems may be likened to the mourner's prayer, the Kaddish, intoned at the graveside, but for those who were shot, buried in mass graves, gassed, and incinerated, there was no such offering of honour or remembrance. Although there is no guarantee that his cries will be heard, the poet has not abandoned or forgotten the victims:

> Vos zaynen gefaln farbrent oyfn shayter
> Mit vundn, vos hobn genetst un geeytert —
> Farbrent [...]
> Baym shayn fun dem blasn, dem shmutskn muld — (1164–67)

> [Those who fell, burnt on the gallows
> With gaping wounds, filled with pus —
> Burnt [...]
> By the light of the pale, the dirty moon —]

Consequently, the moon of Lithuania, the 'muld', celebrated in Fram's earlier poems, becomes a symbol of degradation.

> Farbrent, vayl men hot zay nisht ale bagrobn
> In finstere nekht, ven geklogt hobn ravn
> Mit shive, mit kriye, mit tser nokh der shkhite —
> Farbrent oyf di shayters fun mame-land lite. (1168–71)

> [Burnt without being buried
> In the dark night when the ravens cawed
> With shive, in mourning, with sorrow after the slaughter —
> Burnt on the pyres of motherland Lithuania.]

The two poets' experiences affected their attitudes, evoking Fram's feelings of anger, guilt, and sorrow, and Sutzkever's shame, guilt, and grief. 'Difficult as retelling can be, the opportunity to remember the lost, to have their experiences acknowledged, to hope that some good will come out of it [...] can mean a great deal.'[78] As participant, witness, Sutzkever 'enlists poetry to intervene in public affairs, he creates a '"paradoxical amalgam" between self-focused poetic language and ideological engagement'.[79] In this light, his 'pensive lyric voice can have political implications even when not ideological in register'.[80] While the Brigade tried to save Jewish culture by hiding its treasured documents, only guns and soldiers might have saved the city from destruction.

'[A] simple victim and a leader in heroism',[81] Sutzkever highlighted his personal experience in 'Ikh lig in an oren', 'Der tsirk', and 'A vogn shikh', and also provided proof of genocide. Imagining what might have happened had matters been handled differently beforehand, Sutzkever searched for explanations for his own survival, and his 'poems can function [...] as "spurts of vision" that are effective in their engagement with baffling experiences of suffering'.[82]. Questioning why his family and the Jewish people were decimated, he may have been putting himself in the dock. 'Asking himself what role his poetry could play in a situation [even] where mere survival was everyone's priority',[83] he tried to find meaning in chaos, to distil the suffering and 'trauma of the Jewish world'.[84] Powerless to save his son or his mother, he became 'obsessed with rescuing the dead', to secure for them, at least 'a poetic grave',[85] his heartfelt 'attempt to reinter the dead so as to guarantee them a dignified and enduring memorial'.[86] As poetry's 'hyper-attentiveness [...] allow[s] for reflection on traumatic experiences in a way different from prose',[87] situating the murder of his loved ones at the heart of the matter, Sutzkever's poems 'convey the epiphanic moment of witnessing'.[88] Subsequently, after giving testimony,[89] Sutzkever wrote: 'I feel a tremendous responsibility and I pray that the souls of the martyrs will lament from my words.'[90]

In seeking 'a unique language adequate to unprecedented experience',[91] documenting the occupation and destruction to preserve the history of a people, Fram's and Sutzkever's poems made the plight of the Jews known. They 'illuminated a corpus of "small" life stories from a specific moment in time, both enabling their creation, and then preserving them as objects of historical worth'.[92] Fulfilling the objectives of testimony, these poems voiced his deepest concerns, 'touching on *all* our philosophic questions, all questions of purpose, of right and wrong, of justice, of God';[93] while poetry and testimony on the Shoah may be different genres, one is not more valuable than the other.[94]

As both poets lost members of their close family and communities, their aesthetic representations using armouries of metaphors and images, serve traumatic memory, keeping the Holocaust alive and visible, as they 'clothe adversity in poetic form [and so] immortalize it in an everlasting monument'.[95]

In this vein, at a presentation in Montreal, Canada, in 1959, Sutzkever professed how

> Der koakh un vunder fun dikhtung un fun Yidishn loshn hot zikh antflekt
> far mir der iker in vilner geto. Dort kon ikh beemes gekent zogn: 'hakhayim

vehamoves beyadekh Yidish loshn'. Di shrprakh, mayn Yidish, iz geven der kishuf-panster on velkhn s'hobn zikh opgeshlogn di fayln fun toyt. Mitn lid bin ikh afilu in geto geven a frayer mentsh.[96]

[The power and wonder of poetry and the Yiddish language revealed themselves to me above all in the Vilna Ghetto. There I was able to say truly: 'Life and death are in your hands, Yiddish language'. The language, my Yiddish was the magic armour, which repelled the arrows of death. With my poetry I was a free man, even in the ghetto.][97]

Regarded in this light, '[n]ot only is poetry possible, it is necessary',[98] and Fram's mission, although carried out under different circumstances, endorses these sentiments. 'Despite the risks of distortion and displacement, representations of all sorts [...] remain the only access to historical events.'[99] Hence, Eva Hoffman also encourages the reading of poems of suffering and extremity with sympathy and empathy, to imagine what others feel without diminishment, to imagine the reality of another's situation through their words, reaching towards a community of justice and reason.[100]

Translating personal experience and communal history into a communicable and transmissible form, the Yiddish poems become valuable vessels for bearing witness, and may help to fill in the some of the gaps in the historical records. In that 'memory is important to give meaning to the past and the future',[101] the works of Fram and Sutzkever provide an arena in which we may address Jewish suffering. Although they may only be a partial metonymy for the Holocaust, 'an event that is generally regarded as unimaginable',[102] in resisting amnesia of what once was and is no more, they counteract the complete annihilation of a culture and a people. In that 'extreme violence kills something in addition to people',[103] the poems 'retriev[e] from oblivion the decimated lives and communities [...] of Yiddish-speaking Eastern and Central Europe',[104] and also memorialize them.

Notes to Chapter 6

1. In H. Greenspan and others, 'Engaging Survivors: Assessing "Testimony" and "Trauma" as Foundational Concepts', *Dapim: Studies on the Holocaust*, 28.3 (2014), 190–226 (p. 207).
2. Wirth-Nesher, 'Tradition, the Individual Talent, and Yiddish', p. 3.
3. Ibid.
4. Hirsch and Spitzer, 'Holocaust Studies/Memory Studies', in *Memory: Histories, Theories, Debates*, ed. by Susannah Radstone and Bill Schwarz (New York: Fordham University Press, 2010), p. 404.
5. Natan Levy and Daniel Sznaider, in Hirsch and Spitzer, 'Holocaust Studies/Memory Studies', p. 404.
6. Feinstein, 'Mediums of Memory', p. 201.
7. Ephraim Sicher, 'Introduction', in *Breaking Crystal*, ed. by Sicher, pp. 2–16 (p. 2).
8. Hirsch, cover note for Kaplan, *Unwanted Beauty*.
9. Ibid.
10. Weissman, 'Questioning Key Texts', p. 326.
11. Rothberg, *Traumatic Realism*, p. 60.
12. Abraham Sutzkever, *Di ershte nakht in geto*, pp. 6–10; Schwarz, *Survivors and Exiles*, p. 30.
13. Ibid.
14. Shoshana Felman and Dori Laub in Antony Rowland, *Poetry as Testimony: Witnessing and Memory in 20th Century Poetry* (New York: Routledge, 2013), pp. 21–22.

15. B. Lang in Greenspan and others, p. 197.

16. Wieviorka in Greenspan and others, p. 219.

17. Levy and Sznaider in Hirsch and Spitzer, 'Holocaust Studies/Memory Studies', p. 404.

18. Pollin-Galay, *Ecologies of Witnessing*.

19. (extract), *Dorem Afrike* (January–March 1984), 12. My translation is of this extract, which forms the basis of this discussion. Other translations include Barry Davis: 'The Last Chapter' in his 'David Fram, Yiddish Poet', pp. 48–49; and 'The Slaughter in Lithuania', transl. by Joseph Leftwich, in *The Golden Peacock*, ed. by Leftwhich, pp. 631–32. Copies of Leftwich's translations may also be found in *David Fram Papers*, Folder 17, pp. 1–3, p. 15.

20. L. Goodman, 'David Fram: A Study in Growth'; David Roskies, *Against the Apocalypse: Responses to Catastrophe in Modern Jewish Culture* (Cambridge, MA: Harvard University Press, 1984).

21. Davis, p. 46.

22. Ibid.

23. Max Weinreich founded the Institute in Berlin and Vilnius in 1925 to preserve, study, share, and perpetuate knowledge of the history and culture of East European Jewry worldwide.

24. Mikhail Krutikov, 'Yiddish Literature: Yiddish Literature after 1800', *YIVO Encyclopedia of Jews in Eastern Europe* (29 June 2016) <https://yivoencyclopedia.org/article.aspx/Yiddish_Literature/Yiddish_Literature_after_1800> [accessed 3 July 2020].

25. Justin Daniel Cammy, 'Yung-vilne', *YIVO Encyclopedia of Jews in Eastern Europe* (18 November 2010) <https://yivoencyclopedia.org/article.aspx/Yung-vilne> [accessed 3 July 2020].

26. Wirth-Nesher, p. 5.

27. H. Greenspan in Greenspan and others, p. 210.

28. Similarly, Emanuel Ringelblum's clandestine Oyneg Shabes group collected reports and testimonies about life in the Warsaw Ghetto, the resistance movement, and the deportation and extermination of Polish Jewry. These materials were preserved in three milk cans, two of which were located after the war.

29. Wieviorka in Greenspan and others, p. 207.

30. Valencia, pp. 92–93; Abraham Sutzkever, *Burnt Pearls: Ghetto Poems of Abraham Sutzkever*, trans. by Seymour Mayne (Ontario: Mosaic Press/Valley Editions, 1981), p. 13.

31. Pollin-Galay, 'Avrom Sutzkever's Art of Testimony', p. 25.

32. Lang in Greenspan and others, p. 197.

33. In certain contexts, one would say: 'May their names be erased'.

34. Used as an alternative to Pierre Nora's *lieu*, or site of memory, Hirsch and Spitzer, *Ghosts of Home*, p. xix.

35. Hirsch and Spitzer, *Ghosts of Home*, p. xix.

36. Ruth Wisse, 'Introduction', in Sutzkever, *Burnt Pearls*, pp. 9–18 (p. 14).

37. In *Di ershte nakht in geto*, p. 6.

38. Schwarz, *Survivors and Exiles*, p. 31.

39. Nuremberg Trial Proceedings.

40. All translations of this poem are from Benjamin Harshav and Barbara Harshav, *A. Sutzkever: Selected Poetry and Prose* (Berkeley: University of California Press, 1991), p. 129.

41. Nuremberg Trial Proceedings.

42. Roskies, *Against the Apocalypse*, p. 231.

43. Ibid., p. 227.

44. Rowland, p. 6.

45. Ibid.

46. Schwarz, *Survivors and Exiles*, p. 31 and p. 295.

47. Felman in Rowland, p. 21.

48. Weiss was arrested in May 1949. In February 1950, a court in Würzburg found him guilty of war crimes and sentenced him to life imprisonment. His sentence was suspended in 1970 and revoked in 1977.

49. Valencia, pp. 95–99.

50. Roskies, *Against the Apocalypse*, pp. 231–32.

51. Ibid., p. 231.

52. Ibid., p. 232.
53. Wisse, p. 14.
54. Ibid.
55. Ibid.
56. Nuremberg Trial Proceedings.
57. Pollin-Galay, 'Avrom Sutzkever's Art of Testimony', p. 12.
58. In Valencia, p. 94–95; Sutzkever, *Burnt Pearls*, p. 26.
59. Sutzkever, *Lider fun yam ha-moves fun Vilner Geto, vald un vander*, p. 41.
60. Sutzkever backdated this poem for his own purposes.
61. Harshav and Harshav, *A. Sutzkever: Selected Poetry and Prose*, p. 151.
62. Special squads; Robert Van Voren, *Undigested Past: The Holocaust in Lithuania* (New York: Rodopi, 2011), p. 87.
63. Lithuanian; also Ponary; Yiddish: Ponar.
64. Van Voren, p. 87.
65. Laura Jockusch, 'Justice at Nuremberg? Jewish Responses to Nazi War-Crime Trials in Allied-Occupied Germany', *Jewish Social* Studies, 19.1 (2013), 107–47 (p. 119).
66. Sutzkever, *Di festung lider un poemes: geshribn in Vilner Geto un vald* [The Fortress Songs and Poems: Written in the Vilna Ghetto and Forest] (New York: Yiddisher kultur farband, 1945), p. 62 <http://teachgreatjewishbooks.org/resource-kits/avrom-sutzkevers-lead-plates-rom-printers#resources> [accessed 23 December 2020]. Unless otherwise indicated, translations of 'Di blayene platn fun roms drukeray' are by Neal Kozodoy, in *The Penguin Book of Modern Yiddish Verse*, ed. by Howe, Wisse, and Schmeruk, p. 678.
67. Hirsch, *The Generation of Postmemory*, p. 107.
68. Pollin-Galay, 'Avrom Sutzkever's Art of Testimony', p. 5
69. Wisse, p. 12.
70. Pollin-Galay, 'Avrom Sutzkever's Art of Testimony', p. 5; Roskies, *Against the Apocalypse*, p. 251.
71. 'His arrival in Moscow became a matter of public attention [...], the public understood Sutzkever to be an authoritative witness and treated his verse, speeches, and reportage as testimonial truth', in Pollin-Galay, 'Avrom Sutzkever's Art of Testimony', p. 2.
72. In September 1943, the Ghetto was liquidated and there was no hope. Sutzkever and his wife escaped to the Narocz Forest. There, he gave some of his poems to an escaping partisan. In Moscow, they were passed on to the Jewish Anti-Fascist Committee, drawing attention to the decimation of the Lithuanian Jewish community. Consequently, he and his wife were airlifted to safety from the mass graveyard of the Rudnicki forest.
73. In 'Abraham Sutzkever, "The Lead Plates of the Rom Printers"', *The Yiddish Book Center's Great Jewish Book Teacher Resources* <http://teachgreatjewishbooks.org/resource-kits/avrom-sutzkevers-lead-plates-rom-printers#resources> [accessed 20 June 2020].
74. Pollin-Galay, 'Avrom Sutzkever's Art of Testimony', p. 4.
75. Ibid., p. 5.
76. Pollin-Galay, *Ecologies of Witnessing*, p. 2.
77. Mordechai Zalkin, 'Panevėžys', *YIVO Encyclopedia of Jews in Eastern Europe* (14 September 2010) <https://yivoencyclopedia.org/article.aspx/Panevezys> [accessed 23 July 2020].
78. Greenspan and others, p. 203.
79. Benjamin Harshav in Pollin-Galay, 'Avrom Sutzkever's Art of Testimony', p. 26.
80. Pollin-Galay, 'Avrom Sutzkever's Art of Testimony', p. 26.
81. Pollin-Galay, 'Avrom Sutzkever's Art of Testimony', p. 18.
82. Gubar, p. 7.
83. Valencia, p. 265.
84. Ruth Dorot, *The Art of Time, the Art of Place: Isaac Bashevis Singer and Marc Chagall — A Dialogue* (Brighton: Sussex Academic Press, 2011), p. 79.
85. Wisse, p. 14.
86. Ibid.
87. Rowland, p. 6.
88. Ibid., p. 6.

89. Twenty-four of the most important political and military criminals of the Third Reich were brought before the International Military Tribunal (IMT) by the Allies between 20 November 1945 and 1 October 1946. The Nuremberg indictment mentioned genocide, the extermination of racial, national or religious groups, for the first time in international law.

90. Jokusch, 'Justice at Nuremberg?', p. 120.

91. Sidra DeKoven Ezrahi, *By Words Alone: The Holocaust in Literature* (Chicago: University of Chicago Press, 2008), p. 61.

92. Pollin-Galay, 'Avrom Sutzkever's Art of Testimony: Witnessing with the Poet in the Wartime Soviet Union', *Jewish Social Studies*, 21.2 (Winter 2016), 1–34 (p. 4).

93. Greenspan and others, p. 194.

94. Wieviorka in Greenspan and others, p. 211.

95. Chaim Kaplan in Aaron, p. 9.

96. In Valencia, p. 44.

97. Valencia, p. 45.

98. Efraim Sicher, 'The Holocaust in the Postmodernist Era', in *Breaking Crystal*, ed. by Sicher, pp. 297–328 (p. 299).

99. Ibid., p. 234.

100. Eva Hoffman, 'The Long Afterlife of Loss', in *Memory: Histories, Theories, Debates*, ed. by Susannah Radstone and Bill Schwarz (New York: Fordham University Press, 2010), 406–15 (p. 412).

101. Gubar., p. 20.

102. Feinstein, p. 201.

103. Rafael Lemkin in Pollin-Galay, *Ecologies of Witnessing*, p. 3.

104. Alan Rosen, 'Yiddish and the Holocaust', *In geveb* (August 2015), 1–3 (p. 3) <https://ingeveb.org/chapters/yiddish-and-the-holocaust> [4 September 2020].

CHAPTER 7

Yellow Crucifixion, Yellow Star: Home and the Holocaust in Selected Paintings by Marc Chagall and Poems by David Fram

David Fram's moving poetry and Marc Chagall's evocative paintings reflect a similar, critical time in history. Sharing an Eastern European background, they may be linked through their responses to their losses of Panevezys and Vitebsk respectively. Both were bereaved of home, once by emigration, and then by the Holocaust, and there are also other notable points of connection. While Fram may have encountered Chagall and his paintings in Paris in the 1920s, when he wrote 'es klingt a velt mit bilder fun shagaln' [a world rings with the paintings of Chagall] (11),[1] this discussion does not turn to ekphrasis. Instead, the juxtaposition of their verbal and visual representations may offer 'different versions of the world'.[2]

In their new environments, it was their Jewishness that provided the wellspring for their aesthetics and their worldviews. Hence, the first section of this chapter juxtaposes Fram's poem 'Ikh benk' [I Long] (1931) with Chagall's *I and the Village*[3] and *The Blue House*,[4] in which they expressed their reactions to moving away from home. Thereafter, *Dos letste kapitl* [The Last Chapter] (1947), as well as 'An entfer der velt' [An Answer to the World] (1971), and 'Lesterung' [Blasphemy] (1965), which reflect Fram's ambivalent attitude to faith, fluctuating between disillusionment with and rejection of God and returning to the fold, are placed in conjunction with Chagall's *White Crucifixion* (1938),[5] and *Yellow Crucifixion* (1943)[6] to highlight questions of abandonment of the Jewish people during the Shoah.

Moyshe Shagal was born in the bustling market town of Vitebsk, Belarus, in 1887. Like Fram, he extended his education when he attended secondary school, a choice that was mostly closed to Jews.[7] Almost contemporaries, with roots in Jewish tradition, both received an orthodox religious education. Thus, they observed the Jewish festivals of Rosh Hashanah,[8] Yom Kippur,[9] and Pesach,[10] and maintained traditions such as wearing a *talis*[11] and putting on *tfiln*; both attended *cheder*,[12] as well as *shul*, the synagogue. While Hebrew was their *lashon Ha'kodesh*, the language in which they prayed, Yiddish was their *mameloshn*, their mother tongue, the language used in the day-to-day transactions. They would also both have been familiar with the biblical stricture against taking graven images: while writing brought no conflict to the poet, Fram, for Chagall it was a different story — and he broke the taboo.

The artist's career began formally in 1906, when his mother enrolled him in the art school of the Jewish artist Yehuda Pen, even though an education in this field was an unlikely choice for a Jewish boy from an observant family. In 1911, Shagal left for Paris where he became Marc Chagall, evoking his journey away from his homeland in bright colours in *I and the Village* as he adapted to his new environment. He returned to Vitebsk in 1914, but was then unable to leave because of the outbreak of the war. In 1917, the Pale of Settlement was dissolved, and full citizenship was granted to the Jewish population, so Chagall was permitted to set up his own art school. After the venture failed due to disagreements with Kazimir Malevich, Chagall moved to Moscow in 1920, where he designed sets for the State Jewish Chamber Theatre, then to Berlin, producing etchings to illustrate his autobiography *My Life*.[13] After spending a short time in Paris,[14] where he made his mark on the international scene, he settled in the South of France. He remained there until he was whisked away to safety to America in 1941 under the auspices of Varian Fry's rescue network in Vichy, and with the help of Hiram Bingham, the American vice consul in Marseilles.

Both Fram's and Chagall's works are emotionally charged with memories of the rich culture they had left behind, and comment on their Jewish identity from the vantage point of displacement. Chagall combined traditional themes with experimental styles, fusing fantasy and reality, scattering recognizable objects across his canvas. For example, his grandfather was once found warming himself beside the chimney on the roof and eating *tsimes*.[15] 'Guided by private associations',[16] this image made its way into Chagall's paintings as the iconic fiddler. Fram's poetic style remained traditional, even when transplanted to Africa. Referencing themselves, Chagall includes self-portraits, as in *I and the Village*, and Fram uses the first person singular consistently. As their depictions of their experiences in the shtetl are retrospective, they may also often appear nostalgic. Since their homeland no longer exists as depicted, their works give it an afterlife, a presence in the future — and a future.

In 'Ikh benk',[17] Fram recollects the intimacy of family and his sense of belonging in the village, fields, and forests where he grew up. With the pain of parting still raw, each verse focuses on a different memory of home:

> Ikh benk azoy mid nokh a shtikele shvartse, tsekvolne erd,
> Nokh harbstike regens oyf felder un blotes oyf endlozn trakt,
> Vu shlepn zikh mide, tseveykte, farshpetikte, elnte ferd,
> Mit dorfishn umet balodn un poyerisher pratse gepakt. (1–4)

> [I wearily long for a piece of black, swollen earth,
> After autumn rains on the fields and mud on endless roads,
> Where tired, soaked, late and forlorn horses trudge along,
> Heavy with village sadness and packed with peasant toil.]

The stanza evokes man and beast as they go about their labours, the 'mide, tseveykte, farshpetikte, elnte ferd' [tired, swaying, late and forlorn horses trudge along] (3), contending with natural obstacles and their heavy burdens. The choice of sombre, heavily laden words and the use of long lines emulate the physical exhaustion after the endless 'poyersher pratse' [peasant toil] (4).

> Ikh benk nokh di Yidn fun velder, vi kuperne yodles farpekht,
> Vos shmekn in friyike reykhus fun shvomen un varemen mokh,
> Vos shlepn aheym zikh oyf shabes durkh osyendik-vintike nekht,
> Un garn nokh ruiker shalve fun shverer farmatete vokh. (5–8)

> [I long for the Jews of the forests, solid with firs,
> Smelling of the early scents of mushrooms and warm moss,
> Who drag themselves home for Sabbath through windy, autumn nights,
> Craving tranquillity from the exhausting weekday gloom.]

The poem's traditional four-line stanzas and regular rhyme scheme, and the repetition of the title as the first line of each, draw attention to feelings of loss: 'Ikh benk azoy mid nokh a shtikele, shvartse, tsekvolne erd' (1), 'Ikh benk nokh di Yidn fun velder, vi kuperne yodles farpekht' (5), and 'Ikh benk nokh di teg, ven es gibn di seder avek zeyer gob' [I long for the days when the orchards give up their bounty] (9). During the 'shverer farmaterter vokh' [heavy, exhausting week] (8), in the bleak autumn, the labourers are weighed down by 'dorfishn umet' [village sadness] (4) in their 'groyer, farshvigener velt' [grey, silent world] (16). In winter, the *shtetlekh* were under mud, *blote,* a feature that encapsulates the suffering of the people. However, as they 'shlepn aheym zikh oyf shabes' [drag themselves home for Sabbath] (7), they anticipate their day of rest.

The mood of the poem alters in stanza three, as the poet reminds himself of the benefits of nature's abundance, and the cycle of growth from season to season, when 'gibn di seder avek zeyer gob' [orchards give up their bounty] (9), and the ripe crop ensured that 'kelers farfult mit a vayniker gilderner last' [cellars are filled with their wine-like golden store] (10). As earth and sky conjoin, 'Un zun kumt tsu geyn oyf a vayl vi a zeltener, khoshever gast' [And sun visits awhile, like a rare and honoured guest] (12), the landscape and its inhabitants enjoy the rare and pleasurable warmth, its fruitfulness and productivity.

Nature's bounty, the fertile soil filled with lush fir trees, moss and mushrooms induced feelings of awe, which Fram associated with the presence of a greater being in the lines: 'Dan gloyb ikh ... dan gloyb ikh mit hertser, vos gloybn emunedik-frum, | Vos zaynen mit heylike tfiles vi harbstike kelers gepakt...' [Then I believe ... then I believe with hearts that believe faithfully and piously, | Packed like autumn cellars with holy prayers...] (17–18).

Each vignette triggers memories of the richness and benefits of the poet's early years. No matter what the conditions were, whether favourable or not, and despite the relentless darkness, he remains filled with longing for the familiar, communal way of life, 'In teg fun farlozn di seder ikh benk azoy elntik-shtum, | Nokh Yidn fun pekhike velder oyf soflozn, blotikn trakt' [Now when I have lost those orchards, I long, alone and silent, | For Jews of the fluffy forests and the endless, muddy ways] (19–20). The final verse links the physical location to his emotional state and nostalgia for the once familiar way of life.

Like Fram, who wrote 'Ikh benk' soon after he arrived in South Africa, Chagall painted *I and the Village* shortly after he first left home, creating a record of Vitebsk or Liozno, which was his grandparents' village, from 'a distance of memory'.[18] On the canvas, a large, white, wide-eyed cow stares at the green face of a young man; the two are connected as they face each other, and also through the diagonal line across the green man's nose and behind the cow's nose and mouth. A painted circle encloses both of their mouths and noses, suggesting that they are in conversation. The man is recognizable as a portrait of the artist himself; 'wearing a cross — shows Chagall's effort to accept and identify himself with Christian culture [...]. He also sports a gymnasium uniform hat'[19] rather than a *yarmulke*.[20] Scenes of village life dot the canvas: a domed church, numerous village houses, some of them upside down; a second self-portrait, a diminutive figure, observes the scene from behind the church.

Within the animal's face is another scene with a cow being milked. Lovingly painted, these images evoke the close connection between animal and man, an accepted interdependence in village life. Immediately behind, within a pinkish area, is a small peasant plodding along with his scythe over his shoulder; the woman facing him is rendered upside down. The placement of her arms suggests that she is directing the peasant, but the position of her feet suggests that she may be dancing. In the distance, behind the flat planes of unrealistic colour — red, pink, and purple — little cottages are placed cheek-by-jowl to the church, where Jews and gentiles lived close by for thousands of years. The lack of connection between the objects gives the painting a fragmented quality, which also manifests the dichotomy between Chagall's cosmopolitan French existence and his upbringing.

Chagall's *The Blue House* represents his family home, where 'the village is the centre of the world, and the [house] is the focus of his existence, around which life revolves'.[21] It was 'a peculiar house, very different from all the others because of its extraordinary colour and isolation [...] [which] seems lonely, fragile [...], on the point of collapse'.[22] The colours of this remembered scene and imaginary place, painted at a time when representations of the *shtetl* were rare, are emotive rather than naturalistic. The reference to 'blue' in the title emphasizes the separateness of his home; it may also suggest that he too set himself apart.

In *My Life*, first published in the 1920s, Chagall affirmed how important his hometown was for him.[23] It is often present in the background: when he painted Bella, which he did many times, first as his fiancée and then as his wife, in his flower paintings, the interior scenes, and his multiple biblical works.

One of his most prominent motifs is the Jewish shtetl, and [he] describe[s] everyday life and holidays, the ordinary townsfolk and the more eccentric ones and the wooden huts and synagogues, violinists and rabbis of late nineteenth-century Russian-Jewish small-town life.[24]

In this homely setting, involvement in community events, and performing rituals and offering prayers such as the *Sh'ma*, 'Hear O Israel, the Lord our God the Lord is One', would have been second nature to both Fram and Chagall. However, the genocide challenged both of them in their traditional belief system and orthodox observance. For both artists, these contradictions played out in works that 'represent attempts [...] to explain the metaphysical meaning of suffering'[25] in relation to their religious beliefs or social ideology.

In 'Lesterung', Fram reproaches God for this absence, discontinues observance, and struggles to maintain his faith in the daily rituals. 'An entfer der velt' focuses on the dehumanizing identity patches that the Nazis forced Jews to attach to their outer garments.[26] In *Dos letste kapitl*, he accuses his countrymen of iniquitous deeds, once more deploying images of the yellow star, the columns of people, the gas ovens, the limekiln, and the blackened chimneys to accentuate the dichotomy between the once-felt comfort offered by *talis* and *tfiln*, and the subsequent destruction.

Like Fram, Chagall responded creatively to the Jewish genocide. The painter perceived it to be a result of the abandonment of the Jewish people by God and the world.[27] In addition, he interpreted God's desertion of the Jews as parallel to that of the Jewish Jesus on the cross. Consequently, in *White Crucifixion* and *Yellow Crucifixion*, he appropriates Christian imagery to embody the Jewish tragedy.[28] As he recontextualizes the figure of Jesus of Nazareth in a shtetl, amongst objects of Jewish religious and daily life scattered during an *Aktion* or pogrom, he creates analogies between them. By situating the scriptural scene within a contemporary village, connecting the Crucifixion with the contemporary annihilation of the Jewish people, Chagall provides a controversial double viewpoint, 'remind[ing] us of Christ's Jewishness by integrating him into contemporary Jewish history'.[29]

Where 'folk theodicy'[30] may be described as 'an epiphenomenon of suffering and a strategy for orientation in the midst of a religious or ideological crisis'.[31] Toker comments:

> [a] [...] sense of disgust with the world in which the Nazi atrocities could unfold was the cause of the loss of religious beliefs among some of the victims or at least the cause of the renunciation of the practices associated with religious beliefs.[32]

As 'traditional forms [...] break down when the suffering to which it responds is particularly prolonged and acute, [f]olk theodicy is [...] relinquished along with faith itself'.[33] Although 'people attempted to resist the assault of continuous acute pain on their religious beliefs',[34] this often failed.

Fram's 'An entfer der velt',[35] encapsulates the extent of suffering that may evoke such a reaction. The poem opens with Fram locating himself among the victims, 'Ikh fil, ikh trog oyf zikh tsurik di gele late' [I feel I wear the yellow star once again] (1). The bright yellow of the 'late' [rags] draws attention to the Jewish cohort, and also physically separates them from the Others. As he affirms his connection with his lost community, he also becomes a witness. With or without the 'Jude' imprint, the wearers' fate was certain.

And yet, even when Fram's parents and their community went to their cruel deaths, they sanctified God, and the words of the *Sh'ma* mingled with the smoke of the pyres.[36] Customarily recited twice a day, the prayer has a long tradition in Jewish martyrdom. Rabbi Amnon of Mainz, who intoned it while his flesh was being torn with iron combs because he refused to convert to Christianity, pronounced the last word, 'Eḥad' [One] as he perished.[37]

While the marks of lamb's blood on the doorposts in Egypt signalled the Angel of Death to bypass the Jewish families, the yellow patches mark them for death. In the poet's eyes, they also signify how God and humanity abandoned the Jews: 'Milyonen hobn zikh getsoygn vayter, vayter | Tsum shvartsn eshafot ... oy, gantse zeks milyon!' [Millions were drawn further, further | To black execution scaffolds ... oh, a whole six million!] (18–19). In critiquing humanity's indifference to the tragic loss of his community, the poet delineates how 'meysim kupes-vayz hot men gelozn lign, | Un nokhanand gebrent, geshokhtn un gebrent...' [they left the dead lying in piles | Burning continuously, slaughtered and burnt...] (23–24). The stark yellow stars give the poem a visual focus and a sense of immediacy, as do the deathly kilns. However, their light and heat do not bring hope against the darkness.

In painterly fashion, Chagall responded to the events of *Kristallnacht*[38] with *White Crucifixion*, in which he situates the historical Jesus within the same arena as the shtetl victims. The INRI sign [Jesus of Nazareth, King of the Jews] is translated onto the crossbar into Aramaic: 'Yeshu HaNotzri Malcha Yehudai',[39] and Jesus wears a short headcloth instead of a crown of thorns, and the fringed tallit rather than the traditional loincloth. Evoking Jesus' fate and also that of the Jewish people as a whole, Chagall may be implying his own suffering; he may also have been attuned to guilt at his own absence. In 'violat[ing] narrative logic',[40] the effects of destruction are brought home in this depiction through the 'discontinuities between the individuals and objects',[41] inferring the impact of abandonment and the resulting breakdown of theodicy as well.

> [By] [...] expanding the meaning of the event, not only changing the original biblical image, but placing it in a more clearly modern historical context [the painting indicates] that what was happening in Germany was a recrucifixion of the Jewish Jesus [...]. [Chagall] wanted this message to be understood by the Christian world.[42]

Visually, the white shapes behind the cross expand the cruciform shape and its impact, leading the viewer's eye upwards to the heavenly destination. Around and below, villagers flee holding onto their precious bundles, fragile houses on the left of the canvas are tilted or upside down, and a rowing boat filled with desperate escapees is about to sink with no hope of rescue. On the right side of the Crucifixion, the synagogue goes up in flames revealing the Torah scrolls in the ark; an overturned chair, a torn prayer book, a tall menorah, and a lamp lie scattered on the ground. A lone figure that may remind one of the Wandering Jew 'attempts to escape to the right, carrying his sack on his back. Below him, a mother shields her baby as she too runs away'.[43] On the other side of the cross, three bearded figures try to escape, one of them clutching a Torah scroll. Suggestive, indirect, and allusive, Chagall's works refrain from the specific representation of torture or combat. Instead, Jesus' suffering creates an analogy for individual and communal persecution; representing his singular torment and that of the Jewish victims, the work visually manifests the spiritual tensions between darkness and light.

Chagall's use of the Crucifixion as an archetype in a Jewish context was not new. Other artists who engaged with Christology include Moshe Castel and Reuven

Rubin. David Roskies traces the apocalyptic tradition and the appropriation of the Crucifixion as a universal icon of Jewish catastrophe, highlighting Chagall's representation of Jesus together with Uri Tsvi Grinberg's interpretation.[44] In Grinberg's 'Yiddish "concrete" poem in the form of a cross, titled "Uri-Tsvi before the Cross/INRI", he addresses Jesus as "our brother", a symbol of Jewish suffering, who was hanging on crosses all over Europe for 2000 years'.[45] As Grinberg edited the Yiddish journal *Albatros*[46] in Warsaw and Berlin in the 1920s, which contained many illustrations by Chagall,[47] the latter would in all likelihood have been familiar with the poem.

After the Nazi-Soviet Pact in August 1939, Chagall reworked *White Crucifixion*. He obscured the emblem of the swastika on the armband of a stormtrooper setting fire to a synagogue in the top right-hand corner, as well as the German text 'Ich bin Jude' [I am a Jew] on a placard around the neck of an elderly Jew in the bottom left-hand corner. He did not do this to negate the guilt of the German regime, but rather to place its Russian counterpart as equivalent, and so raise the totalitarian horror of that period — and its specific antisemitic focus — to a more universal plane.[48]

Chagall's internalization of individual and communal persecution was already present many years before the Holocaust:

> '[f]or me, Christ has always symbolized the true type of the Jewish martyr. This is how I understood him in 1908 when I used this figure for the first time [...], it was under the influence of the pogroms. Then I painted and drew him in pictures about ghettos, surrounded by Jewish troubles, by Jewish mothers, running terrified with little children in their arms.[49]

In the early work *Golgotha* (1912),[50] Chagall identifies with the Christ figure by placing his own name above the cross instead of that of INRI, positioning himself at the centre of the scene. Referencing Jesus' disaffection from Jewishness and defamiliarizing both Christian and Jewish imagery also implies the painter's conflicting emotions.

Although Fram's perception that God had forsaken the Jewish people during the Shoah aligned with Chagall's, he was not a Christological poet, unlike 'many modernist writers, [including] Markish [who] incorporated Christological symbolism, especially when treating such expressionist themes as death, sorrow and decline'.[51] However, Fram does highlight the absence of divine intervention; decrying the fact that the Jewish victims' prayers were ignored, 'Lesterung' is predicated on the question, 'where was God...?'[52] The poet cries out: 'Farvos hostu geshvign, Got?' [Why did you keep silent, God?] (51), an accusation that is part of a long Jewish tradition, and calling God to account is a biblical topos. Abraham did so at the time of the destruction of Sodom and Gomorrah, and Moses spoke out on behalf of the Israelites when God intended to destroy them for having worshipped the Golden Calf. Habakkuk questioned God's inexplicable workings and the extent of human suffering: 'O Lord, how long shall I cry, and thou wilt not hear! I cry out to thee of violence, and thou wilt not save!'[53] Rabbi Levi Yitschak of Berdichev, in his 'Kaddish',[54] also challenged Him for punishing His people, despite their commitment to His commandments.

Thus, on behalf of the condemned, Fram asks, 'Un vi a Got fun rakhamim, | Nisht ongetsundn mit a treyst bay zey?' [And as a God of mercy, | Could [You] not have kindled some comfort for them?] (57–58). These lines from 'Lesterung' are reminiscent of Psalm 22, 'Eli, Eli lama azavtani?' [My God, my God, why hast thou forsaken me?] Later, during the war, they formed part of a Yiddish song:

> In 1942 as the bodies were burned, an eye-witness and survivor, Richard Glazer heard a Warsaw opera singer singing in the barracks a Yiddish song based on the psalm, 'My God, My God | Why hast Thou forsaken us?'[55]

Central to Jesus' sorrowful reproach when he was nailed to the crucifix, the final plea is implicit in both depictions.

Interpreting the absence of comfort as an unjust punishment of the faithful, in 'Lesterung',[56] the poet also rebels against Him by putting aside the commandment:[57]

> Di tfiln-zekl hobn lang gefoylt shoyn mayne tfiln.
> Es hot zikh der shel rosh badekt dort mit a grinem shiml,
> Un s'hot mayn talis heyliker farshemt geblibn lign — (42–44)
>
> [The *tfiln* bag and my *tfiln* have long lain untouched.
> And the *shel rosh* has become covered with a green mildew,
> And my holy *talis* has lain shamefully unused —]

Thus, while the poem's 'sonic quality' may evoke the 'rhythms of Jewish liturgy',[58] the poet stopped offering up the obligatory prayers owing to his crisis of belief. However, because the victims themselves continued their observance, Fram also experiences inner conflict and a sense of shame at his own choices:

> Ikh hob mayn altn Got in hartsn merer nit getrogn,
> Un kh'hob zikh keyn al-kheyt fartsitert nit geshlogn,
> [...]
> Hob ikh shoyn merer nit gezogt ma toyvu ohalekho... (35–36, 39)
>
> [I no longer carried my old God in my heart,
> I no longer in trepidation beat *al kheyt*,[59]
> [...]
> I no longer said *ma toyvu ohalekho*.][60]

Accusing God of being complicit and of being on the side of the enemy of the Jewish people, the poet goes as far as to confront Him as the perpetrator: 'Hostu aleyn zey gor gefirt tsu shekhtn in Treblinke' [You yourself took them to be slaughtered in Treblinka] (70), reinforcing this thought in the lines, 'hostu di gaz-oyvns farfult mit mayne brider, | Un hostu dem gzar aroysgelozt — dayn stade tsu farbrenen?' [Therefore, you loaded the gas ovens with my brothers, | And pronounced your decree — to burn your flock?] (77–78). Finding Him blameworthy in these ways, the poet loses his faith and the poem intensifies his sense of betrayal by referring to the Jewish people as once having been His 'stade' [flock] (78). Evoking the previous close and comforting bond between them, this description also echoes Psalm 23, 'The Lord is my Shepherd, I shall not want. He lays me down in green pastures.' The certainty of a dependable God expressed there in the line 'He who keepeth Israel shall neither slumber nor sleep' is a tragic contrast to the hellfire of the *khurbn*.

Oy, Got, ot hostu shoyn gezen, vi iz avek tsuzamen
Tsum shayter-hoyfn nokhamol dayn gantser groyser kool,
Un zikh gelozn far dayn shem fartsukn fun di flamen —
Fun vanent s'hot aroysgeshpart der letster Sh'ma Yisroel... (79–82)

[Alas, God, now you have seen how together they have gone
To the pyre-mounds once again, your whole great community,
And they let themselves be gobbled up by the flames for the sake of
Your [God's] name —
Where they sighed the final *Sh'ma Yisroel*...]

Perishing *al kiddush Hashem*, sanctifying God's name, the martyrs reinforce their unique relationship with Him. This dirge may also be read within a tradition of mourning literature, which 'began with the Book of Lamentations'.[61] Their final prayer goes up in smoke with them and the poem becomes their final Kaddish,[62] a poignant memorial.

Chagall's *Yellow* Crucifixion, painted in 1942 after the sinking of the *Struma*,[63] when news of genocide was spreading in the free world, also distils tragedy into 'images at once immediate, simple, and symbolic to which everyone could respond'.[64] The work draws attention to the fact that 'the Jewish Jesus with his covered head and fringed garment is also a Christian'.[65] Although Christ's phylacteries are correctly bound around his head and arm, he wears his fringed *talis* as a loincloth instead of a mantle, and is nailed to the cross, not praying in the synagogue. Illustrating the destruction of a pogrom, 'the [...] smaller "explanatory" scenes around the crucified figure [are] integrated [...] into the landscape, so that it seems that both they and Christ inhabit the same time and space.'[66] Although 'conceptual rather than realistic, each detail may be quite realistically depicted';[67] affirming Jesus' Jewishness, it also suggests his abandonment of it — and perhaps Chagall's as well.

A ladder creates a second focal point, situated at the centre and at an angle. Associated with the biblical narrative of Jacob and the angels connecting heaven and earth, it is usually considered a symbol of divine support. However, here it floats away or seems to be falling, or is perhaps being deliberately moved away. Like the image of Jesus on the cross, it hangs in limbo; offering no support, it may also imply a schism between man and God. The cross is placed close to the suspended, open Torah, which covers Jesus' right arm. This conjoining of Judaic and Christian iconography and the fact that they are given equal painterly weight suggesrs their continued dialogue and/or conflict. However, the fractured effect is 'underscored by the impossible proportions', and with 'no realistic transition',[68] they remain 'unassimilated into an explanatory plot'.[69] As the archangel blows the horn for the Day of Judgment, the ship sinks and burns on a fiery sea, and the refugees drown.[70] This cacophony of fragments does not 'represent one momentary experience but involve[s] different modules from various times and places'.[71] By exceeding conventional limitations of Holocaust representation, Chagall links images and symbols ambiguously across the canvas to evoke disaster and chaos instead of balance and comfort.

Emphasizing colour's crucial role, the yellow background aesthetically denotes space and unifies the whole, thus conjuring a 'combination of beauty and horror'.[72] The contrast with the spewing black smoke sets up a 'startling relationship between formal beauty and abhorrent function'.[73] Despite, or because of, the disturbing disjuncture created by its disruptive composition, and transgressive[74] use of the aesthetic elements of line, shape and space, as well as images and colour, a painting of this 'horrific subject ... resulted in [something that] might be called "aesthetically beautiful"',[75] which is an unsettling paradox.

Similarly evocative of loss, the broken Jewish ritual objects included in Fram's 'Dos letste kapitl'[76] are reminiscent of the images scattered across Chagall's canvases:

> Ot ligt a farblutikter vaybersher yakl,
> Ot trogstu di hemder fun undzere zeydes,
> Vos oysgeton hostu fun zeyere layber.
> Ot trogn mit khutspe atsind dayne vayber,
> Di tsirungen fun mayn gehargeter bobn,
> Vos unter mayn shvel du host tsinish bagrobn. (60–65)

> [Here lies a bloodied woman's jacket,
> Here you wear the shirts of our grandfathers,
> Which you stripped from their bodies.
> Here your wives wear now with impertinence,
> The jewellery of my murdered grandmother,
> Whom you cynically buried at my lintel...]

The aggressive verbs 'oysgeton' [stripped], 'gehargeter' [murdered] and 'bagrobn' [buried] intensify the horror as the murderers parade in the victims' clothes:

> Aikh ze fun a yidishe kale,
> Ot ze ikh a shtraymel, a yidishe hitl
> Un ot iz a vayser, a heyliker kitl.[77]
> Ot valgert zikh elnt a zilberner bekher
> Fun velkhn mayn tate gemakht hot nokh kidesh...[78] (69–73)

> [I see the veil of a Jewish bride.
> Here I see a fur hat, a Jewish hat.
> And here is the holy white robe.
> Here lies in desolation a silver goblet
> With which my father made Kiddush...]

Representing their murdered owners, the veil once worn by a bride, and the fur hat donned by the groom are reminders of valued individuals and intimate moments. Not just a collection of random detritus, each object represents someone who cherished it and whose life was enriched by it. The 'shleyer' [veil] (67) and 'shtraymel' [fur hat] (70) signify an active orthodox way of life, and the 'kitl' [holy white robe] (71) and the cup of wine embody previous rhythms of births and marriages, synagogue and family rituals — metonymical memorials to those who perished. Like the fragmented books, chair, table, and menorah that Chagall scattered across the canvas, where Jews take flight, holding onto their precious bundles, Fram's series of broken images draws attention to their plight. The disregard for and destruction of these artefacts evoke the loss of an entire community and a culture.

When Jewish Lithuania was destroyed, the sun, the honoured guest of 'Ikh benk' also disappeared. Thousands were locked in synagogues and set alight, or shot in the forests and buried in mass graves.[79] Nothing remained except 'meysim, harugim un kupes mit beyner' [murdered, the dead and piles of bones] (49) in a blood-soaked land. *Dos letste kapitl* is as 'deeply bitter about his homeland as his former love [for it] once was'.[80]

Afterwards, Lithuania welcomed the Russian conquerors as liberators,

> [Vayl itster men ken zikh gevis shoyn fartroyn
> Di ale derleyzer, di ale bafrayer:
> Di zun fun dem groysn, dem roytn oktober.]
> (*Dos letste kapitl*, 1089–91)
>
> [But we can now trust
> All our saviours, the liberators,
> The sons of the great, red October.]

Like much Yiddish poetry of the time, the poem idealizes the Soviet Union: the scale of Stalin's reign of terror — including the persecution and murders of Jews and others, and the 'acts of judicial murders'[81] of the Yiddish poets Peretz Markish, Itzik Fefer, and Dovid Hofshteyn in August 1952 — was only revealed after his death in 1953.

By the time Chagall's Vitebsk was liberated in 1944, it had been razed to the ground. Of its population of 170,000, there were only 118 survivors.[82] Over the years, the town continued to provide source material for Chagall's art, appearing in many oil paintings, sketches, and gouaches. Chagall transformed the Belarus he remembered into 'a fantastical vision and at the same time froze it in time like a memory, filled out with his own imaginative motifs rooted in memories and dreams, the unseen and the irrational'.[83] An etching for Chagall's memoir *My Life* includes the figure of a man with a row of houses on his back — Chagall carried Vitebsk with him wherever he went: 'I didn't have one single picture that didn't breathe with your spirit and reflection.'[84]

He also continued to paint crucifixions after the war, distilling his interpretations of the events and effects of 'the trauma on the Jewish world'[85] in the belief that these visual images would be 'the most effective means to convey his distress at the annihilation of Jewish life in Europe'.[86] With their incorporation of a Christian symbol to represent the Jewish *khurbn*, *White Crucifixion* and *Yellow Crucifixion* each emerged as 'a work of Jewish martyrology that transforms the crucifixion into an emblem of contemporary [Jewish] tragedy'.[87] These paintings 'address [Christians] in their own symbolic language'[88] in order to explain the deeper meaning of [Holocaust] events to them. By 'portray[ing] Jesus as a suffering man and Jew, rather than as Christianity's divine figure of redemption and salvation',[89] Chagall hoped to appeal to Christian viewers[90] to show follow their value system of goodwill towards all men, and to encourage their empathy for the Other, the Jewish victims, through self-identification. However, placing the icon of Jesus on the cross together with the Nazis' prey, affronted many Jewish viewers;[91] by subverting Judeo-Christian iconography, Chagall violated the normal Jewish boundaries of what was considered an acceptable representation of their genocide. Flouting Jewish lore, the iconoclastic paintings 'smack of conversion to Christianity, even if their Christian symbolism is inverted and freed from Church dogma'.[92] He wrote, '[n]o world conferences will be successful until the Jewish people are taken off the cross on which they were crucified for 2000 years.'[93]

Although Chagall and his wife Bella left in 1922, after the Soviet Union was formed, and received official permission to do so, he was regarded as a defector. As a result, he noted his 'intense, specific and long-lasting censorship of his own free expression',[94] afraid of retaliation against his two sisters and their families who remained behind, as well his friends and colleagues involved in cultural pursuits there.[95] As this situation 'tied his hands',[96] his choice to paint Jesus the Jew to represent his people's suffering instead of depicting German and Soviet atrocities directly may also be related to this fear.[97] Fearing for his own life, he returned to the Soviet Union only once, in 1973. Whatever the reason, in seeking 'a unique language adequate to unprecedented experience',[98] to depict the unimaginable, and represent the unrepresentable, Chagall makes use of disjunctive, fragmented imagery, moving away from classical elements such as balance, proportion, and the harmony of 'an unreconstructed return to an idealized version of beauty'.[99] Thus, as Kaplan suggests that Holocaust representation is best served by 'ambiguous, diverse, complicated, [and] open-ended' qualities[100] of these mute images captures the viewers' attention and may offer an antidote.

In different circumstances, when Fram wrote against Lithuanian perpetrators in 1947, he could do so openly: he had no surviving family in the Soviet Union, and writers in South Africa enjoyed 'a paradoxical freedom', where Yiddish could function as a 'demisecret code', free from political regulation.[101] However, as with Chagall, his estrangement from ritualized religion was also seared with questions about suffering: 'if he had any faith at all it was in a residual romanticism that trusted — potentially — in the redeeming power of love.'[102] In his confusion, he wrote, 'Ikh veys nisht vemen ikh zol betn — | tsu betn dikh, tsi betn got'[103] [To whom shall I address my yearning — I know not whom — to God or thee] (7–8).[104] Consequently, he instead dedicated his cycle of poems 'Lider tsu a froy aza vi du' [Songs to a Woman such as You],[105] to an unknown woman whom he cherished. This includes 'Friling' [Spring]:[106]

> Hot friling farshept
> Mit zayn eydeln tsvit.
> S'hot sheyn der orandsh, der milgroym,
> Der apelboym ergets geblit. (1–4)

> [The spring began to blossom
> with the scent of apple and lemon
> the orange poured gold
> in the golden day.][107]

All his senses are stirred by the warmth and fragrance surrounding him, so that he feels nourished: 'Bliyen mit gloybn, mit yugnt, | Mit varemer, zuniker freyd — ' [Blossoming with belief | With warm, sunny satisfaction] (7–8).

Whereas he had once associated nature's bounty with a 'derbarmikter Got' [beneficent God] (15),[108] here his spirit is uplifted by the woman's warmth: 'Trinken di bisem farshikurt | Vos roykhln zikh fun ire hor' [To be drunk with her nectar | tossed in the softness of her hair] (13–14). Disillusioned with religious rituals and feeling that his people had been abandoned in their plight, he seeks and finds some relief elsewhere. 'Un khotsh a vayl fargesn | Dem emes fun nikhterer vor' [And for a moment to forget and be forgiven | Released from my suffering] (15–16). Alive with passion, typical of Fram's lyric art,[109] these lines evoke his connection to nature as well as to her: 'zi iz gekumen mikh treystn | mit laykhte, mit zunike trit' [She came to console me | with light, with sunny steps] (23–24).

Had Fram returned home, he would have found everyone gone; his mother, Shifra Mina, father Yoysef Ber, his sister Esther together with the rest of his community were murdered by the Nazis' Lithuanian henchmen in the Panevezys death camp in June 1942.[110]

> Un eyner aleyn do on shvester un brider
> On shakres, on mayriv, on shabes, on kidush,
> On hartsikn prostn un tayern yidddish —
> Iz shver dokh tsu lebn un shver iz tsu zayn do.
> (*Dos letste kapitl*, 1148–51)

> [And I am here alone, no sister, no brother,
> No Jewish children, no Jewish songs.
> No morning prayers, no evening prayers, no Sabbath, no Kiddush
> No warm welcome in clear Yiddish.
> It is difficult to live, difficult to be here.][111]

Fram's sixty-eight-page classic, *Dos letste kapitl*, which evolved over the war years, was instrumental in his being proposed for the Nobel prize for literature.[112] Using Yiddish allowed him to highlight the guilt of his former countrymen in Lithuania without fear of censorship or retribution, 'providing an important window onto a period in which unrestricted access to archives remained unusual',[113] unlike his peers who had remained in Soviet Russia, most of whom perished. By memorializing the fate of his silenced people, Fram's poems also functions as testimony.

Because 'the Nazis planned that there would be no Jewish survivors to tell the tale (the story Himmler said would never be written)',[114] the need to record what happened was and remains urgent. Fram and Chagall's Holocaust-inflected works reference trauma narrative;[115] responding to the destruction on the killing fields of Eastern Europe, their interpretations and outcomes were influenced by their choice of words and paint respectively. By locating Jews at the centre of their works representing singular Jewish subject matter, the artist and the poet affirmed their deep connection to their roots emotionally, psychologically, and spiritually. Giving 'voice to a would-be silenced culture which continues to assert its continuities',[116] they may elicit empathy, anger, or incredulity. 'Despite the risks of distortion and displacement, representations of all sorts [...] remain the only access to historical events.'[117] In exploring Fram's verbal imagery together with Chagall's symbols, the hope is to provide fruitful insights, encouraging us 'to know the apocalypse, express it, mourn it, and transcend it'.[118]

Fram and Chagall's works also counteract our contemporary concerns with distortion, denial, and forgetting. Where metaphor transforms the painful past, such 'attempts to represent horror [...] can encourage complex forms of memory work and enhance Holocaust remembrance'.[119] Addressing current anxieties related to such questions such as 'What if no one remembers?' and 'What happens when there is no one left to remember?', they may influence the reader and viewer's understanding of significant and traumatic events. Through their aligned sensibilities and resonant themes, the 'intertwining of the everyday and the extreme',[120] both poet and painter warn us against abandoning the victims once more.

Notes to Chapter 7

1. 'Fareltert' [Obsolete] (1929), *Lider un poemes*, pp. 85–86.
2. W. J. T. Mitchell, *Iconology: Image. Text. Ideology* (Chicago: The University of Chicago Press, 1986), p. 38.
3. Marc Chagall, *I and the Village (The Village and I)*, 1911, oil on canvas, 192.1 × 151.5 cm, The Museum of Modern Art, New York.
4. Marc Chagall, *The Blue House*, 1917, oil on canvas, 66 × 97 cm, Musée d'Art Moderne et d'Art Contemporain, Liège, Belgium.
5. Marc Chagall, *White Crucifixion*, oil on canvas, 154.3 × 139.7 cm, Art Institute of Chicago.
6. Marc Chagall, *Yellow Crucifixion*, 1942, oil on canvas, 140 × 101 cm, Musée National d'Art Moderne — Centre Pompidou, Paris.
7. Benjamin Harshav, 'Chagall, Marc', *YIVO Encyclopedia of Jews in Eastern Europe* (15 December 2010) <https://yivoencyclopedia.org/article.aspx/Chagall_Marc> [accessed 17 December 2020].
8. Jewish New Year.
9. Day of Atonement, Day of the Fast.
10. Passover, when it is customary to eat unleavened cakes, rather than bread.
11. Prayer mantle.
12. Hebrew school.
13. Marc Chagall, *My Life*, 3rd edn (New York: Orion Press, 1960).
14. Peretz Markish translated Chagall's autobiography *My Life* into Yiddish in Paris during the mid-twenties, and Chagall illustrated the cover of the Yiddish literary journal *Khalyastre* [Happy Gang], edited by Markish and Oyzer Varshavsky, with an image of the three of them climbing the Eiffel Tower.
15. Sabbath dish of carrots and potatoes.
16. Benjamin Harshav, *Marc Chagall*, p. 52.
17. *Lider*, p. 89.
18. Benjamin Harshav, *Marc Chagall*, p. 41.
19. Ibid., p. 62.
20. Skullcap. Hebrew: kipah.
21. Dorot, p. 35.
22. Ibid, pp. 27–28.
23. Chagall in Dorot, p. 11.
24. Dorot, p. 35.
25. Leona Toker, 'Folk Theodicy in Concentration Camps: Literary Representations', in *Knowledge and Pain*, ed. by Esther Cohen and others (New York: Rodopi, 2012), pp. 197–214, (p. 197).
26. Dating back to medieval times, this symbol of humiliation also took the form of an armband or a patch on the back. It was often imprinted with the identifying term 'Jude' [Jew].
27. The topic of the Allies' awareness of what was happening to the Jews of Europe and their failure to intervene goes beyond the scope of this study.
28. S. T. Goodman, *Chagall*, p. 57.
29. Avram Kampf, *Chagall to Kitaj: Jewish Experience in 20th Century Art* (London: Humphries, 1990), p. 84.

30. Ibid.
31. Ibid.
32. Toker, p. 197.
33. Ibid.
34. Ibid.
35. *Dorem Afrike* (July–August 1971), 50.
36. Cf. Chapter 5, note 9, and discussion.
37. *The Complete ArtScroll Machzor, Rosh Hashanah*, ed. by Rabbi Nossen Scherman and Rabbi Meir Zlotowitz (New York: Mesorah Publications, 2001), p. 480. See Chapter 6, note 85, and Chapter 5, note 12.
38. The Night of Broken Glass took place across Germany and Austria on 9 to 10 November 1938. Now categorized as a massive pogrom, this was an officially orchestrated destruction of Jewish homes, synagogues, and shops. The Nazis also imprisoned thousands of Jews.
39. Ziva Amishai-Maisels, 'Chagall's White Crucifixion', *Art Institute of Chicago Museum Studies*, 17.2 (1991), 138–53, 180–81 (p. 139).
40. Gubar, p. 166.
41. Benjamin Harshav, *Marc Chagall*, p. 60.
42. Amishai-Maisels, p. 143.
43. Ibid.
44. Roskies, *Against the Apocolyps*e, p. 269.
45. Benjamin Harshav, *Marc Chagall*, p. 218.
46. *Di khalyastre*, the group of Yiddish Expressionist poets, who also published the journals *Khalyastre* and *Literarishe Revi* [Literary Review] in Paris.
47. Harshav, *Marc Chagall*, p. 218.
48. Paul Trewhela, 'Chagall and the Murdered Poets', *Jewish Affairs*, 75.3 (Winter 2020), n. p. <https://www.sajbd.org/media/chagall-and-the-murdered-poets> [accessed 19 December 2020].
49. Chagall in L. Leneman, 'Marc Chagall wegen zeine Christus-figuren als Symbol fun Yidishe martyrertum' [Marc Chagall on his Christ-figures as Symbols of Jewish Martyrdom], *Undzer Wort* [In Yiddish], 22 January 1977, p. 4; in Amishai-Maisels, p. 143.
50. Marc Chagall, *Golgotha*, 1912, oil on canvas, 46.4 × 55.3 cm, Collection of Ruth O'Hara, New York.
51. David Shneer, 'An Introduction. *My Name is Now*: Peretz Markish and the Literature of the Revolution', in *A Captive of the Dawn: The Life and Works of Peretz Markish (1895–1952)*, ed. by Joseph Sherman and others (Oxford: MHRA and Maney Publishing, 2011), pp. 1–15 (p. 6).
52. Toker, p. 197.
53. Habakkuk 1. 2.
54. Cf. Chapter 5.
55. Sicher, 'Introduction', p. 38.
56. *A shvalb oyfn dakh*, 127–29; (extract), *Dorem Afrike* (May–June 1965), p. 3; part of a longer poem, 'Ma tovu ohalekho Yankev' [How Goodly Are Thy Tents, O Jacob].
57. 'And thou shalt bind them for a sign on thy hand, and they shall be for frontlets between thine eyes' (Deut. 6. 4–9).
58. Sherman, 'Singing with the Silence', p. 44.
59. 'For the sin wherein we have sinned...': refrain on the Day of Atonement, see Rabbi Nossen Scherman, *The Complete ArtScroll Machzor: Yom Kippur* (New York: Mesorach Publications, 1986), pp. 94–97.
60. Prayer said on entering the synagogue, Num. 24. 5.
61. *From a Ruined Garden*, ed. and trans. by Kugelmass and Boyarin, p. 6.
62. The Mourner's Prayer intoned for the dead at the graveside, for eleven months thereafter in the synagogue, and on the *yortsayt*, the anniversary of the day of death.
63. The doomed steamship, carrying 768 Jewish refugees from Nazi-occupied Europe to Palestine, was torpedoed by a Soviet submarine in March 1942.
64. Jackie Wullschläger, *Chagall: A Biography* (New York: Knopf, 2008), p. 4.
65. Ibid.

66. Ibid.
67. Ibid., p. 60.
68. Ibid.
69. Gubar, p. 166.
70. The scene is perhaps subversively reminiscent of Pieter Breughel's *Landscape with the Fall of Icarus*.
71. Benjamin Harshav, *Marc Chagall*, pp. 41–42.
72. Simone de Beauvoir in Lanszmann, p. iv.
73. Wendy Joy Kuppermann in Feinstein, 'Mediums of Memory', p. 212.
74. Matthew Boswell, *Holocaust Impiety in Literature, Popular Music and Film* (London: Palgrave Macmillan, 2012).
75. Feinstein, 'Mediums of Memory', p. 210.
76. *Dos letste kapitl* (London: Narod Press, 1947): Fram gives 1945 as the date he completed writing the epic (p. 68). Unless otherwise indicated, the discussion is based on the extract 'Dos letste kapitl', *Dorem Afrike* (January–March 1984), 12. Also see Chapter 6.
77. White garment worn by many religious Jews on Yom Kippur, the Day of Atonement; also the garment in which every Jew is buried.
78. Blessing over wine and bread made every Friday night.
79. Yehuda Bauer, *A History of the Holocaust* (Connecticut: Watts, 1982), p. 198.
80. J. M. Sherman, '"David Fram"'.
81. Sherman in Chana Kronfeld, 'Murdered Modernisms: Peretz Markish and the Legacy of Soviet Yiddish Poetry', in *A Captive of the Dawn*, ed. by Sherman and others, pp. 186–206 (p. 186).
82. Wullschläger, p. 4.
83. Ibid., p. 141.
84. Ibid., p. 29.
85. Dorot, p. 79.
86. S. T. Goodman, *Chagall*, p. 51.
87. Wullschläger, p. 381.
88. Amishai-Maisels, pp. 150–51.
89. Wullschläger, p. 381.
90. Catherine Quehl-Engel, 'Modern Jewish Art and the Crucifixion: A Study in Appropriation', *Soundings: An Interdisciplinary Journal*, 80.1 (Spring 1997), 132–52 (p. 140).
91. Quehl-Engel, p. 140.
92. Ibid.
93. Harshav, *Marc Chagall*, p. 218.
94. Chagall in Trewhela, n. p.
95. A number of his friends and peers, including Markish, were murdered in 1952.
96. Chagall in Trewhela, n. p.
97. Trewhela, n. p.
98. Ezrahi, p. 61.
99. Kaplan, *Unwanted Beauty*, p. 12.
100. Ibid., p. 2.
101. Rosenblatt, p. 53.
102. Sherman, 'What Balm for the Heart...?', p. 11.
103. *A shvalb oyfn dakh*, p. 13. 'Ikh veys nisht vemen ikh zol betn' [I do not know whom to ask] is the poem's first line; it has no title.
104. 'Untitled', trans. of 'Ikh veys nisht vemen ikh zol betn' [I do not know whom to ask] by Rochelle Mann, *Jewish Affairs*, 48.3 (Spring 1993), 83.
105. *A shvalb oyfn dakh*, pp. 9–32.
106. Ibid., p. 9.
107. 'Spring', trans. by Marcia Leveson, *Jewish Affairs*, 16.2 (September 1991), 83.
108. 'Ikh benk', *Lider*, p. 89.
109. Sherman, 'What Balm for the Heart...?', p. 10.
110. Testimony submitted by Fram's nephew Itamar Borowitz, testimony documents no. 633259, 6332600, 6332601, *Yad Vashem* <https://yvng.yadvashem.org/index.html?language=en&s_

id=&s_lastName=Fram&s_firstName=&s_place=&s_dateOfBirth=&cluster=true> [accessed 19 December 2020]. Fram's daughter Shifrah Mina was named for his deceased mother. A custom amongst traditional Jews, this tangibly affirmed his connection to his family.

111. Trans. by Davis, p. 46.

112. Joseph Sherman, 'Literature: Yiddish and Hebrew', in *South African Jewry: A Contemporary Survey*, ed. by Marcus Arkin (Cape Town: Oxford University Press, 1984), p. 156.

113. Rosenblatt, p. 53.

114. Sicher, 'The Holocaust in the Postmodernist Era', p. 306.

115. Cathy Caruth, *Unclaimed Experience: Trauma, Narrative and History* (Baltimore: Johns Hopkins University Press, 1996).

116. Rothberg, p. 276.

117. Ibid., p. 234.

118. Roskies, *Against the Apocolypse*, p. 310.

119. Ibid.

120. Ibid.

CONCLUSION: REVITALIZATION, PRESERVATION, AND MEMORIALIZATION

This study establishes the aesthetic and cultural value of David Fram's poems, bearing in mind the broader question 'Who Will Write our History?'[1] In doing so, it illuminates the richness of Yiddish literature and culture of Eastern Europe and its offshoots in South Africa. By drawing attention to this small but significant area, and by relating Fram's oeuvre to other aspects of literary and cultural interest, this research goes some way towards the perpetuation, preservation, and continuity of the vibrant culture of Yiddish far from its original locus.

Fram's education, devotion to learning, and his exile gave him the wherewithal to become a writer. He was not part of any 'school of writing [...], [but] was an individualist with his own specific vision of life, his own interpretations of it, and his own reaction to it'.[2] A teller of tales, a 'dertsayler',[3] Fram's explorations included lyrics and epics that reflect the circumstances of a particular individual in a specific time and place, bringing together diverse strands of literary individuality and influence, the poet's personal worldview, and his struggles with belief.

His wanderings, loss of family and community, and interactions in his environment evoked his poetic search for meaning. Constantly on the move, unable to return home but not belonging where he was, 'his loneliness',[4] his 'aynzamkeyt'[5] was heightened by his desire to be elsewhere — '[u]n zukhn nokh trayst in ergets andershvu'.[6] Embodying a sense of place rooted in language and routed through memory, his poetry narrates his unique journey as an insider and an outsider. Offering different ways of seeing the Jewish immigrant and the Black Other as more than the stereotypes of commonplace prejudices, the poems confirm the impact of migration and also the significance of a minority literature within that of the dominant culture in Lithuania and South Africa.

After the destruction of its cultural and linguistic centre,

> post-war Yiddish study has had a sense of urgency about it, from the taping and documenting of the survivors to the monumental efforts to create archives, libraries, and electronic databases of the writings produced in worlds erased by violence, neglect, or indifference.[7]

It was in this context that Fram's second collection, *A shvalb oyfn dakh*, was launched at the Connoisseur Hotel, on Tuesday, 2 November 1983. Coinciding with his 80th birthday, the function was sponsored by the South African Jewish Trust. Joseph Sherman was the driving force behind its editing and publication,[8] and he confirmed the collection's value.[9]

However, language communicates best when it can rely on a broad background of understanding in society and on readers' familiarity with a wide range of texts, written and oral, fiction and folklore, essays, ideology, and philosophy. Today, 'little of this can be assumed in the reader of Yiddish',[10] and 'compared with its pre-war breadth and diversity, post-war Yiddish culture was perceived as an epilogue, a mere shadow and deplorable remnant, and thus much less significant'.[11] As a 'generation has arrived for whom Yiddish is not a native language, and where a Yiddish cultural atmosphere is an object of study rather than a lived occurrence',[12] it has 'different conceptualizations of the language than for those who grew up in a Yiddish speaking environment, let alone those from the shtetl itself'.[13]

Because it is no longer the vernacular for readers and students in the secular environment, there is an urgent need for the translation of Yiddish literature, to provide access to its historical and cultural richness. In bringing Fram's poems into the consciousness of the reading public, and making them available through my transliterations and translations, the hope is to contribute to the understanding of these concerns in a broader context.

In a marriage of opposites, with Fram inhabiting 'a culture of diversity and simultaneity, diasporically Jewish and national citizen at once',[14] Lithuania remained his emotional home, but as he began to 'notice Africa, Africa began to dominate his poems'[15] and 'he was inspired and determined to go along that path.'[16] In doing so, he became 'progenitor of the Yiddish lyric in a new centre, South Africa',[17] the 'progon fun der yiddisher lirik in a nayem tsenter — Dorem Afrike'.[18]

Nevertheless, even then, those other spaces filled his imagination, and he used his mother tongue to preserve their cherished memory. Seeking 'balm for the heart',[19] solace, possibility, and hope, 'Oyf mayn dakh hot amol nokh gesvistshert a shvalb' [Once a Swallow Twittered on my Roof][20] illustrates how his longing for the familiar landscape of home and its vanished world remained constant:

> Un di lonkes bashotn mit tsheredes shof,
> Un di oygn fun likht ikh farzhmure oyf halb,
> Un es khapt mikh arum aza gliklekher shlof, —
> Oyf mayn dakh hot amol nokh gesvistshert a shvalb... (17–20)
>
> [And the meadows were shaded with flocks of sheep,
> And I half close my eyes against the bright light,
> And I am seized by such contented sleep, —
> Once a swallow still twittered on my roof...]

Fram never returned to Lithuania, and through memories of *di alte heym*, his poetry became both relic and reliquary of a culture. It also contributes important contemporary insights into the Holocaust in the face of widespread distortion and denial. Embedded in the personal and historical past, his responses to the *khurbn* resist the erasure of a particular heritage. The inscription on Fram's tombstone represents his exile, holding a deep memory of what he left behind and acknowledging his meaningful contribution to South African Yiddish literature.[21]

Affirming the valuable contribution of Fram's poems to South African literature and history, and to the field of Yiddish literature and Jewish studies as a whole, this study retrieves and recuperates them to enhance remembrance.[22] Where the 'ethical act is to never forget so the burden of memory is passed on',[23] this testament contributes to the current 'mammoth effort to preserve Yiddish literature'[24] for future generations.

Notes to the Conclusion

1. Samuel Kassow, *Who Will Write Our History? Emanuel Ringelblum, the Warsaw Ghetto, and the Oyneg Shabes Archive* (Bloomington: Indiana University Press, 2007).
2. Fayvl Zygielbaum, 'David Fram's 60th birthday in Salisbury', *Zionist Record and South African Jewish Times*, 23 August 1963, n. p.
3. Niger, p. 616.
4. Sherman, 'What Balm for the Heart...?, p. 11.
5. Zygielbaum, 'Tsu Dovid Frams avekforn', p. 23.
6. Ibid.
7. Wirth-Nesher, 'Modern Yiddish Literary Studies', p. 213.
8. W. Levick, 'A Personal Appreciation of David Fram', *Jewish Affairs*, 36.9 (September 1983), p. 36.
9. Joseph Sherman, 'On Publishing the New Anthology', *Jewish Affairs*, 38.9 (September 1983), 37. Sherman's foresight also enabled the archiving of Fram's papers at the Benson Library at the University of Texas, Austin. Microfiche files are available.
10. B. Harshav and B. Harshav, *American Yiddish Poetry*, p. 9.
11. Lipphardt, p. 80.
12. Krutikov, 'Yiddish Studies from a New Perspective', p. 2.
13. Ibid.
14. Zemel, p. 177.
15. Ravitch, 'Dovid Fram un zayn lider', p. 59.
16. Ibid..
17. Ibid.
18. Niger, p. 616.
19. 'Vert den gringer derfun', trans. by Amelia Levy in L. Goodman, 'David Fram: A Study in Growth', p. 30.
20. *A shvalb oyfn dakh*, p. 67.
21. The inscription on David Fram's tombstone in West Park Jewish Cemetery reads:

    Dovid Fram, nifter 25 tamuz 5748. Geboyren in Ponevezh 14-tn oktober 1903. Geshtorbn in Yohanesburg 10stn yuli 1988. Poet liriker, idiliyen-shrayber in a zaftikn litvishn idish arayngebrakht dorem afrike in der idisher literatur. Es troyern ale libheber fun idishn vort [David Fram. Yiddish poet. 14 October 1903–10 July 1988. Born in Ponevyzs, died in Johannesburg. Lyrical poet and writer of idylls who brought tender Lithuanian Yiddish into South African Yiddish literature. Sadly missed by all lovers of the Yiddish word].

22. The establishment of Holocaust and Genocide Centres in Johannesburg, Cape Town, and Durban in South Africa are part of this drive.
23. Peterson, p. 179.
24. Wirth-Nesher, 'Tradition, the Individual Talent, and Yiddish', p. 8.

POEMS BY
DAVID FRAM

The YIVO system has been used for Yiddish. Hebrew words
have been transliterated using the Yiddish system.

Fun tate-mames yidishe

Di kinderlekh fun der ershter yidisher folksshul
in Yohanesburg-geheylikt

1   Fun tate-mames yidishe, vos hobn zikh geshemt
Mit yidish un fun yidishkayt geven azoy farfremdt —
Ikh hob aykh, libe kinderlekh, tsum ershtn mol derzen,
Un s'hot a fayer heyliker in hartsn zikh tsebrent...

5   Ir hot in yidish poshetn tsezungen ayer freyd,
Zikh gloybike, tsufridene in karahod gedreyt,
Un s'hot geklungen kishefdik der kindisher gezang,
Nokh vos ikh hob an elnter gebenkt vi ir fun lang...

9   Ikh hob gebenkt an elnter, un dokh hob ikh gevust,
Az s'tsaplt zikh a heylikayt bay yedern in brust:
— Dos yidish, vos es zaftikt zikh oyf lipelekh bakheynt —
Fun vos me hot aykh, kinderlekh, fun kindvayz on antveynt.

13   Pionern hobn oysgeleygt far aykh a heln veg —
Tzu firn aykh dermunterte tsu yon-tevdike teg:
Dan hot mayn simkhe oyfgebroyzt mit ayerer tsu glaykh.
Az voyl iz mir, o kinderlekh, tzu freyen zikh mit aykh!

Lider, p. 77

From Jewish Parents

Dedicated to the children of the first
Yiddish folk school in Johannesburg

1   From Jewish parents who were embarrassed
     By Yiddish and were so estranged from *yiddishkayt* —
     I have noticed you, dear children, for the first time,
     And a holy flame has flared up in [my] heart...

5   You sang out your joy in simple Yiddish,
     And faithfully in contentment twirled the circle dance,
     And the childlike singing rang out enchantingly,
     For which, like you, I have forlornly longed for ages...

9   I have longed forlornly, and yet have I known,
     That a holiness quivers in each and every breast:
     — That Yiddish, so juicy on charming little lips —
     From which they weaned you away, children, from infancy.

13   Pioneers set out a bright path for you —
     To lead you with spirits raised to festive days;
     Then my joy welled up together with yours.
     How happy I am, oh children, to rejoice along with you!

Ikh benk

1   Ikh benk azoy mid nokh a shtikele shvartse, tsekvolene erd
Nokh harbstike regns oyf felder un blotes oyf endlozn trakt,
Vu shlepn zikh mide, tseveykte, farshpetikte, elnte ferd,
Mit dorfishn umet balodn un poyerisher pratse gepakt.

5   Ikh benk nokh di yidn fun velder, vi kuperne yodles farpekht,
Vos shmekn in friyike reykhus fun shvomen un varemen mokh,
Vos shlepn aheym zikh oyf shabes durkh osyendik-vintike nekht,
Un garn nokh ruiker shalve fun shverer, farmaterter vokh.

9   Ikh benk nokh di teg, ven es gibn di seder avek zeyer gob,
Un s'vern di kelers farfult mit a vayniker gilderner last,
Un himlen, zey vern alts nenter un lozn tsu dr'erd zikh arop,
Un zun kumt tsu geyn oyf a vayl vi a zeltener, khoshever gast.

13   Un dan vern shtiler di reges, nokh shtile fun leydikn sod,
Nokh shtiler fun dorfishn elnt oyf harbstik-farlozenem feld.
Tsevakst dan in vareme hertser a groyser, derbarmiker Got,
Un shpreyt aza mekhtikn gloybn oyf groyer, farshvigener velt.

17   Dan gloyb ikh ... dan gloyb ikh mit hertser, vos gloybn emunedik-frum,
Vos zaynen mit heylike tfiles vi harbstike kelers gepakt...
In teg fun farlozn di seder ikh benk azoy elntik-shtum,
Nokh yidn fun pekhike velder oyf soflozn, blotikn trakt.

Lider, p. 89

Mayn opfor

1   Dos hemd — atsind gedenk ikh nokh — mayn shvester hot geneyt.
Derken ikh ire kleyne shtekh, di forzikhtike net.
Zi hot mit shtiler hartsikayt un benkshaft es baveyt
In lange, lange ovntn farzesn zikh biz shpet.

5   Un nokhdem hot mayn mame shtil a pekele gemakht,
Dort pomerantsn ongeleygt un tsukerlekh farpakt.
Gedenk ikh, aza kleyninke in harbstikn farnakht
Fardayget mikh aroysbagleyt tsum breyt-tseleygtn trakt.

9   Mayn tate iz geshtanen mid mit dine, lange hent,
Dem vaysn kop aropgelozt, on verter un on reyd.
A shkie hot a blutike in hartsn zikh tsebrent,
Un s'hot a nakht a finstere unz alemen tsesheydt.

13   Un kh'hob in nakht in harbstiker farlozn zey aleyn,
Tseshnitn hot mayn shtume harts a trukn-sharfer vey,
Un s'hot a vildn shpar geton mit trern a geveyn —
Farshtikt in triber elntkayt an elntn geshrey.

17   Un do, in vayter Afrike, iz veytogdik un shver,
Durkh benkenish geleyterter farvoglt in der fremd...
Mayn shvester hot mikh oysgeputst mit shmekedikn hemd,
Un mame hot aroysbagleyt in veg mikh mit ir trer.

Lider, p. 14

I Long

1 I wearily long for a piece of black, swollen earth,
For autumn rains on the fields and mud on endless roads,
Where tired, soaked, late and forlorn horses trudge along,
Heavy with village sadness and packed with peasant toil.

5 I long for the Jews of the forests, pitch-dark like copper firs,
Smelling of the early scents of mushrooms and warm moss,
Who drag themselves home for Sabbath through windy, autumn nights,
Craving tranquillity from the heavy, exhausting week.

9 I long for the days when the orchards give up their bounty,
And the cellars are filled with their wine-like golden store,
And skies draw closer, stooping down towards the earth,
And sun visits awhile, like a rare, honoured guest.

13 And then the moments become quieter, even more still than empty orchards,
Even quieter than village desolation in the autumn-abandoned field.
And growing then in warm hearts, a great, merciful God,
Spreads a mighty belief on a grey, silent world.

17 Then I believe ... then I believe with hearts that believe faithfully and piously,
Packed like autumn cellars with holy prayers,
Now, when I have lost those orchards, I long, alone and silent,
For Jews of the fluffy forests and the endless, muddy ways.

My Departure

1 The shirt — I still remember — sewn by my sister.
I know her tiny stitches snug and neat.
Made while sitting in quiet diligence alone
For long, long evenings until late.

5 And after that my mother quietly made a parcel
Packed with oranges and sweets.
I remember, such a tiny woman in the autumn evening,
As she anxiously escorted me to the wide, far-reaching road.

9 My father stood wearily with thin, long hands,
His white head bowed, without words and silent.
A bloody sunset burned in [our] hearts,
As a dark night separated us all.

13 And in that autumn night I left them on their own,
My quiet, severed heart is full of pressing, sharp pain,
And many lonely tears we moan —
Pierced by dismal loneliness we cry out desolately.

17 And here, in far-off Africa, in pain and hardship
I am an exiled stranger filled with pure longing...
My sister dressed me in a sweet-smelling shirt,
And mother accompanied me along the path, crying.

Mayn mame hot mir tsugeshikt a kishn

1   Mayn mame hot mir tsugeshikt a kishn —
        A grus a heymisher fun benkendiker Lite!
        Do in Afrike, in enger kaferite.
        Oy, ven zi volt epes fun dem visn! ...

5   Mayne lange teg un zunike baginens,
        Kh'hob akhzaryesdik farkirtst zey un farshnitn,
        Un hakhnoedik, tsufridn un farlitn,
        Kafers muz ikh shmutsike badinen.

9   Zaynen zey atsind mir nont azoy gevorn,
        Glaykh vi oreme un leydndike brider,
        Oykh azoy vi zey — farshvigener un mider
        Tseyl ikh ovntn tsuzamen shoyn in yorn.

13   Tseyl ikh glaykhgiltik a shtumer yedn ovnt
        Vi blumen harbstike fun gertener gerisn;
        Mayn mame hot mir tsugeshikt a kishn —
        Durkh vayse vintern di federn gekhovet.

                                    Lider, pp. 18–19

My Mother Sent Me a Cushion

1   My mother sent me a cushion —
     A homemade greeting from yearning Lithuania!
     Here in Africa, in the crowded concession store.
     Oy, if she only had an inkling about it! ...

5   Through long days and sunny dawns,
     I have cruelly deprived and suppressed them,
     And servile, content and patient,
     I must serve dirty black customers.

9   I have now become so close to them,
     Just like poor and suffering brothers,
     Also just like them — more silent and tired,
     I have already counted my nights in years.

13   Indifferent I count each night in silence,
     Like autumn flowers torn from the gardens;
     My mother sent me a cushion —
     The feathers gathered through winters white.

Iz vos?

1   Iz vos, oyb gelebt kh'hob amol in der vayter un shtiler Samare
Un nokhdem megulgl gevorn aleyn tsu di breges fun Lite,
Un itst — shoyn in Afrike fremder, vu s'shmekt mitn zamd fun Sahare,
Mit trukene zunen farbroynte un shteynerne felzn tseglite?

5   Iz vos, oyb es hobn gehodevet mikh ven der Volges tsegosene breges,
Un s'hobn farvigt mikh di lider fun berdike, mide 'batrakes'?
Az s'hot mikh mayn goyrl farbundn mit troyer fun blutike reges,
Vos zaynen gerunen in khoyshekh, vi ayeter fun ofene makes...

9   Iz vos-zhe, oyb ikh hob farzindikt baym lebn di heylike klorkayt fun shneyen,
Dem kupernem harbst bay di taykhn, dem shikern vinter tseglitn?
Un itst oyf farzhaverte gruntn, fartserte fun brenike veyen, —
Di oytsres fun gilderne harbstn un zilberne vinters tsebitn?

13   Iz vos-zhe, oyb s'hot zikh in Afrike fremder fartoplt mayn leydn in tsveyen,
Fargresert di atsves in hartsn, der elnt farshvign gevorn...
Ikh veys dokh: di teg vi fartsaytn, zey kumen un geyen, fargeyen,
Un s'klaybn zikh shtile mes-lesn un bindn tsunoyf zikh in yorn...

17   Iz vemenen art es, a shtayger, az emetser veynt, a fartserter,
Az emetser benkt in der finster nokh lider fun Volger 'batrakes'?
Iz vemenen art es, a shtayger, az hele fartrikenen verter,
Un s'rinen tseveytogte reges, vi ayeter fun ofene makes? ...

21   S'iz gornisht ... s'iz gornisht ... ikh veys es; — der emes iz shreklekh far eynem.
Di teg, vi zey zaynen gegangen, fargeyn veln vider in vaytn.
Un ikh vel nokh voglen a mider oyf shtoybike vegn on keynem,
Un efsher nokh Afrikes elnt oyf topltn elent tsebaytn.

Lider, pp. 16–17

So What?

1   So what, if I once lived in distant and silent Samara
And after that, transformed, I landed up alone on the shores of Lite,
And now — in strange Africa, which smells of the sand of Sahara,
Browned by the sun and stony glowing cliffs?

5   So what, if I was raised when the Volga overflowed its banks,
And the songs that lulled me to sleep were those of bearded, weary farm labourers?
And what if my fate was linked with sadness of bloody moments
That curdled in darkness, like the pus of open abscesses...

9   So what, if I sinned in life against the holy clarity of snow,
The copper autumn by the rivers, a drunkard heating the winter?
And now on rusted soil, devoured by burning pain, —
The treasure of golden autumn exchanged for silver winters?

13   So what, if in the strangeness of Africa my suffering has doubled,
The sadness in my heart is increased, the loneliness is silenced...
I know: as in times past, the days come and go, and pass on,
And the silent days and nights collect and bind the years together...

17   So who cares at all, for instance, if someone weeps, brokenly,
If someone is filled with longing in the dark for the songs of the Volga
farm labourers?
And who cares at all, for instance, how harsh a place it is, if clear, dry words,
And painful moments ooze, like pus from open abscesses? ...

21   It's nothing ... it's nothing ... I know this; — the truth is frightening for all.
The days as they have gone by, again will pass by into the distance.
And I will still roam on wearily, alone on dusty roads,
And still perhaps exchange Africa's desolation for twice the loneliness.

Efsher

(A fragment fun a greserer poeme.)

1   'Shver iz di rege fun tsesheydung,
Yener tog vert epes leydik,
Yene sho vert oysgehoylt,
Yene reges shmartst un groylt...
5   Vet di benkshaft shtendik rinen? —
Veln oyf fremdn breg
Oyfgeyn freylekhere teg? —
Vet men epes vos dergreykhn? ...
Ot der alter frage-tseykhn
Vert fun mir oyf s'nay geshtelt
In der pustkayt fun der velt...

9   Do hob ikh ober tsebaytn
Naye heym oyf fremde vaytn
Vider fun dos nay gedarft.
S'hot der veytog zikh farsharft
13   Yener shverer, temper veytog —
Letster grus fun letstn shneytog,
Tshemodanes, kishns, rimens —
Alts fun lange rayzes simens —
Plonterst zikh in pek un shtrik.
Veyst: — nishto shoyn keyn tsurik...

19   Hinter zikh farbrent di brikn.
Itster fort men naye glikn,
Naye glikn zukhn vu,
Efsher arbet, broyt un ru.
23   Efsher, efsher, ver ken zogn...
Halt den umetum in klogn
Groyser tsar fun yedn land? —
Kh'bin an alter emigrant —
27   Darf men pruvn, darf men zukhn,
Un di hundert toyznt skrukhn
Mitn gantsn shvern shrek
Oyf mayn nayem, vaytn veg
Zaynen shoyn nit vert keyn kimer...
32   S'iz di velt punkt vi dayn tsimer:
Yedn tog der balebos
Ken dikh heysn geyn — iz vos?' ...

35   'Amol, mit zekhtsik yor tsurik
Iz men gekumen zukhn glik
Oyf hayntikn bavustn rif.
Men iz gekrokhn in der tif,
Gezukht mit groyse, zhedne oygn
40   Dos gold, vos s'hot tsu zikh getsoygn,

Perhaps*

(A fragment of a longer poem.)

1   'Heavy is the moment of parting,
       That day becomes somewhat empty,
       That time becomes hollow,
       Those minutes sting and horrify...
5   Will the longing always ooze? —
       Here on foreign shores
       Will happier days arise? —
       Will one accomplish anything?...
       So will the same old question
       Be put to me anew
       In the emptiness of the world...

9   Here I had to exchange
       My new home for foreign distances,
       Yet again had to start anew.
       The pain has become sharper,
13   That heavy, blunt pain —
       The last farewell of the last snow-day,
       Suitcases, cushions, straps —
       All signs of long journeys —
       Entangled in parcels and string.
       You know: — there is no going back...

19   I burned the bridges behind me.
       Now one travels to new fortunes,
       New fortunes looked for somewhere,
       Perhaps work, bread and rest.
23   Maybe, maybe, who can tell...
       Endlessly everywhere lamenting
       Great sorrows in every land? —
       I am an old immigrant —
27   One must try, one must search,
       And the hundred thousand shudders
       With full and heavy fear
       On my new, long way
       Are not worth the effort...
32   The world is exactly like your room:
       Each day the owner
       Can tell you to go — so what?' ...

35   'Once, sixty years ago
       They came seeking happiness
       On today's famous reef.
       They crawled in the dark depths,
       Searching with big, greedy eyes
40   The gold that lured them,

* The line numberings and verse breaks are Fram's.

Getsoygn vi mit a magnet
Fun kraln, derfer un fun shtet
Dem sharlatan un karyerist
Dem Yidn, kafer un dem krist,
Dem groysn, vildn eyrev rav,
Vos hot do ayngeshpart un brav
Fun ershtn elntn getselt
Azh oysgeboyt a gantse velt,
Un s'lebn hot derlangt a shlog
In likht fun groysn, heln tog.

50   Ikh perzenlekh halt gevis,
Az tomid unter dayne fis
Muztu hobn festn grunt:
Nisht zayn heymloz vi a hunt,
Nisht tsebaytn itlekh mol
55   Dayn balibtn barg un tol,
Dayn shtikl erd, vos dir iz nont,
Zol zayn, dayn kleynem horizont,
Dayn heym, dayn svive, un dayn dakh,
Dayn eygene farshemte sprakh,
60   Dayn altn shokhn lebn dir, —
Zayn gute tsi zayn shlekhte tir,
Dayn boym, dayn groz, dayn vald un feld —
Oyf keyne oytsres fun der velt...
Ikh halt gevis, punkt vi der beym
65   Muztu farblaybn in dayn heym, —
Meg es zayn kleyn, meg es zayn groys, —
Nor koym men rayst dem vortsl oys
Oyf naym bodn tsu farflantsn,
Dan kenstu opvelkn ingantsn,
Vayl, gevis, oyf fremder erd
Vestu blaybn nisht dernert.

72   Un dortn, vu du bist geborn,
Dortn leb oys dayne yorn,
Dort elter zikh un shtarb.
A yede blum hot dokh ir farb,
A yeder mentsh hot zayne zitn.
77   Zol zayn afile — host gelitn,
Host aleyn tsvishn faynt
Farbrakht dayn nekhtn un dayn haynt,
Ober vish nit op dem shpur
Fun dortn, vu dem vikl-shnur
Dayn mame hot far dir geviklt.
83   Vu heymish iz der alter brikl
Geshtanen oyfnemen dikh greyt
Un heymishkayt un vareme freyd,
Un hartsikayt fun nonter svive,
In simkhes groyse un in shive, —
In tsar fun shive-zitser shtile,

Drew them like a magnet
From kraals, villages and from cities
The charlatan and careerist
The Jew, kaffir and Christian,
The great, wild riff-raff
Who had here stubbornly and bold
From the first lonely tent
So built a whole world,
And life delivered a blow
In light of great, bright day.

50   I personally believe,
That always under your feet
You must have solid ground:
Not be homeless like a dog,
Not to change every time
55   Your beloved mountain and valley,
Your piece of earth, which is dear to you,
Should be your little horizon,
Your home, your surroundings and your roof,
Your own embarrassing language,
60   Your old neighbour beside you, —
His good or his bad door, —
Your tree, your grass, your forest and field —
For any treasures of the world...
I insist, exactly like the tree
65   You must stay at your home, —
Whether it be small or big, —
Even if one pulls out the roots
To plant them in new places,
Then you can blossom fully,
Because, certainly, in strange places
You will remain unsustained.

72   And there, where you were born,
Live out your years,
There grow old and die.
As each flower has its colour,
Each person has his mannerisms.
77   Let's say — even if [you] suffered,
[You've] been alone amongst foes
Spent your yesterdays and your todays,
But don't wipe away the tracks
From there, where your swaddling was
In which your mother wrapped you.
83   Where familiar is the old bridge
Standing ready to welcome you
And homeliness and warm joy,
In hearty and in close surroundings,
In great celebrations and in mourning, —
In sorrow of silent mourners

In heylikayt fun frumer tfile
90   Tsedavente fun alte doyres
Bay yortsayt-likht un hele menoyres —
Vu groye, oreme khalupes
Hobn zikh gefreyt mit khupes,
Mit zate tumldike brisn,
Un vu men hot shabosim zise
Farfult mit heylikn bitokhn —
96   Dervart durkh groye indervokhns
Tsu bentshn, vi gebentshtn broyt
Biz shtiln onkum funem toyt...'

Dorem Afrike (August 1949), 21

Oyf mayn dakh hot amol nokh gesvistshert a shvalb

1   Oyf mayn dakh hot amol nokh gesvistshert a shvalb,
Un in shtub hot geshmekt mit tsufridenem broyt,
Un in shtal hot der friling geborn a kalb,
Un in kleyt hot gefoylt nokh faryoriker kroyt...

5   Umetum, yeder trot, yeder eyntsiker shpan
Hot gekvoln mit zun un geotemt mit freyd.
Oyfn taykh iz gefaln farnakht a tuman,
Un mit varemer erd hot fun felder geveyt...

9   Un in sod hot gebenkt der farshikerter bez,
Un in vald iz shoyn trukn gevorn der mokh.
Ale tishn gegreyt mit ladishes un kez,
Un mit varemen broyt oyf a gliklekher vokh...

13   Ot azoy hot in khate di shefe gekvelt:
Fule donitses milkh, fule sloes mit shmant.
Un es tunkt zikh in gold dos farakerte feld,
Vos gebentsht hot mit zriye di poyershe hant,

17   Un di lonkes bashotn mit tsheredes shof,
Un di oygn fun likht ikh farzhmure oyf halb,
Un es khapt mikh arum aza gliklekher shlof, —
Oyf mayn dakh hot amol nokh gesvistshert a shvalb...

A shvalb oyfn dakh, p. 67

In holiness of observant prayers
90 Prayed by older generations
By anniversary candles and bright candelabra —
Where grey, poor shacks
Enjoyed and celebrated weddings,
With satisfying, noisy circumcisions,
And where sweet Sabbaths were filled
With holy confidence —
96 Awaited through grey weekdays
To bless, like blessed bread
Until the quiet coming of death...'

Once a swallow twittered on my roof

1 Once a swallow twittered on my roof,
And from the house came the aroma of satisfying bread,
And in the stall the spring bore a calf,
And in the shop still rotted last year's cabbage...

5 All around, every step, each and every stride
Enjoyed the sun and breathed in happiness.
At dusk a mist fell on the river,
And with warm earth a whisper from the fields...

9 And in the orchard the intoxicated lilac was filled with longing,
And in the forest the moss was already dried out.
All the tables were bedecked with jugs and cheese,
And with warm bread for a happy week...

13 And here in the cottage abundance flourished:
Full milk pails, full gallipots of sour cream.
And the ploughed field was dipped in gold,
Which peasant hands blessed with sowing,

17 And the meadows were shaded with flocks of sheep,
And I half close my eyes against the bright light,
And I am seized by such contented sleep, —
Once a swallow twittered on my roof...

Nokh vos zol ikh forn?

1   Nokh vos zol ikh forn, un vu zol ikh forn,
Az s'zaynen farkirtst mayne vegn gevorn,
Az s'zaynen gevorn farshnitn di vaytn,
Un kh'veys nisht oyf vos kh'vel mayn elnt tsebaytn.

5   Kh'vel efsher a mol nokh a ru vu gefinen,
Un s'vet nokh a shprits ton mit freyd a baginen;
Un efsher vet merer un shtarker nokh vey ton
In fremde merkhokim un leydike breytn?

9   Ikh veys, ikh vel keyn zakh nisht kenen farmaydn,
Un umetum vartn di zelbike leydn.
Ikh veys es, avade, nishto vos tsu gloybn
Un vandern vider mit trukene shtoybn.

13   Un vandern vider mit tunkele vegn...
Nishto vu tsu geyn un bay vemen tsu fregn;
Nishto vos tsu zukhn in leydike vaytn.
Ikh veys nisht, oyf vos kh'vel mayn elnt tsebaytn...

Lider, p. 24

In tsveyen

1   Fun rusisher rakhves tsu Afrikes umet,
Fun vayse midboryes un glimike shneyen —
Tsu zunike vayten fun eybikn zumer,
O, filt men zikh elnt in tsveyen!

5   Un benkenish vayse oyf vegn tsegosn,
Oyf blutike gruntn farzhavert tserunen,
Un ovntn kurtse vi knoytn farloshn,
Fartriknt fun gliike zunen...

9   Un goysese shkies — on glokn-geklangen
Mit eybiker shtilkayt un langvayl tsetrifn —
Mit benkenish tsarter un tribe farlangen,
Vi elnt-farblonzhete shifn...

13   Un hartsike lider fun volger galakhn
Tsezingn do rekords in eynzame shtiber.
Mit eybikn benken fun rusishn[*] shlyakhn —
Dan shvimen di breges ariber.

17   O, Afrikes umet mit Ruslands georemt,
Der umet fun shvaygn in blutike veyen —
In shikere nekht fun farshikertn dorem,
Do filt men zikh elnt in tsveyen...

Lider, p. 7

[*] The Yiddish should be 'rusishe', but it appears as 'rusishn' in Fram's original.

Why Should I Leave?

1 Why should I leave and where shall I go,
When my options have been shortened,
And when the places are limited?
I don't know what I'll get in place of my loneliness.

5 Perhaps I shall still find rest some place,
And there will still be spray of joy at dawn;
And perhaps it'll hurt more and ever more strongly
In distant places and empty spaces?

9 I know, there is nothing I'll be able to prevent,
And everywhere there awaits the same suffering.
I know this for sure, there is nothing to believe in,
But to carry on wandering with dry dust;

13 And carry on wandering on dark roads...
Nowhere to go and no one to ask;
Nowhere to look in empty distances.
I don't know what I'll get in place of my loneliness...

Twofold

1 From Russian expansiveness to Africa's sadness,
From white deserts and gleaming snow —
To sunny distances of everlasting summer,
Oh, one feels the loneliness doubly!

5 And white longing spilt out on roads,
On bloody ground rusty and dissolved,
And short evenings extinguished like wicks,
Dried out by glowing suns...

9 And dying sunsets — without the ringing of bells
With eternal silence ragged and wearisome —
With delicate yearning and bleak longing,
Like lonely and lost ships...

13 And hearty songs of Volga priests
Records playing brightly here in lonely houses.
With constant longing for Russian paths —
Then the banks flow over.

17 Oh, Africa's sadness made poorer with Russia's,
The loneliness of keeping quiet in bleeding pain —
In drunken nights of the intoxicated south
Here one feels the loneliness twice over...

In an afrikaner baginen

1   S'iz zunik un s'iz loyter der frimorgn.
    Ekh, vos hele, shtralndike zun!
    Un azoy bafrayt fun dayges un fun zorgn —
    Kvoktshet ergets-vu a leygedike hun,
5   Un stayes-vayz in luft tsefliyen vayse toybn —
    A fokh, a patsheray, un fligl shotndike veyen,
    Un s'gist zikh on der vayn in grine troybn,
    Un royte kavones in feld dergeyen.
    Un shiker iz di luft fun tsaytikdike peyres.
10   A lid, a brumeray, a shire farn boyre
    Fun tsarte flaterlekh, fun babelekh, fun flign...
    Un s'shpreyt zikh oyset vayt a nign —
    Het-vayt, oyf stoygn shmekedikn hey, oyf lonkes plikhevate
    Un felder genetsn un pyetshenen zikh zate
15   Mit korn baykhikn, mit gilderdikn veyts, mit shvere miles.
    Fun regn un fun toy batrifte tfiles
    Trikenen zikh shtil oyf grine lonke-lipn,
    Un shtiklekh shtraln breklen zikh un zipn zikh un zipn...
    Oy, s'iz gut! S'iz zunik-hel. S'shmekt in vayse epel,
20   In tropns zun, in frishn, kiln nepl,
    In grozn bliike, in faykhte roses...
    Un vayt tseklingen zikh betsiber koses:
    — A klung, a shprung, a tants oyf feste gruntn,
    Oyf kraytekher tsepreyet un tsevaremt,
25   Un s'shpritst-aroys a freyd an erdishe fun untn.
    Un tife himlen hobn zikh oyf erd derbaremt: —
    A shmir, a shot, a glants fun toyznt zunen!
    Tsegist zikh klorer shayn oyf felder gantse emers
    Un vert in shtrayfelekh, in ritshkelekh, in shnirelekh tserunen
30   Un klingt zikh op in gold mit kishefdikn zemer.
    Un s'kvelt a hele freyd in tsapldike brustn:
    — A shire, a geveyn, a loybgezang dem boyre!
    In kholel friikn mispalel zaynen kustn
    Un beymer knokhike balodene mit peyres.
35   S'iz groys di shtume freyd bay shrotsim un bay mentshn,
    Un shrayen vilt zikh, shrayen fun hispayles!
    Frum mispalel zayn un davenen un bentshn
    In di zunike, di oysgehelte vayles!
    Temp aroysshrayen mit ale dayne glider
40   Di freyd tsekhlinete, vos rizelt zikh in gufn,
    Un a fal ton tsu der mame-erd anider
    A tsetumlter, farshikert begilufn,
    Un zikh durkhmishn mit erd, mit leym, mit royte gruntn,
    Mit shefe erdisher, vos shpart aroys fun untn,
45   Mit bloyen himl-shayn, vos breklt zikh fun oybn,
    Un zikh aleyn mit eygenem geshrey fartoybn!
    Un zol zikh vayt der oysgeshrey tsetrogn
    Het-vayt, oyf kupes hey, oyf shmekedike felder.
    Un ophilkhn in shvaygenish fun velder
50   In di zunike, di loytere fartogn.

Lider, pp. 74–76

In an African Dawn

1   It's a sunny and clear early morning.
Oh, what a radiant, full-rayed sun!
And so, free of worries and cares —
A laying hen clucks nearby,
5   And white doves fly up in flocks —
A flap, a beating, and shadowy wings fanning the air,
And wine pours from green grapes,
And red watermelons ripen across the field,
And the air is drunk with ripening fruits.
10   A poem, a hum, a song of praise for the Creator
From soft butterflies, from beetles, from flies...
And melody spreads far and wide —
Far across the fragrant haystacks, over bald meadows
And fields yawn and indulge themselves until satiated
15   With potbellied rye, with golden wheat, with heavy *mielies*.
From rain-and dew-spattered prayers
Drying lightly on green lips of fields,
And bits of sun-rays shred and screen and sift...
Oh, it's good! It's sunnily bright. It tastes of white apples,
20   In drops of sun in the fresh, cool haze,
In blooming grasses, moist with dew...
And in the distance scythes ring out loud:
— A ring, a jump, a dance on firm ground,
Warmed on sweaty herbs,
25   And there sprays out an earthy joy from underneath.
And deep skies have compassion for the earth: —
A smudge, a shadow, a radiance of a thousand suns!
Full buckets glow and pour out on the fields
And vanish in little stripes, in rivulets, in threads
30   And ring out in gold, in enchanted melody.
And bright joy and delight well up in quivering breasts:
— A song of praise, a lament, a hymn for the Creator!
Early, in the void, the bushes pray
And gnarled trees laden with fruit.
35   Great is the silent joy in insects and with people,
And one wants to shout and scream in rapture!
Pray piously and worship and bless
In the sunny brightened moments!
Bluntly shouts out with all your limbs
40   The unbridled joy that gurgles up inside,
And falls down to mother-earth beneath
Confused, intoxicated with joy,
And wallowing in the earth, with clay, with red soil,
With earthy abundance, that pushes up from beneath,
45   As blue heaven-splendour, which crumbles from above,
And deafens one with one's own cry!
And so that the cry carries far
Far, over the heaps of hay, over sweet-smelling fields.
And resounds in the silence of the forests
50   In the sunny, the clear dawns.

Fun shop tsu shop

(A fragment fun a greserer poeme)

1 Azoy a gantsn tog — fun shop tsu shop —
 Iz er arumgegangen betlendik a dzhob —
 A shtikl arbet zol men im vu gebn.
 Er iz geven yung un kreftik vi an ayzn
5 Un dafke hot zikh im gevolt nokh lebn,
 Tsu shtarbn vet er tomid dokh bavayzn —
 Un tzulib vos, lemoshl, zol er dos shoyn shtarbn,
 Un vern oyf der velt bay alemen fargesn?
 Ot poshet tsulib dem, vayl er vil mer nit esn?

10 Eh-eh, a narishkayt, er iz nokh nit keyn oysgedilter sharbn,
 Dos volt bay im geheysn glat a meshugas,
 Er vet fardinen nokh avu nit iz zayn shtikl broyt...
 Un ot, er loyft arum a gantsn tog azoy fun gas tsu gas
 Un s'shrayen zayne groyse oygn shrekevdik aroys mit noyt:

15 'Vork, ay vont tu vork, may bas, ay vont a dzhob' ...
 Nor keyner ruft zikh oyf zayn betenish nit op —
 Derlangt men mernit shtil a shokl mitn kop:
 Neyn, nito keyn arbet do, farshteyst? — Neyn! ...
 Un vider veys er vayter shoyn nit vu tsu geyn,
20 Er iz shoyn do kimat bay alemen geven
 Er hot azoy fil gute, vayse mentshn shoyn gezen
 Un keyner hot zikh iber im a hungerikn nit derbarmt.
 Mashmoes, keyner darf nit hobn do zayn pratse un zayn shveys.
 Dervayl hot zikh der afrikaner halber tog tsevaremt,
25 Di groyse zun hot zikh tsegosn oyf der erd. S'iz heys,
 S'iz likhtik oyf der velt fun ot der groyser zun,
 Es ken dokh zayn azoy min gut un ongenem un voyl...
 Nor vos kumt im aroys, a shteyger, fun derfun,
 Az s'kukt fun zayne oygn alts aroys nokh der groyl,
30 Un s'triknt im di shpayekhts azh fun hunger in zayn moyl?
 Iz kayklt er zikh iber shtot a gantsn tog,
 Punkt vi a shvarster knoyl
 Un benkt farkhalesht nokh a bisl proste 'mili-pap' —
 Di tsayt gedenkt er shoyn nit ven er hot dos gliklikher gehat —
35 Ekh, volt er zikh veln onesn atsind mit dem tsu zat
 Khotsh vu nit iz a bisele fun dem bakumen, ot azoy, a kap,
 Dos shepn shporevdik mit alemen fun heysn blekh
 Dos aynkaykln in zayne shvartse hent s'zol vern shvarts vi pekh,
 Un nokhdem leygn dos mit groys hanoe in zayn moyl...

Dorem Afrike (July–September 1984), 29

From Shop to Shop

(A fragment of a longer poem)

1   A whole day like this, from shop to shop —
He went round begging for a job —
Hoping someone would give him a bit of work somewhere.
He was young and strong as iron

5   And yes, he still wanted to live,
There would always be a time to die —
And for what reason, for instance, should he die now,
And be forgotten by everyone in the world?
And simply for this reason, that he doesn't want to eat any more?

10   Eh-eh, a foolishness, he is not yet a dried-out skull,
That would have seemed plum crazy to him,
He will still earn his piece of bread anywhere he can...
And yet he hurries around like this the whole day from street to street
And his huge eyes cry out terrified with fearful need:

15   'Work, I want to work, my boss, I want a job'...
But no one responds to his begging —
Giving him nothing more than a quiet shake of the head: —
No there is no work here, understand? — No! ...
And once again he does not know where to turn,

20   He has already been to almost everyone,
He has already seen many good white people
And no one yet has taken pity on him in his hunger.
Presumably no one here needs his labour and his sweat.
Meanwhile the African noon has warmed up,

25   The great sun has poured out on the earth. It's hot,
The world is made bright by this great sun,
There could be so much that is good and appealing...
Only of what benefit is this to him, for instance, from this,
When still the horror looks out from his eyes,

30   While the saliva dries in his mouth from hunger?
And he wanders around the city the whole day,
Like a black ball
And starving longs for a bit of simple *mielie pap* —
He does not remember the last time when he happily had it —

35   Ekh, how he would like to eat his fill of it now
Or where he could come by a little bit of it, oh, here's a taste,
To scoop up carefully from a hot tin with everyone
Rolling it in his black hands so it becomes as black as pitch,
And then putting it in his mouth with great pleasure...

Tsu di shvartse

1   Hot keyn moyre un antloyft nisht fun mir, shvartse,
     Nisht dershrekt zikh far dem bleykh fun mayn gezikht.
     S'klemt a vey oykh vi bay aykh bay mir in hartsn,
     Un ikh vart azoy vi ir oyf ayer likht...

5   Ikh farshtey aykh, un ikh trog mit aykh tsuzamen
     Ayer freyd un ayer shvaygndike payn.
     Un nisht shuldik iz gevezn ayer mame,
     Vos der tog hot aykh geshonken tsufil sheyn.

9   Un nisht shuldik zaynen oykh geven di yorn,
     Vos tsetrift hobn mit tropns heler zun.
     Ver iz shuldik den in dem, az s'iz gevorn
     Ayer brust azoy geshmidt, vi fun tshugon?

13 Ver iz shuldik, un tsu vos zol dos unz arn,
     Az di hoyt bay aykh iz shpigldik un shvarts?
     — Az in gufim in farlitene un dare
     Tsaplt oykh bay aykh a blutik-royte harts!

17 Un ir trogt in zikh vi mir di zelbe leydn,
     Un oykh ir farshteyt, vos shlekht iz un vos gut...
     Un ven emetser zol ayer layb tseshnaydn —
     Oykh fun shvartser hoyt a rizl ton vet blut!

21 Un ven emetser zol ayer payn barirn,
     Vet ir oyftsaplen mit shtumpikn geshrey;
     Un, avade, oykh vi mir vet ir dershpirn
     Tif in hartsn aza brenendikn vey!

25 Un, avade, oykh vi unz vet aykh fardrisn,
     Vos me shtroft aykh azoy veytogdik un shver,
     Un farshvign, un farlitn, un farbisn
     Oykh in ayer oyg tsebrent zikh dan a trer...

29 Zaynen shuldik, zaynen shuldik, di mes-lesn,
     Vos farsmalyet hobn shvartser ayer hoyt?
     — Az ikh ken nisht un ikh vil aykh nisht fargesn —
     Ayer shvere, ayer shtikndike noyt! ...

33 To antloyft nisht un antloyft nisht fun mir, shvartse,
     Nisht dershrekt zikh farn bleykh fun mayn gezikht.
     S'klemt a vey oykh vi bay aykh bay mir in hartsn,
     Un ikh vart azoy vi ir oyf undzer likht.

                                        Lider, pp. 19–21

To the Black Man

1   Do not be afraid and do not run away from me, black man,
     Do not be afraid of the paleness of my face.
     There is a choking pain in my heart as there is in yours,
     And I wait for your light just like you...

5   I understand you, and I carry with me like you
     Your happiness and your silent pain.
     And your mother was not guilty,
     That the day gave you too much beauty.

9   And the years too were not guilty,
     That dripped like drops of clear sun.
     Who is guilty then that it happened
     Your breast was smelted so, like cast iron?

13   Who is guilty, and why should this bother us,
     That your skin is mirror-like and black?
     — If within the suffering and slender body
     And in you there also beats a blood-red heart!

17   And you carry within you like me the same suffering,
     And you too understand, what bad is and what good...
     And if someone were to cut your body —
     Also from black skin blood would trickle!

21   And if someone would touch your pain,
     You would quiver with a dull cry;
     And, surely, like me, you would feel
     Deep in your heart such burning pain!

25   And, surely, also like us it would bother you,
     That they punish you so painfully and hard,
     And silent, and suffering, and grim
     That in your eye too there burns a tear...

29   Are they guilty, are they guilty, the days and nights,
     That have scorched skin to black?
     — That I cannot and do not want to forget you —
     Your heavy, your oppressive need! ...

33   Do not run and do not run away from me, black man,
     Don't be afraid of my pale face.
     My heart too is clammed up with pain like yours,
     And I am waiting like you for our light.

Matumba

1 Matumba iz gekumen fun vaytn kral,
Er iz gekumen dinen zayne vayse balebatim.
Ergets-vu in a vinkl fun Transval
Iz gebliben zayn royte, leymene khate.

5 Matumba hot gelozn dray vayber
Tsu pashen in kral zayne ki,
Zey hobn ale dray gehat shvartse layber
Un groyse brustn — azh bald biz di kni...

9 Un di rukns bay zey flegn glantsn
Vi di hintns bay tayere ferd,
Ven Matumbas vayber flegn zikh aveklozn tantsn
Flegt mamesh tsitern unter zeyere pyates di erd.

13 Di brasletn, di fis-bend, di drot
Farviklte heykh biz di knekhlekh,
Flegn avektrogn itlekhn trot
Mit geklang fun di sherblekh un blekhlekh...

17 Un gelekhter tsemisht mit geveyn,
Oystantsn flegn farshikert di vayber,
Ay, flegn damolst blanken zeyere vayse tseyn,
Un gebrit hobn heys zeyere nakete layber.

21 Hot take Matumba merer keyn zakh nisht gedarft,
Er iz gevezn tsufridn mit dem vos er hot shoyn gehat,
Er hot gevust az er hot zayne vayber shtark holt
Un shlofn hot er gekont mit zey tsu zat.

25 Nor dokh hot Matumba oykh gut gevust,
Az zayn libste vayb iz bay im Sesula,
Ekh, flegt im reytsn ir nakete, shvartse brust —
Ir boykh azoy rund, azoy shtayf, nokh gor vi a bsule.

29 Far ir hot er gantse tsvelf oksn
Gegebn ir taten 'lobola',
Un itst iz bay im zi gevoksn
Vi a zeltener ferd in stadole...

33 Volt dokh altsding geven azoy voyl,
Ven nisht di minhogim fun vaysn —
Hot do ober punkt vi a koyl
Gedarft im an umglik tseraysn...

37 Matumba hot nisht gevust dem vert fun gold,
Gold iz bay im geven punkt vi 'mili-pap' tayer,
Hot er shoyn ober dray yor gehat nisht getsolt
Dem vaysn bos zayn farsholtenem shtayer.

41 Iz far Matumban gebliben nor eyn zakh,
Eyn eytse hot er bloyz gekont gefinen:
Farlozn zayn altn, heymishn dakh
Un avekgeyn in shtot ergets-vu dinen.

Matumba

1   Matumba came from a distant kraal
He came to serve his white bosses.
Somewhere in a corner of Transvaal
His red, clay hut remained.

5   Matumba left three wives
To look after his cattle in the kraal,
All three had black bodies
And big breasts — almost right down to their knees...

9   And their backs would shine
Like the hindquarters of precious horses,
When his wives began dancing
The earth shook beneath the soles of their feet.

13   Their bracelets, the foot-bands, the wire
Twisted high around their ankles,
Would reverberate with each step
With the sound of metal shards and tin...

17   And laughter mixed with crying,
In the intoxicated dancing of his wives,
Oy, then their white teeth shone,
And their naked bodies burned.

21   And actually Matumba needed nothing more,
He was happy with what he already had,
He knew that he loved his wives greatly
And he could sleep with them to his fill.

25   But Matumba also knew full well,
That his favourite wife was Sesula.
Ah, how her naked, black breast would tease him —
Her round belly, so firm, still as a maiden's.

29   For her a whole twelve oxen
He gave her father *lobola*.
And now she flourished with him
Like a rare horse in the stable...

33   Everything would have been just fine,
If not for the customs of the whites —
But here came just like a bullet
A misfortune to tear him apart...

37   Matumba did not know the value of gold,
Gold was to him worth exactly the same as *mielie pap*,
So that for three years he had not paid
His accursed tax to his white master.

41   So for Matumba only one thing remained,
Only one remedy he could he find:
To leave his old, homely roof
And go away to town to work there.

45   Ale dray vayber hot Matumba gelozn bay zikh aheym,
      Oy, hot er zikh biter mit zey dan gezegnt,
      Es hot im oysgekukt shver un faryosemt der leym
      Oyf di trukene, vayte, farzhaverte vegn.

49   Un ot zaynen shoyn bald dray yor avek
      Vi er hot gedint in shtot zayne vayse balebatim.
      Langvaylik hot er dortn getseylt zayne teg
      Un on oyfher gebenkt nokh zayn khate.

53   In shtot hot er far zikh keyn zakh nisht gedarft, —
      Bloyz optsoln vos gikher dem shtayer,
      Zayn 'assegai' hot er shoyn lang nisht gesharft,
      Un in hartsn gebrent hot a fayer...

57   Dort vayt, ahinter dem leydikn bush,
      Dort ligt vu zayn khate farlozn,
      Er volt zikh atsinder ahintsu tsufus
      Mit di leymike vegn gelozn.

61   Zayne heyse dray vayber avade ver veys,
      Vos es tut dortn itster Sesula,
      Ir zol gor nisht trefn, kholile, keyn beyz: —
      Er't betn dem royfe a sgule...

65   Un amol iz gevezn er brav un gezunt —
      A leyb hot er dan azh gekont dokh tseraysn,
      Itst ligt er azoy vi a kretsiker hunt
      Un klaybt breklekh fun tish bay dem vaysn...

69   Ekh Matumba, Matumba, — s'iz avade nisht gut
      Dayn harts iz gevorn kleyn un fartsoygn,
      Un s'hot in di odern zayne gezotn zayn blut —
      Un mit trern gebrent zayne oygn...

73   To zol er khotsh platsn fun shvern geveyn, —
      Er volt zikh aleyn itst derkoylet.
      Nor neyn, er vet loyfn — antloyfn aheym
      Vi nor es vet oyfgeyn der moyled...

77   Dervayl muz er shtiln zayn bitern gal, —
      Er't betn baym royfe a sgule.
      Ver veys vifl mayl s'iz der veg tsu zayn kral, —
      Oy, Sesula, Sesula...

81   Iz Matumba gevorn farshrumpn fun tsar,
      Er hot zikh ingantsn gebitn,
      Gedint hot er erlekh zayn vaysn har,
      Gedint im getray un farlitn.

85   Nor poshet er hot nisht gekont farshteyn,
      Farvos zayn 'misis' hot im gekimert keseyder,
      Oftmol er hot zi baym shpigl aleyn
      Gezen in ir tsimer on kleyder.

45 All three wives Matumba left at his home,
    Oy, how bitterly he bade them farewell,
    The clay seemed so heavy and abandoned to him
    On the dry, distant, rust-coloured roads.

49 And so three years soon went by
    As he served his white bosses in town.
    Tediously he counted his days there
    And without respite he longed for his hut.

53 In town he needed nothing for himself
    Only to pay off his tax the more quickly.
    He had not sharpened his assegai in so long,
    And in [his] heart there burned a fire...

57 And in the distance behind the empty bush,
    There lay his desolate hut,
    He would now have left on foot
    On the empty clay roads.

61 Of his three devoted wives who knew,
    What Sesula was doing there now,
    May no evil happen to her, heaven forbid: —
    He would ask the doctor for a remedy...

65 And once he was bold and healthy —
    He could then have ripped a lion apart,
    Now he lies like a mangy dog
    And collects scraps from the table of the whites...

69 Oh, Matumba, Matumba, — it's really not good,
    Your heart has become small and tightened,
    And the blood in his veins seethed —
    And his eyes burned with tears...

73 Then although he could have burst with heavy lament, —
    He could on his own have slit his throat.
    But no, he would run — run away home
    As soon as the new moon would rise...

77 Meanwhile he must still his bitter gall, —
    He would ask the [witch] doctor for a remedy.
    Who knows how many miles it is to his kraal, —
    Oy, Sesula, Sesula...

81 Matumba became shrunken with grief,
    He became completely changed,
    He has honestly served his white master,
    Served him faithfully and patiently.

85 He simply could not understand,
    Why his missus bothered him constantly,
    Often he saw her alone at the mirror
    Saw her in her room without clothes on.

89   Dan flegt er in foderhoyz vishn dem shtoyb,
      Un zi — ire hor flegt zi kemen,
      Halb-naket un reytsnd azoy vi a leyb —
      Zi flegt zikh far im gornisht shemen...

93   Un tsaytvayz flegt zi in shtayfn korset
      Farshnureven hart ire brustn,
      Dan flegt er arayngeyn farbetn dos bet
      Nokh varem fun tayve un glustn...

97   Hot dan shoyn Matumba fun gornisht gevust, —
      Geshtanen far im iz Sesula,
      Es iz mernisht vayser gevesn ir brust, —
      A brust aza shtayfe un fule...

101   Un eyn mol in friling hot er bay ir tir
      Gevart vi a khaye farborgn,
      Er hot zikh meshuge gevorfn oyf ir
      Un hot zi shir-shir nisht dervorgn...

105   Azoy, az es iz shoyn gevorn tsu shpet
      Tsu betn, tsu shrayen, tsu rufn,
      Es hobn getsaplt zikh damolst in bet,
      Farkhalesht tsvey nakete gufim.

109   Tsvey kerpers tsemisht hobn vays zikh un shvarts —
      Fargesn hot er fun zayn 'misis',
      Un s'hot nokh a tsayt zayn farblutikte harts
      Geshprungn, getsukt vi in gsises.

113   Nisht lang hot Matumba itst vartn gedarft
      In friling, vos halt nokh in blien,
      Er hot zayne shpizn shoyn mer nisht gesharft, —
      Avek iz er shtil tsu der tlie.

117   Un keyner hot im tsu zayn mise bagleyt,
      Tsum vint nor er hot zikh getulyet,
      Fartsitert, gefaln, Matumba is toyt,
      Eh, eh, Sesula, Sesula!

A shvalb oyfn dakh, pp. 85–88

89   Then he would be dusting in the forehouse,
        And she — she would comb her hair,
        Half-naked and alluring as a lion —
        She was not embarrassed before him...

93   And at times she would in a taut corset
        Tightly lace up her breasts,
        Then he would go in and straighten the bed clothes
        Still warm with passion and lust...

97   And then Matumba knew nothing at all, —
        In front of him stood Sesula,

        It was only her breasts that seemed whiter, —
        Breasts so firm and full...

101   And once in spring by her door
        He waited like an animal concealed,
        He madly threw himself at her,
        And he almost choked her...

105   And so, when it became too late
        To ask, to scream, to call,
        There squirmed together then in bed,
        Two naked bodies in a faint.

109   Two bodies entwined white, and black —
        He forgot about his missus,
        And after a while his bloodied heart
        Sprang, twitched as in a death throe.

113   Not for long did Matumba have to wait
        In the spring, while it was still blooming,
        He could no longer sharpen his spears, —
        He went quietly to the gallows.

117   And no one accompanied him to his death,
        He could only cling to the wind,
        Trembling, fallen, Matumba is dead,
        Oh, oh, Sesula, Sesula!

Matatulu

I

1   A mentsh.
    A mentsh hot zikh getulyet vi a khaye tsu der erd.
    Er iz gelegen oysgetsoygn inem heysn bush,
    Er hot di glider zayne ale naygerik baklert:
    'Ho, a runde kni, a flinke, shpirevdike fus,
    A hant a kreftike — gezunt un shtark.'
    Fun hintn tapt er on zayn festn kark,
    Gegosn fun eyn shtik azoy vi tshugun,
    Un s'trinkt zikh azh in freyd zayn tsapldike harts:
    Ho, vi gut, vi varem s'iz di groyse zun.
10 Zayn kerper naketer iz glantsik, fet un shvarts,
    Bashmirt mit reynem oyl fun shmekedike flantsn.
    A mentsh. Ot vi a khaye fray er ken zikh itst tsetantsn,
    Er ken tseshpringen zikh mit hefkerdikn shprung,
    Er ken zikh mitn shtroys farmestn in gelaf.
    Er filt zikh groys. Er filt zikh kinderish un yung.
    Er hot dem koyekh funem oks, di flinkayt fun zhiraf,
    Un fun der malpe hot er ir naivn seykhl.
    Derfar farmogt er do arum di gantse velt.
20 Er ligt. Zayn ponem iz bagosn mit a breytn shmeykhl,
    Zayn brust — zi vakst, zi otemt un zi kvelt.
    Zi gist zikh on mit heyser, tsapldiker freyd,
    Er bedarf do gornisht inem bush; keyn shukh, keyn kleyd;
    Zayn beged* iz di fel fun a shakal.
    Zayn hoyz — on dort der erdisher rondavel.
    Dort ligt zayn heymisher, zeyn benkendiker kral
    Dort viklt oys di zun a knoyl mit gilderdikn bavl,
    Dort brent der zamd di grobe, tantsndike pyates,
    Dort shtinkt in mist, in roykh, in sharfn shveys,
30 Vos shpart aroys fun yene niderike khates.
    Der groyser tog iz foyl un umdertreglekh heys,
    Azoy min heys az smalyet poshet op di shvartse hoyt.
    Es brent di trikenish biz kiln oyfdernakht.
    Un er? Er ligt in bush aleyn un trakht.
    Er trakht atsind fun zayn farlibter moyd,
    Fun ire tayvedike, groyse tsitsn,
    Vos hengen shver arop, vi bay a ku der ayter...
    Ho, er klert a sakh in yene foyle hitsn,
    Er klert un dremlt ayn un kholemt azoy vayter...
40 Zayn markh iz nokh nisht sharf un rirevdik genug,
    Es kumt im on nokh shver dos seykhldike klern.
    Un dokh iz er far zikh hamtsoedik un klug,
    Er kortshet nokhanand zayn niderikn shtern,
    Nor mer farlozt er zikh oyf zayn farshpitstn khush —
    Punkt vi es tut der leyb, der odler, di pantere.
    Ho, der afrikaner vilder, shvaygndiker bush!

---

* 'levush' is used instead of 'beged' in the version in *A shvalb oyfn dakh*

Matatulu

I

1   A man.
    A man nestled like an animal into the earth.
    He lay stretched out in the hot bush,
    He considered his limbs with curiosity:
    'Ho, a rounded knee, a swift, muscular foot,
    A sturdy hand — well and strong.'
    From behind he touches his firm neck,
    Poured from one piece like iron,
    And his beating heart drinks with sheer pleasure:
    Ho, how good, how warm is the great sun.
10 His naked body is shiny, fat, and black,
    Smeared with pure oil from aromatic plants.
    A man. Just like a free animal he can now dance around.
    He can jump around with gay abandon,
    He can compete with the ostrich.
    He feels his greatness. He feels like a child and young.
    He has the strength of an ox, the agility of a giraffe,
    And the monkey's innocent intelligence.
    Therefore here he owns the whole world.
20 He lies. His face is filled with a broad smile,
    His chest — it heaves, it breathes, and it swells.
    It fills with warm, quivering joy,
    He needs nothing more in the bush, no shoe, no garment;
    His garb is the skin of a jackal.
    His house — is a mud rondavel.
    There lies his homely longed-for kraal
    There the cluster of golden threads of the sun grows,
    There the sand burns the big, dancing feet,
    There it stinks of dung, of smoke, of sharp sweat,
30 That emanates from lowly huts.
    The great day is lethargic and unbearably hot,
    So hot that it almost singes the black flesh,
    The dryness burns until the coolness of the night.
    And he? He lies alone in the bush and thinks.
    He thinks about his beloved lass,
    Of her voluptuous, great breasts,
    That hang down heavily like cow's udders...
    Ho, he thinks a lot in that sluggish heat,
    He thinks and dreams and dreams again...
40 His mind is still not sharp and nimble enough.
    He finds clear thinking difficult.
    And yet he is resourceful and clever,
    He scratches his low brow over and over,
    But relies the more on his sharpened intuition,
    Exactly like the lion, the eagle and the panther.
    Oh, the wild silent African bush!

Baynakht gefint er do zayn veg nokh di tseblite shtern,
Baytog dershmekt er zayne trit oyf vayte oysgeleygte mayln,
Zayn kral derkent er tomid nokh dem heysn shtoyb...
50   Un vi geshikt es flien zayne sharfe fayln,
Ven er lozt girik zikh avek do nokhshpirn zayn royb,
Ven er yogt nokh mit 'assegai' un blankn shpiz
A tsiterdikn hirsh, vos falt farblutikt in di derner.
Ho, s'iz groys di freyd — a shprung, a tsi, a ris,
Er heybt di khaye oyf bagaystert far di herner
Un shlept zi inem kral arayn dan, vi a gvar.
Ho, er ken zikh gut, der shtarker Matatulu.
Er veys zikh vi azoy tsu hitn fun gefar,
Un shtolts iz er bay zikh, vi shtolts es iz a Zulu,
60   Vi shtolts es iz der leyb — zayn afrikaner shokhn
Vos ligt in hoykhn groz un loyert nokhn bok...
Es shrayt fun im aroys zayn broyziker nitsokhn,
Ho, der groyser, likhtiker, der afrikaner tog!

II

Nisht vayt fun ot dem plats gefint zikh zayn rondavel.
Di zun, zi viklt alts nokh knoyln zilberdikn bavl,
Zi viklt nokhanand, keseyder, on a sof,
Matatulu khapt zikh itster oyf tsufridn fun zayn shlof,
Vi s'khapt zikh oyf di kleyne malpe in di tsvaygn,
Un loyft oyf gikh farshpetikter aheym.
70   Er iz itst ongelodn mit a shvern shvaygn,
Er hot zikh oysgerut in 'bush-feld' vi der beym,
Nor epes filt er vi es kitslt im in mogn —
Der hunger hot in im tsereytst zikh vi a beyzer hunt.
Un er vert epes mitamol azoy min umruik, tsetrogn.
Hagam in algemeyn, er filt zikh gut, tsufridn un gezunt,
Der zelbiker, der groyser Matatulu —
Dokh shpirt er itster vi es kumt do epes mit im for:
Er benkt geferlikh nokh zayn naketer, tsereytster bsule.
Ayede khayele in dzhungl, veys er hot zayn por.
80   Es hot di shlang afile zikh gefunen do a vayb.
Nor er? Es loyert iber im fun lang shoyn aza shvere klole
Es kvelt a glustenish a zhedne in zayn layb,
Un s'matert im keseyder der gedank: 'lobola.'
Ir tate fodert dokh far ir fun khosn gantse fertsn oksn,
Fun vanet zol er nemen dos aza rekhush?
Az shtendik iz er do a vilder vi der leyb gevoksn,
Un mitamol es vert im epes umetik in bush,
Azoy min umetik, az s'nemt im shtikn azh in kel...
Balekt er zayne grobe lipn mit zayn feter tsung,
90   Fargartlt zayne breyte hiftn mit a dine fel,
Un ongeshpitst un flink, er tut a veykhn shprung
Un trogt zikh vi der hirsh, het vayt, in vildernish avek.
Dervayle geyen oyf in bush di nekht mit naye teg,
Un vider kumen nekht mit kile, durshtike levones,

At night he finds his way by the blossoming stars,
By day he senses his way across the wide-open miles,
He always recognizes his kraal through the hot dust...
50 And as, once shot, his sharp arrows fly,
When he keenly tracks his prey,
When he pursues with his assegai and shiny spear
A quivering deer, that falls bloody into the thorn bushes.
How great is the joy — a jump, a pulling, a tearing,
He grabs the animal by its horns with excitement
And drags it to his kraal, like a strong man.
Oh, he knows himself well, the powerful Matatulu.
He knows how to heed danger,
And proud as he is, as proud as a Zulu,
60 As proud as the lion — his Afrikaner neighbour
That lies in the high grass and stalks the buck...
His bubbling triumph bursts out of him,
Oh, the great, light, African day!

II

Not far from that place is his rondavel.
The sun still moves behind clusters of silvery cotton,
It moves constantly, consistently, without end,
Matatulu wakes up satisfied from his sleep,
As the small monkey stirs in the branches,
And hurries home, late.
70 He is now laden with a heavy silence,
He has rested in the Bushveld like the tree.
But now he feels how his stomach rumbles —
The hunger growls in him like an angry dog.
And becomes suddenly unsettled, weighed down,
Still on the whole, he feels good, satisfied and well.
The same, the great Matululu —
Yet now he feels that something is happening within him,
He pines deeply for his naked, exasperated maiden.
Every animal in the jungle, he knows, has his partner.
80 Even the snake has found himself a wife.
Only him? A heavy curse lurks over him,
There wells up an eager longing in his body,
And the thought bothers him constantly, *lobola*.
Her father demands for her from her groom fourteen oxen,
From where can he get such riches?
Since always he has grown wild like a lion,
And suddenly he becomes saddened in the bush,
So lonely, that it is as if his throat constricts...
He licks his broad lips with his fat tongue,
90 Girds his broad hips with a thin skin,
And alert and agile, he gives a gentle jump
And bears himself like a deer, far away, into the wilderness.
Meanwhile the nights in the bush follow new days,
And once again nights come with cool, thirsty moons,

Matatulu loyft geshvint, vi fayl fun boygn,
Di durkhgeyer bagrist er ale 'sakebona'
Un shlingt shtokhim gantse mit tseglite oygn,
Un trogt zikh flink mit laykhtn, tanstndikn trot,
Az zayne pyates rirn koym vos on di erd.
100   Er loyft bagaysterter tsu yener groyser shtot
Fun vos er hot azoy fil vunder shoyn gehert.
Er veys fun altsding, Matatulu, ho, er veys,
Er vet di vayte shtot atsind a zikherer gefinen,
Un s'rint in heysn tayneg zaynem iber im der shveys.
Ho, er vet shoyn itster dort oyf oksn zikh fardinen,
Er vet dort arbetn, nisht lebn merer punkt vi der volf fun royb,
Er vet dort onklaybn 'lobola' far zayn bsule,
Un s'heybt zikh hinter im gedikht der heyser shtoyb,
Ho, gezunter, yunger, shtarker Matatulu!

III

110   In shtot hot Matatulu, mit der tsayt, gebitn zikh ingantsn.
Der bush, di vayte stepes oysgeleygte zunike un fraye, —
Dort vet er shoyn far di levones merer zayne tents nisht tantsn,
Er tulyet zikh atsind tsu zikh aleyn fun shrek vi a faryogte khaye: —
Im dem groysn Matatulu, vos hot mit leybn zikh farmostn,
Far vemens gvure s'hot der kral amol der gantser zikh geshrokn, —
Bahandlen zayne vayse balebatim vi a hunt a prostn.

Ho, er trogt shoyn hoyzn, dakht zikh, mit a hemd, mit zokn,
Un vestlekh hot er azoy fil,
Un shvere umbakveme shikh...
120   Un dokh, khadoshim lange horevet er oyf der kikh,
Zayn modne arbet vaybershe gefalt im azoy shver,
Er ken aleyn zikh poshet nit derkenen ver er iz: —
Ot ligt er — oyf der erd, a groyser mentsh, a riz,
Un shayert nokhanand dem shpilevdikn dil.
Er shayert gut, er shayert mit hasmode es zol blankn.
Iz vos? Vet er mit dem dergreykhn ven nit iz zayn tsil? —
Ot git men esn im do kloymersht vi a krankn,
Vosi? Er iz den shvakh, er filt zikh nit gezunt,
Er hot zikh den far emetsn baklogt?
130   Farvos bahandlt men im vi a prostn hunt:
Men shrayt, men zidlt im, men traybt arum, men yogt,
Far yeder kleynikayt — men musert un men shtroft...
Tsi veysn zey den nisht, az s'iz zayn yikhes groys,
Az loyfn flink hot er amol gekont — nokh flinker farn shtroys,
Un itst? Er filt zikh umruik afile ven er shloft.
Ho, zey zaynen vild di vayse mentshn do in shtot,
Er kon zey zikher keynem nisht farshteyn...
Hot er zikh ayngenuret in zikh, vi in feld der krot,
Un iz geblibn shtil, farshvign un aleyn.

140   Er tut zayn arbet gut, farlitn un geduldik,
Er shayert tep, er halt di tsimern do tsugeklibn, reyn,

Matatulu runs fast like an arrow from a bow,
He always greets the passers-by with a *sakebona*,★
He swallows landscapes with fiery eyes,
And carries himself agily with light, dancing steps,
So that the soles of his feet barely touch the ground.
100 He runs excitedly to that big city
About which he has heard so many wondrous things.
He knows about everything, Matatulu, oh, he knows,
He will confidently find the distant city now,
And the sweat pours from him in hot pleasure.
Ho, he will now tend the oxen there,
He will work there, live no more like the wolf from prey,
There he will gather the *lobola* for his maiden,
And behind him gathers the thick hot dust,
Ho, healthy, young, strong Matatulu!

III

110 In the city, over time, Matatulu changed altogether.
The bush, the wide plains, spread out sunny and free, —
There he will never again dance his dances before the moons,
He curls into himself now, alone in fear like a pursued animal: —
He the great Matatulu, who competed with lions,
For whose strength everyone at the kraal was once afraid, —
Treated by his white employers like a common dog.

Oh, he soon wore trousers, it seemed, with a shirt, with socks,
And he also had many vests,
And heavy uncomfortable shoes...
120 And yet, for long months he toiled in the kitchen,
He finds his strange, womanly work so hard,
He himself does not recognize who he is: —
There he crouches — on the ground, a big man, a giant,
And scrubs the playful floor repeatedly.
He polishes well, he shines diligently so that it glows.
So what? Will he accomplish anything with this when it is not his goal? —
Here they give him food as if he were an invalid,
So what? Is he weak and does he not feel well,
Did he complain to anyone?
130 Why do they treat him like a common dog:
They shout, they curse him, they drive around, they chase,
For any small thing — they reproach and they punish...
They do not know of his great pedigree,
That once he could run agilely — even faster than an ostrich,
And now? He feels uneasy even when he sleeps.
Ho, they are bizarre, these white people in the city,
He can surely understand none of them...
He curled up into himself, like a mole in the field,
And he remained quiet, silent and alone.

140 He does his work well, carefully and patiently,
He scrubs pots, he keeps the rooms neat, clean,

★ English: 'Hello'.

Er blaybt di balebatim zayne, dakht zikh, gornisht shuldik,
Farkert — keseyder shmeykhelt er mit zayne vayse tseyn
Un vayzt far alemen zayn knekhtishe hakhnoe,
Ayedern badinen iz er tomid greyt,
Er hot dokh alemol fun dem aza min kindishe hanoe
Es kvelt dokh dan in im aza naive freyd —
A knekht. Farlitn shvaygevdik, dershrokn, vi a knekht,
Es rint dos lebn zayns azoy min shtil, ayntonik...
150   Un in di tife, shvartse, afrikaner nekht,
Nemt Matatulu shpiln umetik oyf zayn harmonik,
Er tsit keseyder, shoen-lang a langvaylikn nigen,
Azoy vi voyen volt fun vaytn a shakal,
Biz vanent umetik er vert in nakht aleyn farshvign,
Un dremelt ayn farbenkter nokh zayn kral...

IV

Derfar a zuntog filt zikh Matatulu gliklekh.
Er shteyt oyf fri. Der toy oyf bleter tsapelt nokh un trert.
Di zun heybt nor vos on tsu krishlen zikh in gliderdike shtiklekh
Un s'shit zikh oys mit fuler shefe oyf der erd.
160   Dem tog er hot far zikh biz oyf der nakht a frayen.
Es iz im gut. Fun tayneg vil zikh Matatulu azh tseshrayen,
Er vil zikh itst avektrogn het vayt foroys
Tsu yenem rand, vos hot zikh dortn hel azoy tseviklt.
Dan firt er forzikhtik zayn 'baysikl' aroys,
Vos glanst in zun vi shpogl-nay, baniklt,
Batsirt mit glezlekh kolerley, mit groyse, blankendike knep
Arumgezetst dem oysgeputstn zotl,
Un lozt zikh in eyn otem flink avek tsum step.
Er trogt zikh vi a vint, meshuge, oyver-botl,
170   In eyn minut un durkhgeshnitn hot er shoyn di lange gas,
Es shpreytn zikh far im shoyn vider opgebrente pleynen.
Nor in geayl fargest er alemol aheym zayn pas,
Er kon zikh nokh biz haynt tsum pas nisht tsugeveynen...

Vosi? Vos darf er den mit zikh dos shtikl narishe papir?
Darf den mit zikh arumtrogn a pas der ber,
Tsi efsher ken der helfant zikh on dem nisht ton keyn rir,
Der leyb, der krokodil, der bufl-oks? — Un er? ...
Farvos zol er dos erger zayn far zey?
Lemay zol men im shtendik darfn hitn?

180   Un vi a khaye brumt er demolst oys zayn finstern geshrey: —
Ho, er ken zayn gut, er ken zayn frayndlekh un farlitn,
Nor ven men darf, dan ken er groyzam shteln zikh antkegn,
Er ken farteydikn zikh vi di vilde shlang...
Azoy iz Matatulu vider do in bush gelegn,
Gelegn umetik, gelegn zeyer lang,
Un vider tif in zikh fartayeter getrakht.
Dervayl hot shoyn di zun zikh ayngetunkt in blut —
Der ershter simen fun a heysn oyfdernakht,
Un s'hot oyf mayln vayt di trikenish gerut...

He owes his masters, nothing, it seems,
On the contrary — he always smiles with his white teeth
And displays to everyone his slave-like servility,
He is always ready to serve everyone,
He had always gained from these a childlike pleasure
That there rose in him such naive joy —
A slave. Long-suffering, silent, afraid, like a servant,
His life seeps away so quietly, monotonously...

150   And in the deep, black African nights,
Lonely, he starts to play on his harmonica,
He plays, for hours on end, an incessant melody,
Like the distant howl of a jackal,
Until sad and alone he becomes quiet in the night,
And dreams with longing of his kraal...

IV

Therefore, on Sunday Matatulu felt happy,
He rose early. The dew quivered still like tears on the leaves.
The sun has just begun to shimmer in glowing fragments
And pours out with full abundance on the earth.

160   That day he was free until the night.
He felt good. He wanted to cry out with pleasure,
He wanted to go forward far away
To that ridge that unfurled over there so clearly,
Then he carefully took his bicycle out,
That shon, brand-new, nickel-plated, in the sun,
Adorned with all sorts of glassy lights, with great shiny buttons,
Surrounding the decorated saddle,
And left in one breath for the plains.
He went like the wind, madly, demented,

170   In one minute he cut through the long street,
Where the burnt plains spread ahead of him again.
Except that in his haste he always forgot his pass at home,
Even until today he could never get used to it...

What is it? Why does he need that stupid paper?
That he needs to carry around the pass, the (bug)bear,
As if the elephant cannot move without it,
The lion, the crocodile, the buffalo-ox? — And he? ...
Why should it be worse for him than them?
Why should they always have control over him?

180   And like an animal he roars out his dark cry: —
Ho, he can be good, he can be friendly and patient,
But when necessary, he can stand up against them strongly,
He could defend himself like the wild snake...
That is how Matatulu stayed again in the bush,
Remained lonely, lay very long,
And again, deep in himself secretly thought.
In the meanwhile, the sun itself had become dipped in blood —
The first sign of a hot evening,
And for miles around the dryness rested.

V

190   Dan vert er plutsim umruik un aylt zikh shoyn aheym.
Er hot a gantsn tog farbrakht a shtoybikn, a heysn...
Es brent mamesh der veg fun roytn, zhaverdikn leym.
Nor Matatulu shtelt zikh op nokh oyf a vayle in 'lokeyshn'
Dort hot er fraynd. Es vilt zikh im atsind abisl reydn —
Mit eygene iz dokh gor an ander zakh...
Un vider ken er zikh mit zey a lange tsayt nisht sheydn:
In shtot bay zayne vayse balebatim? — Ho, er leydt a sakh,
Er tsit di teg zayne farhorevet vi fun gedikhter smole,
Er shayert tep, er kokht, er vasht. Ho, a meshugas...
200   Un far zayn moyd — er hot nokh alts nisht keyn 'lobola' ...
Nor do dermont zikh plutsim Matatulu on zayn pas.
Es iz shoyn shpet. Der khoyshekh vert gedikht.
Er zet in finsternish far zikh a shvern tseykhn...
Er flit oyf gikh. Es rint der heyser shveys fun zayn gezikht,
Er vil vos gikher itst zayn nakhtleger dergreykhn,
Fun vaytn zet er shoyn di likht fun shtot tseshpreyte vi a nets.

Un ot — er iz shoyn nont. Sakhakl nokh eyn gesl...
Un plutsim, a bafel in nomen fun gezets:
Vu flitstu, tayvel eyner? ... shtey, dayn 'speshl',
210   Un Matatulu falt tsetumlter oyf dr'erd arop,
Er filt oyf zikh a drikndike, shtarke hant.
Dos heyse blut derlangt a shpar tsu im in kop:
Er, gefangen vi a tkhoyr ot do oyf eygn land?
O, neyn. Er vet di bushe nisht fartrogn.
Un vi a leyb tsereytster git er zikh a ris.
Men nemt im vi a vilde khaye iber ale gasn yogn.
Umzist — es zaynen flink nokh zayne shtarke fis...
Nor mitamol — a knal. In finsternish a fayerdiker shos...
S'iz Matatulu oyf der erd glaykh vi a leyb gefaln.
220   Un bislekhvayz es gist zikh oys fun im zayn blutiker fardros...

V

Azoy flegt er amol zikh yogn nokh shakaln
Arum zayn shtiln kral in shvaygndikn bush
Un brengen zey tsutrogn far zayn bsule.
Der letster tsapl mit zayn toyter fus.
Ho, gezunter, sholtser, yunger Matatulu.

Dorem Afrike (December 1953), 17–19

V

190 Then he quickly became unsettled and hurried home.
He had spent the whole dusty, hot day...
The way burned with red, rusted clay.
But Matatulu stopped for a while in the 'location'.
There he has friends. He wants to chat a little —
With close friends it is another matter entirely...
And once more he cannot part from them for a long time:
In town with his white bosses? — Ho, he suffers much,
He drags through his days tempered as from thick tar,
He scrubs pots, he cooks, he washes. Ho, a madness...
200 And for his lass — he still does not have any *lobola*...
Now suddenly Matatulu remembers his pass.
It is already late. The darkness becomes thick.
He sees in the darkness ahead a bad sign...
He runs fast. The hot sweat pours from his face,
He wants the faster now to reach his night's bed,
In the distance he sees the lights of the city spread out like a net.

And here — he is already near. Only one more street...
And suddenly, an order in the name of the law:
Where are you rushing, you devil? ... stop, your 'special',
210 And confused Matatulu falls to the ground,
He feels a strong, oppressive hand on him.
Hot blood rushes to his head:
He, trapped like a skunk here in his own land?
Oh, no. He cannot endure the shame.
And like a provoked lion he tears himself away.
They chase him as if he were a wild animal through the streets.
In vain — his strong feet are still fleet...
But suddenly — a bang. In the darkness a fiery shot rings out.
Matatulu's body falls to the ground just like a lion.
220 And slowly his bloody trouble pours out...

V

So once did he chase after jackals
Near his quiet kraal in the silent bush
And carrying them, brought [them] for his maiden.
The last shudder of his dead foot
Oh the healthy, proud, young Matatulu.

Burn

(A fragment fun a greserer poeme aroysgegebn oyfn
tsentn yortog fun der Dorem Afrikaner Republik.)

Mit halbn tog — gekumen iz a fule shtub mit gest;
Di burn in garniters oysgeputst,
Mit breyte hit un hengendike grobe hent.
Di vayber zaynen do gezesn mat
Mit kerpers ongegosene mit schmalts,
Mit fete geyders un mit fule brist,
Azoy, az shver gevezn iz tsu geben zikh a rir;
Un s'hot geshpilt der alter gramafon
Fun s'nay, shoyn efsher fun tsentn mol
10   Dem zelbikn, dem gut-bakantn vals.
Di vayber hobn ongekvoln azh
Fun der mekhayediker, emeser muzik
Un tsugetupet mit di fis,
Un tsugeshoklt mit di shvere kep,
Un s'hot zikh zey gekhalesht geyn a tans!

Di mener hobn tsugekukt tsu dem
Un oykh zikh gutmutik farbrakht.
Men hot geredt in prostn Afrikaans.
Di nayes zikh dertseylt fun oyfn land,
20   Un shtilerheyt geshmuest politik,
Un nokhamol Pol Krugern dermont:
Ot dos gevezn iz a braver man —
Nishto haynt nokh eyner tsu im! ...
Fargangen zaynen yene yorn, yo ...
A shod ... di Englender, zey lozn nit tsuru,
Me vet zey bald shoyn gor aroystraybn fun land.
Nor neyn, s'iz Afrike batrift mit zeyer blut ...

Un itster zaynen zey faranen do a sakh.
Gedenken zey nokh ale yene tsayt,
30   Ven s'iz geven a vildernish arum.
Un tomer hot a bur gefirt amol a gast
Tsu zikh arop in farm —
Hot dos gedoyert mamesh gantse teg...
Me fort, me fort, un s'nemt keyn sof afile nit tsum shlyakh.
'Var iz di plats?'
Flegt yener naygerik shoyn ton a freg.
'Da — bu — u — u' — Flegt men im dan a vayz ton mit der hand:
'Es iz shoyn nont, on dortn. Kan yey sin?'
Nor s'hot zikh alts nokh keyn zakh nit gezen,

40   Un oftmol flegt men opgeyn gantse nekht ...
Nor haynt iz shoyn an ander tsayt.
Zey konen shoyn a sakh epes vos ton.
Di kafers vet men oysshisn vi hint ...

Farmers (Afrikaners)

(A fragment of a longer poem published on the
tenth anniversary of the Republic of South Africa.)

At midday — there was a full room of guests;
The farmers dressed up in their best outfits,
With broad hats and hanging, huge arms.
The wives sat there listlessly
With bodies covered in fat,
With fat chins and full breasts,
So that it was difficult to move;
And the old gramophone played
Anew, perhaps for the tenth time
10   The same, the well-known waltz.
The women enjoyed so much
The pleasurable, authentic music
And tapped their feet,
And kept time with their heavy heads,
And they longed to go and dance!

The men looked on at this
And also enjoyed themselves good-naturedly.
They spoke in simple Afrikaans.
Told the news of the land,
20   And quietly spoke of politics,
And mentioned Paul Kruger once again:
— Now that was a brave man —
Today there is no one like him! ...
Those years are passed, yes, ...
What a pity, the English, they don't leave us alone,
We will soon drive them from the country.
But no, Africa is steeped in their blood...

And now there are many of them here.
They all remember that time,
30   When there was a wilderness around.
And if sometimes a farmer would bring a guest
To his farm —
It really took many days...
One went on, one continued, and the dirt road never ended.
'Where is the place?'
Someone asked curiously.
'Up there' — Someone pointed with his hand:
'It is near, just there. Can you see?'

40   And many nights would pass...
But today it's a different era.
They could still do a lot.
They could shoot the kaffirs like dogs...

Un me vet kemfn nokh far zeyer folk un shprakh ...
Gevis vet men nokh oyfton epes ... yo ...
Azoy hobn di burn zikh getreyst,
Gezupt di kave fun der flakher shal,
Zikh tsugehert geshmak tsum gramafon
Un emese hanoe do gehat.

50   Der balebos farroykhert hot a Holender tsigar,
Traktirt mit dem tsufridn zayne gest.
Men hot genumen azoy forzikhtik zayn gob
Mit tsvey fargrebte finger in der hant,
Mit derekh erets un mit opshay, vi a zakh,
Far vos me hot a gevaldikn respekt.
Un nokhdem hot men dos azoy min gut bakukt,
Derlangt a lek dem shpits mit naser tsung
Un take zikh bagavert bay derbay,
Un vishndik di sline fun der lip,
60   Gants aynfakh mitn arbl pidzhak.
Hot men farkhlinet zikh mit shmekedikn roykh.

Di paypn hot men oysgebitn glaykh
Oyf ot dem khoshevn un tayern antik;
Un s'iz gevorn ongeroykhert bald
Mit aza bitern, gedikhtn tshad
Di gantse benkendike shtub.

Azoy hot men in eynem zikh farbrakht,
Gemitlekh in der yon-tevdiker ru,
Un keyner hot afile nit bamerkt,
70   Vi s'hot getsoygn zikh der zumerdiker tog,
Getsoygn zikh mit aza foyler hits
In droysn biz dem kiln oyfdernakht.

Dorem Afrike (May–June 1971), 13

And they would struggle still for their folk and language...
Surely they would still do something ... yes ...
That is how the Boers comforted themselves,
Sipped coffee from the shallow saucer,
Listened with pleasure to the gramophone,
And enjoyed it very much.

50   The boss smoked a Dutch cigar,
Offered one to his guests with satisfaction.
They took his gift carefully
With two huge fingers of the hand,
With politeness and with appreciation, like something
For which they had the utmost respect.
And after that they examined it so well
Licked the tip (of the cigar) with a wet tongue
And they was really slobbering in the process,
And wiped the saliva from their lips,
60   Quite simply with the sleeve of the coat.
They drooled with enthusiasm in the aromatic smoke.

The pipes were exchanged at the same time
With the reckoning of expensive antiques;
And it became smoke-filled soon
With such bitter, thick fumes,
The whole enviable house.

That is how they all passed the time together
Companionably in celebratory rest,
And nobody even noticed
70   How the summer day passed,
Played out with such a tiring heat
Outside until the coming of the cool evening.

Dimantn

1   Brilyantn — du zest zey, mayn kind oto-do? —
Zey zaynen far mir in a finsterer sho
Bashafn gevorn durkh hent umbavuste...
Durkh leydike teg un durkh ovntn puste,
5   Mit girikayt sharf, vi di sharf fun a shverd,
Men hot zey gegrobn fun finsterer erd, —
Far mir un far dir zey gezukht, vi du zest.
Un itst zeyer glants, zeyer kalter, er prest
Keseyder mit tifer, farborgener moyre,
10   Er prest dikh un drikt mit aza more-shkhoyre,
Mit kaltkayt fun toyter, fargliverter kelt...
Er prest azoy shver in der fremd fun der velt: —
Nisht varem, nisht heymlekh, mit durshtiker kine...
Der glants fun brilyantn, — di fayerlekh grine,
Di fayerlekh royte, di gele, di bloye,
Vos tsindn zikh, dakht zikh, vos tsindn zikh toyen
Oyf lonkes, ven s'heybn on seder tsu blien
Un shvalbn, ven s'kumen di ershte tsu flien
Mit likhtike grusn fun freyd un yetsire, —
20   Dan zestu di dimantn kalt, vi zey frirn
In eygenem fayer, — in grinem un bloyen
Vos brent, dakht zikh, varem azoy vi di toyen
In likhtikn friling oyf likhtike grozn...
Nor neyn, zeyer fayer du kenst nisht tseblozn
Far mide neshomes, — neshomes vi mayne,
Neshomes fartrakhte, un yunge vi dayne,
Vos zukhn un benken, un filn, un lekhtsn —
Neshomes farfulte mit veytok un krekhtsn,
Vos veynen in velt vi der elnter vint, —
30   Neshomes fun mentshn, vos lebn vi hint...
Brilyantn — far dir kh'hob, mayn kind, zey gezukht,
Far dir kh'hob a lebn zey zhedne geklibn...
Es hot zikh mir lignerish tomid gedukht,
Az du vest vi ale zey tsiterik libn.
Derfar hob ikh shtendik far dir zey gehit,
Ikh hob nor in dimantn finster gegloybt,
Far zey hob ikh shtil vi a betler geknit
Un oftmol afile dem tayvl geloybt...
Vayl zey zaynen tayer un mekhtik, un shtark.
40   Far zey boygt di velt ir farmatertn kark,
Zey kenen bafrayen un kenen farshklafn,
Zey kenen tseshtern un kenen bashafn,
Zey kenen derhoybn un vider tsebrekhn...
Derfar hob ikh keseyder geklert un gerekhnt,
45   Barekhnt di shteyner tsum vifltn mol,
Getseylt zey, gekheshbnt farshtikt oyfn kol,
Farzorgt zey gevaremt in buzem bay mir,
Zay zhedne gekhovet, gevisht un sortirt
In tsimer bay shverer, farshlosener tir,

Diamonds[*]

 1   These brilliants, you see them, my child, do you see —
For me they were made and created for me,
By unwilling hands in the darkness of night,
While digging with greed and with a grasping eye,
Through evenings empty and unending days,
Exploring and sifting deep-down underground,
For me and for you they were sought and were found.
And now they are glittering, icy and cold,
With fear and with horror that are hidden and deep,
And holding you tight in their deadening grip.
10   The coldness of death is their glittering shine,
The frightening cold of unnamed horror,
Their fires that glimmer in many a colour
With green and with red, and with yellow and blue,
And sparkle on mornings with light like the dew,
On meadows in spring, or on blossoming trees,
The diamonds' fires are cold, and it seems
As if they were freezing in their own gleams,
But trembling with zeal I have guarded with care,
My treasures of stones, of the rough and the rare.
20   And trusting forever their power concealed,
I kept them for you as a gift and reward,
For them like a beggar my knees I have bent,
And even the devil I've praised as a saint,
Because they are powerful, precious and dear,
For whom all the world is bowing with fear.
Accounting for every and each of the gems,
I counted them quietly and many a time,
Counting with cunning and counting again,
And tenderly wiping off traces of dust,
30   And putting them back in their places with care,
I fed them with looks that were hungry with lust.
The stones were my thoughts, and my dreams through the night,
And stricken with terror I held in my hands
The diamonds, burning, bewitched in their light.
Locked in by doors that were bolted and barred,
My fingers touched softly the diamonds all,
And stroking them, counting, alone in the hall,
While safe amidst safes of cold iron and steel —
Myself I got stronger and hardened and hard.

[*] This is Fram's own translation, which is much shorter than the original Yiddish poem, and forgoes line-by-line translation (*David Fram Papers*, Folder 11, pp. 409–11)

50   Mit finger fartsitert zey heylik barirt
      Un gliklekh gevezn fun itlekhn rir...
      Mayn lebn fun zey hob ikh bloyz nor getrakht,
      Ikh hob fun di shteyner gekholemt baynakht,
      Dershrokn gehit zey durkh loytere teg,
55   Durkh shoen, ven zun hot mit gold mikh geblendt,
      Un tomid gevaksn iz greser di shrek,
      Ven dimantn hobn bay mir in di hent
      Mit fayerlekh kalte farkisheft gebrent...
      Un ven kh'fleg ahinter farriglte tirn
60   Di dimantn harte mit veykhkayt barirn,
      Un gletn, un tseyln zey lang a farshparter
      In tsimer tsvishn di ayzerne shranken, —
      Flegt shtendik mayn harts vern harter un harter,
      Un punkt vi a khalef flegt nemen dan blankn
65   Mayn blik der tsekokhter bay mir in der oygn.
      Ikh hob di brilyantn getseylt un gevoygn,
      Un kelter, un beyzer mayn harts iz gevorn,
      Biz ikh hob derfilt durkh tsendliger yorn,
      Az ikh bin gevorn ingantsn farshteynert, —
70   Un elnt in velt kh'bin farblibn aleyn nor,
      Aleyn in der velt a farshtikter vi Shaylok
      Hob ikh mayne oytsres dershrokn gehit,
      Un alts vos s'iz zindik gevorn iz heylik,
      Ven s'hobn di shteyner mayn moyekh gebrit...

75   Ikh hob a farshemter zikh oyfgehert shemen,
      Gezen hob ikh zikh umetum nor aleyn,
      Nor groylik flegt vern, ven ikh fleg farnemen
      In ovntn shpete fun vint dem geveyn.
      Der vint oyf farlozene, elnte pleynen
80   Far mir flegt keseyder dan veynen un veynen.
      Tsi s'iz geven friling, tsi s'hobn geblit shoyn
      Di karshn in seder bay poyershe ploytn,
      Tsi s'iz geven zumer mit gilderne hitsn,
      Tsi harbst hot di beymer geforbn in roytn,
85   Tsi vinter afile geyogt hot mit shneyen
      Un vays un geheylikt farhilt ale shlyakhn, —
      Dos hot shoyn fun lang-on mikh oyfgehert freyen,
      Ikh hob vi a mentsh nisht gekont merer lakhn,
      Ikh hob nisht gekont merer gloybn un libn —
90   Di ale gefiln kh'hob lang shoyn farlorn,
      Di dimantn hob ikh nor kalte geklibn
      Un durkh zeyer fayer farfrorn gevorn...
      Durkh doyres, durkh gantse yorhunderter hobn
      Fartsveyflte mentshn di shteyner gegrobn,
95   Fun finstere griber, fun erdishe tifn, —
      Zey zoyber gevashn, geputst un geshlifn,
      Gemostn, gevoygn, geshatst zeyer vert, —
      Milyonen tsu zikh in di hoyfns farshart,
      Vi yenem tsu narn keseyder geklert
100   Un zikh un dem tsveytn gebloft un genart...

40   From weighing and sorting the wealth of my jewels,
The sight of my eyes becomes sharpened and cruel
Until after years that are passing, I feel
That hard like a stone I am growing myself,
And that in the world I am one and alone.
And lonely alone like a Shylock reborn,
I treasure my secrets with terror unceasing —
And everything evil seems sacred and pleasing,
Since burned is my brain with the treacherous jewels,
So great was my shame that I no longer felt shame.

50   Wherever I looked, it was always the same:
The mirrors and walls they shadowed and haunted,
Myself I saw only and nothing but me,
The winds that were blowing through evenings late,
They sounded as if they were weeping aloud,
So lonesome across the deserted dark lanes,
Yet neither in springtime the blossoming trees,
Nor heat of the summer, so golden and bright,
Nor autumn leaves' red, nor winter's snow-white
That sacredly covered the plains and the fields —
60   They long ceased to gladden my sorrow and grief.
And laughter I lost, and love and belief.
Collecting the diamonds cold and unceasing,
Myself in their fires I was steadily freezing.
For ages and centuries, deep with despair,
Have humans been digging for treasures unknown.
And clearing from darkness and cutting them bare,
They polished and washed them and made them glare.
And measuring, weighing, assessing their worth,
They heaped in the millions the money they brought,

70   By fooling themselves and deceiving their friends.
More brilliant than starlight and brighter than sun
The stones seemed to burn in their cold frozen hands.
Whoever they were who have touched them one time:
The dealer or agent, the miner or cutter,
The thief just released, and the man from the gutter,
The cheats and adventurers, hunting for chances —
They were all inflamed with the glimmering glances
That flowed from the cold and adored ornament.
Since then and forever they cursed their own fate,

80   And felt in their misery abandoned and lost.
In the winds that were blowing, in sunsets unfolding,
Sailed merchants from countries all over the world.
From far away cities of far continents,
From London, New York, from Antwerp and Rome,
From India and Egypt and China they came,
To buy and to sell and to bid and to game.
They traded and cheated and changed and exchanged...
Allured and enticed by the glittering gems,
Their hearts were hardened and frosty still more,

Der diment hot heys zeyer tayve gehitst,
Far zey hot er hel vi a shtern geblitst,
Un azh fun der zun hot er heyser gebrent
In zeyere karge, farfroyrene hent.

105 Un ver s'zol nisht zayn dos: — a soykher a shtayfer,
A mekler, a 'kliver', fun Holand a shlayfer,
A dimentn-greber fun Afrike vayter,
A ganev, nor okorsht fun tfise bafrayter,
A shvindler a fremder mit khutspishe blikn,
110 Vos hot zikh gelozn nokh finstere glikn,
A hur fun Pariz, tsi fun London a dame: —
Bay alemen flegn di oygn tseflamen
In shayn fun di kalte, brilyantene tsirung.
Un ver s'flegt nor kumen mit dem in barirung
Flegt blaybn farshteynert, farklemt un farglivert: —
Di dame, der soykher, der tremp un der 'kliver', —
Zey flegn shoyn blaybn oyf eybik farlorn
In tsar fun farsholtene leydike yorn...

Zey hot shoyn in lebn keyn zakh nisht gekimert,
120 A khuts der brilyantener, bloylekher shimer,
A khuts vi in shteyn di bahaltene flekn:
Der 'glets', der 'pikey' oyfn zoybern tovl, —
Far dem nor zey flegn zikh hitn un shrekn,
Azoy vi es shrekt zikh in shive der ovl,
Azoy vi es shrekn zikh tsaytike grozn
In harbst farn sharf fun di poyershe serpn.

Un vintn zey hobn in shkie geblozn
Un hendler fun Indye, fun Roym un Antverpn,
Fun Vin un Pariz, fun Nyu York, Argentine,
130 Fun London, Brazil, fun Egiptn un Khine,
Fun ale fir ekn, fun ale fir kantn, —
Zey hobn gekoyft un farkoyft di brilyantn,
Gehandlt, geshvindlt, geyogt un gelyaremt,
Un s'hot zey der diment gereytst un gevaremt,
135 Gereytst un gevarmt, un shtarker gefrorn
Mit prostikn fayer di hertser di harte,
Vos zaynen alts kelter, farglivert gevorn
Durkh fayern falshe un funken genarte.
Un vintn, zey hobn in shkie geblozn,
140 Un s'hobn getsitert di tsaytike grozn
In blank fun di koses un poyershe serpn.
Un London, Pariz, un Nyu York un Antverpn
Gekoyft hobn shteyner, getoysht un farbitn,
Geganvet karatn fun erlekhe sholn,
Un hobn keynmol nisht bamerkt vi gelitn
Arum hobn mentshn fun hunger geshvoln,
Fun krankayt tsegrizhet, fun veytog tsefresn,
In eygenem elnt farshtupt un fargesn —
Di mentshn, zey hobn durkh teg nisht dernerte

90   With fires unreal and sparks that were lying.
     But still they were changing and selling and buying
     And stealing the carats from innocent scales —
     And never they noticed those others who bore
     With pain and with patience their suffering lot,
     And swollen from hunger and touched with disease
     Were unknown and wretched and forgotten and lost —
     But they, they saw only the diamonds they knew,
     With tears in their eyes that were glistening like dew,
     In evenings late and in autumn belated.

100 For whom, my dear child, has your father with care,
     For whom has he saved all that colourful ware,
     And hoarded with warmth all the treasures, for whom?
     For sinister women in harems of gloom,
     For prostitutes lingering in the streets of the city,
     For ladies in noble salons,
     And for the pretty and young lusting harlots of old growing men;
     For hideous traders, for kings and for courts,
     For bankers and barons, for courts and for lords?
     With them he was trading and dealing — your dad,
110 For them he has always been bowing his head,
     To them he has looked with the eye of a slave.
     And cashing the dollars and pounds,
     He has been the servant of murder, of theft and of sin.
     But then at the end I was handing as gift
     To you, my dear child, all my wealth and my gains,
     You did not accept them, but took them to pieces
     And threw them away in the winds and the rains.
     In vain have the miners been digging so hard
     In darkness of night and in dangerous ditches.

120 In vain have the cutters been proving their skill;
     In vain was I sharing in swindle and theft.
     Now in the autumn I am lonely and empty,
     Remaining alone with the valuable stones —
     And still I shall guard them with worry and will.
     No longer for you I shall need them and hoard them,
     And yet as before I shall weigh them and count them,
     Not sharing the shame and the fear that you feel,
     For people who suffer with love and with faith,
     Believing in beauty and glory and grace —

130 It was so before and so will remain.
     But you who rejected my gifts and my gains
     And threw them away to the winds and the rains —
     Relieved from the curse of the glittering stone,
     The greatest of treasures in life you have won.

150   Gezen bloyz dimantn in oygn fartrerte,
       In trern, vi toyen, vos vern farloshn
       Fun shpetikn vint in a shpetikn osyen...

       Un itster, far vemen, mayn kind, hot dayn tate
       Gekhovet di vayse un bloye karatn,
       Far vemen hot er zey gevaremt, far vemen? —
       Far vayber fun tunkele, zate haremen,
       Far zoynes fun shtetishe likhtike gasn,
       Far eydele dames fun raykhe salonen
       Azoy vi di hurn in nakht oysgelasn,
160   Far miese sokhrim, far melokhim un tronen,
       Far kepsvayber yunge fun alte magnatn,
       Far lordn, bankirn, un grafn, baronen,
       Mit zey hot, mayn kind, dos gehandlt dayn tate,
       Far zey hob ikh tomid mayn kop dos geboygn,
165   Geshlept zikh tsu zeyere shleser di zate,
       Gekukt zey farshklaft vi a hunt in di oygn,
       In zeyere simkhes hob ikh zikh bateylikt,
       Geven a farmitler fun ganeyve un mordn,
       Un kh'hob zeyer zind, zeyer tume geheylikt
170   Far funtn un dolers fun sokhrim un lordn...

       Un haynt, ven far dir kh'hob gebrakht mayn farmegn, —
       Hostu im tseshmisn in harbstikn regn,
       Du host nisht genumen, du darfst im nisht hobn:
       Umzist hobn greber di shteyner gegrobn,
       Fun finstere griber, fun erdishe tifn,
       Umzist hobn shlayfers zey gute geshlifn,
       Umzist hob ikh zikh in ganeyve bateylikt
       Un heslekhe tume in lebn farheylikt,
       Atsind inem harbst bin ikh umetik eyner
180   Geblibn aleyn mit di tayere shteyner,
       Ikh vel zey nokh hitn mit klem un mit veytik,
       Nor du host avade, mayn kind, zey nisht neytik,
       Du darfst zey nisht hobn, du vilst zey nit nemen
       Du vest mit di dimantn mayne zikh shemen
       Zikh shemen far mentshn, vos leydn un gloybn
       In libe un sheynkayt. Tsu zey zikh derhoybn
       Hostu zikh gevis — nisht azoy vi dayn tate,
       Vos hot nor gevoygn di shvere karatn,
       Getseylt zey, gekheshbnt, gegloybt in zey heylik
190   Un durkh zey gelitn, geveytogt vi Shaylok,
       Nor ikh vel nokh vayter di dimantn klaybn, —
       Azoy iz geven un azoy vet shoyn blaybn,
       Nor du host dem diment dem grestn bakumen —
       Ikh hob dir gegebn, nor du st'nit genumen,
       Ikh hob dir gegebn mayn gantsn farmegn,
       Hostu im tseshmisn in harbstikn regn,
       Bist raykher, avade, mayn kind, fun dayn tatn,
       Fun yene farsholtene, reyne karatn...

                                   A shvalb oyfn dakh, pp. 64–68

Undzere kedoyshim

1   Nokh aykh, ir brider mayne, hob ikh haynt gerisn krie —
Dem sharf fun heysn meser bizn layb mit veytik ayngeshnitn
Es shteyt nokh far di oygn mayne yene shvartse tliye
Oyf velkher ir hot ayer toyt oyf kedushe eybiker tsebitn.

5   Ikh ze aykh nokh, ir kedoyshim heldishe, ir geyt tsu der akeyde
Mit festn trot, derhoybene fun shrek, baloykhtn mit a shmeykhl
Azoy vi s'volt farbay a frume, shtralndike eyde
Fun yidn gloybike tsu Gots gebentshtn heykhl.

9   Ikh ze aykh nokh, giboyrim yidishe, gehangene fun sheker,
Fun sine un fun has, un khayishe retsikhes
In blutikn geklang fun shrayendike gleker
Ven s'filt der talyen oys zayn merderishe shlikhes...

13   Ikh ze aykh nokh far zikh ir mutike derleyzer,
Farshlefert vi in shlof durkh mamisher yenike,
Azoy min shtil un reyn, on tsorn, on gebeyzer,
Vi Got volt aykh gekusht mit getlekher neshike.

17   Vi Got volt aykh geshikt tsu lebn vayter eybik.
Gelaytert ze ikh aykh, vi durkh a loyterer yerie.
Mispalel zayn mayn folk far aykh vet frum un gleybik
Un undzer grester shtolts — iz itster ayer tliye.

21   To rut in ayer shlof, ir yidishe giboyrim,
Di kedushe hilt aykh ayn azoy vi tsu neile.
Farovlt vet di velt far aykh nokh faln koyrim
Un betlen farn toyt vet zi bay aykh mekhile.

25   Un ir bay undzer folk farblaybn vet ir heylik!
Oy vey, lemay bin ikh nisht eyner fun der eyde!
Mit velkher kh'volt gevolt zikh teyln ayer kheylek
In shtolts tsuzamen geyn mit aykh tsu der akeyde.

Dorem Afrike (March–April 1969), 170

Our Martyrs

1 For you, my brothers, I have rent my garment today —
The sharpness of the burning knife cut through to the body in pain
Those black gallows still remain before my eyes
On which your death was changed into eternal martyrdom.

5 I see you still, you heroic martyrs, you walk towards the sacrifice
With steadfast step, elevated in terror, illuminated with a smile
As if a pious, radiant congregation of faithful Jews
Were passing by [on their way] towards God's holy temple.

9 I see you still, Jewish heroes, strung up because of lies,
In malice and hatred, and savage murder
In bloody peals of screaming bells
When the hangman fulfils his murderous task...

13 I see you still before me, you courageous redeemers,
Drowsy as if in sleep after a mother's suckling,
So quiet and clean, without wrath, without anger,
As if God would have kissed you with a divine kiss.

17 As if God would have sent you to live again forever.
Clearly I see you as through a transparent curtain.
Praying my people for you, observant and believing
And our greatest pride — now is your gallows.

21 So rest in your sleep, you Jewish heroes,
Sanctity envelops you as if it were *Ne'ila*.
Bereaved the world will still prostrate itself before you
And beg forgiveness of you for this death.

25 And you will remain holy among our people!
Oh, woe, that I am not one of that congregation!
With whom I would have wanted to share your destiny
And proudly walk together with you to the sacrifice.

An entfer der velt

(Araynfir fun a greserer arbet.)

1   Ikh fil, ikh trog oyf zikh tsurik di gele late.
Fun vaytn knoylt zikh nokh fun kalkh-oyvn der roykh,
Vu s'hot zayn letstn Sh'ma Yisroel oysgelebt mayn tate,
Vu s'hot mayn mame oysgehoykht ir letstn hoykh,

5   Vu brider zaynen tsu dem toyt farlitene gegangen,
Vu oyfhelekh geshtelt hobn in vakl zeyer shtiln trot,
Farviklte in hartsike, in mameshe gezangn,
Zey zoln farn shtarbn khotsh nit veynen — o mayn Got!...

9   Un kh'ze nokh haynt un fil nokh dem gehenem
Fun gornisht-lang fargangenem amol,
Ven laykhtste shtrof gevezn iz: — 'farbren im',
Dos iz der psak — dem henkers shvartser kol —

13 Hot men keseyder unz gehargt un gevorgn, —
Vos greser s'iz der mord — alts freylikher iz zey.
Es hot zey nit geshtert di hele shayn fun morgn,
Es hot zey nit geshtilt der groylikster geshrey...

17 Azoy zaynen gegangn yidn tsu dem shayter —
Fun Varshe un Pariz, fun Kovne un fun Bon.
Milyonen hobn zikh getsoygn vayter, vayter
Tsum shvartsn eshafot... oy, gantse zeks milyon!...

21 Oyf dem — di gantse velt gekukt hot un geshvign,
Geshtanen glaykhgiltik mit aropgelozte hent,
Un meysim kupesvayz hot men gelozn lign
Un nokhanand gebrent, geshokhtn un gebrent...

25 Biz vanen s'hot a nes unz oysgeleyzt, bafrayte,
Es hot bavizn zikh an oysgeshtrekte hant.
Mit hofn un mit treyst, mit zeungen banayte
Zi hot unz drayst gefirt tsurik tsu undzer land.

29 Di oysbahaltene in derfer un in shtetlekh,
Vos oysgehit zey hobn zikh fun merderisher shverd —
Gegangen zaynen shtolts mit tfiles frum un getlekh
Geratevet fun toyt — bazetsn undzer erd.

33 Un do iz dos geshen — men hot genumen boyen,
S'hot yederer gevolt zikh oyslebn in freyd...
S'iz erd gevorn faykht, bafrukhpert fun di toyen,
Vos ayngezapt hot zat do yeder boym un kveyt.

37 S'hot oyfgelebt a folk fun akerer un zeyer,
Men hot gepashet shof, men hot geshnitn broyt
Un yidn fun der vayt, vi durkhn midber-geyer —
Zikh oyfgehert tsu shrekn hobn farn toyt.

41 Dos iz dokh zeyer heym, zey veln zikh bashitsn,
Vi heldn zaynen greyt — mit zeyer shveys un blut

An Answer to the World

(Introduction to a larger work.)

1 I feel, I wear the yellow star once again.
 In the distance there still billows the smoke from the limekiln,
 Where my father lived out his last *Sh'ma Yisroel*,
 Where my mother breathed her last breath of air,

5 Where brothers went to their death with resignation,
 Where infants trod their quiet shaky steps
 Enwrapped in moving, in motherly songs,
 They would not cry out before dying — oh my God!...

9 And I still see today and still feel the hell
 From the recent past of not long ago
 When the lightest penalty was: 'burn him' —
 That is the judgement — the hangman's black voice —

13 They constantly killed and choked us, —
 The greater the killing — the happier they are.
 They did not care about the clear gleam of morning
 The most appalling scream did not disquiet them...

17 Thus did the Jews go to the pyre —
 From Warsaw and Paris, from Kovne and from Bonn.
 Millions were drawn further, further
 To black execution scaffolds ... oh, a whole six million! ...

21 On this — the whole world looked on and kept silent,
 Stood by indifferent with hands hanging at their sides,
 And they left the dead lying in piles
 And burnt them continuously, slaughtered and burnt...

25 Until a miracle redeemed us, freed us,
 An outstretched hand appeared.
 With hope and with comfort, with renewed visions
 It took us boldly back to our land.

29 Those concealed in towns and villages,
 Who were protected from the murderous sword —
 Proudly went with prayers pious and divine
 Saved from death — settled our land.

33 And here it happened — they began to build,
 Each one wanting to live their life in joy...
 Earth became moist, made fruitful by the dew,
 Which each tree and blossom absorbed.

37 And there rose to life a people, ploughmen and sowers,
 They tended sheep, they cut bread
 And Jews from afar, like desert wanderers —
 Stopped fearing death.

41 This is now their home; they will defend it,
 Like heroes they are ready — with their sweat and blood

Un zol es dunern un flakern un blitsn —
S'vet keyner ayntsoymen nit kenen zeyer mut...

45   Di felder fridlekhe genumen hobn blien,
Mit groyser likhtikayt gekumen iz der tog,
Di likhtikayt fun zayn, di oysshtralung fun Tsien,
Geheylt hot undzer vund, geshtilt hot undzer klog...

49   Azoy hot men gefilt, azoy hot men farshtanen:
Der faygnboym in ru vet vaksn bay dayn tir.
Men vet shoyn blaybn do, men vet nit geyn fun danen,
Men vet zikh funem ort atsind nit ton keyn rir.

53   Di reshtlekh fun a folk, der iberblayb fun pleyte
Vet opvaksn tsurik un lindern dem brokh...
Un himlen iber unz gekukt hobn derfreyte
Mit shabesdiker ru oyf pratse fun der vokh...

Dorem Afrike (July–August 1971), 50

And should it thunder and blaze and flash —
No one will be able to contain their courage...

45   The peaceful fields began to blossom,
In great brightness the day has arrived,
The brightness of being, the radiance of Zion,
Healed is our wound, silenced is our lament...

49   This is how we felt, this how we understood it:
The fig tree will grow restfully at your door.
Here we will remain, we will not depart from here,
From this place now we will never move.

53   The remnant of a people, the remaining survivors
Will grow back and soothe the catastrophe...
And heavens above us looked down delighted
With sabbath-like rest after the toil of the week...

Dos letste kapitl

(Fragment fun der poeme, geleyent fun Ruvn Ziglboym oyfn Fram-
ovnt, vos der 'Jewish Trust' hot ayngeordnt lekoved
Dovid Fram tsu zayn akhstikst geboyrntog.)

1   Geshen iz dos lang shoyn, fartsaytn, nit itster:
   A Yid iz gekumen fun veg a farshvitster
   In eynem a tog fun a zunikn tamez.
   Di erd iz gelegn bagosn mit flamen
   Fun gilderner hits un fun gilderner shefe
   Un breyt hot di erd ire orems tseefnt,
   Azoy vi a mame, hot dan farn Yidn,
   Zi hot zikh derfreyt mitn gast mitn midn.
   A Yid iz gekumen dan shtil un farmatert,
10   Un s'hot aza freyd in zayn hartsn geflatert:
   Di erd iz im lib un der himl iz bloy im,
   Do lebn besholem vet er mit di Goyim,
   Zey veln im ale derkenen, dem altn,
   Er vet zikh mit keyn zakh fun zey nit bahaltn,
   Er vet zey bagrisn fun vaytn un noentn...
   Un s'vinken derhoybn tsu im horizontn
   Mit heymisher ru, balebatish mit verde —
   Tsu im, tsu dem Yidn oyf litvishe erdn.
   Oyf litvishe erdn, vi groys s'iz der khidesh!
20   Der Yid hot farflantst dort a lebn in Yidish:
   Shabosim, yon-toyvim, havdoles un kidesh!
   Barmitsves un khasenes, zilberne menoyres
   Un bekhers, un koyses far simkhes un brisn —
   Geburtn fun naye, fun yidishe doyres, —
   Un zmires tsezungn bay vareme tishn
   Mit tishtekher klore oyf shabes farshpreyte,
   Mit likht in di laykhter un khales gegreyte.
   Mit tishtekher vays, vi mit shneyen bashneyte.
   Un fraytig-tsunakhtn, di likht oyf di tishn,
30   Zey flegn tsebrenen mit heylikn tsiter.
   In fraytig-tsunakhtn in yidishe shtiber,
   Zey loykhtn mit gloybn un varemkayt liber.
   Es hot zey dos gloybn geshtarkt un gemutikt.
   Un ven s'hobn Yidn afile geblutikt,
   Ven s'hot zey di noyt vi a khalef geshnitn —
   Azoy vi a khalef, a blutike britve,
   Zey hobn geshtarkt zikh un hobn gelitn,
   Gelitn, oyf erdn fun heymisher Litve.
   A Yid iz gekumen amol in der Lite,
40   Der Yid iz gevezn mayn zeyde, mayn tate,
   Es hobn getsoygn zikh lonkes tseblite
   Un felder mit broytn — tsekvolene, zate —
   Di ale khidushim, di ale geshtaltn,
   Vos hobn gelebt dort a gliklekhn lebn,
   Zey zaynen shoyn dortn atsind nishto mer.

The Last Chapter

(Fragment of the poem, as read by Reuven Zygielbaum at the Fram
Evening convened by the Jewish Trust in honour of
David Fram's eightieth birthday.)

1   It happened a long time ago, once, not now:
A Jew came along the road all sweaty
On one sunny *Tamuz* day.
The earth was flooded with flames
Of golden heat and gilded abundance
And then the earth spread her arms wide,
Like a mother, for the Jew,
Delighted with the guest, though exhausted.
A Jew arrived then quietly and wearily,
10   And such great joy fluttered in his heart:
The earth was fond of him and the heavens blue,
Here he could live in harmony with the Gentiles,
They would all acknowledge him, the ancient one,

He would not hide anything from them,
He would greet them from near and from far...
And horizons winked at him politely
With homely calm, respectable and worthy —
To him, to the Jew on Lithuanian soil.

On Lithuanian soil, how great the surprise!
20   The Jew implanted there a life in Yiddish:
Sabbaths, festivals, *havdolah* and *kiddush*!
Bar mitzvahs and weddings, silver candelabra
And chalices and goblets for celebrations and circumcisions —
For the birth of new, Jewish generations, —
And Sabbath songs sung at warm tables
With clean cloths spread out for Sabbath,
And candles in the candlesticks and brides ready prepared.
With white tablecloths, as if covered with snow.
And on Friday nights, the candles on the table,
30   They would burn with holy shimmer.
And Friday nights in Jewish homes,
They light up with belief in loving warmth,
Belief strengthened them and gave them courage.
And even when there were Jews who were bleeding,
When need cut into them like a slaughter knife —
Like a slaughter knife, a bloody razor,
They strengthened themselves and they suffered,
Suffered, on the soil of homely Lithuania.

Once a Jew arrived in Lithuania,
40   That Jew was my grandfather, my father,
Blossoming meadows stretched out
And fields of bread — overflowing, satiated —
All these wonders, all these figures,

Dort trogt zikh arum itst a leydiker yomer,
A yomer fun kreyen vos pikn di beyner
Un s'feln dort ale, ale — nishto iz shoyn keyner
Bloyz meysim, harugim un kupes mit beyner,
50   Afile on kadish, on treyst, on baveyner
Mayn Lite, mayn heymland, vi ken ikh dos gloybn,
Az du host di Yidn bay zikh dort geshokhtn,
Du host zey dervorgn,
Mit dayne farblutikte negl atsinder,
Du host zey dershtikt — dayne eygene kinder!
Di hent dayne zaynen mit blut haynt bagosn,
Dos blut vest shoyn keynmol fun zey nit farvashn,
Es hot zikh in dir dayn bizoyen farloshn
Un s'zaynen farfoylt itst mit mord dayne gasn.
60   Ot ligt a farblutikter vaybersher yakl,
Ot trogstu di hemder fun undzere zeydes,
Vos oysgeton hostu fun zeyere layber.
Ot trogn mit khutspe atsind dayne vayber,
Di tsirungen fun mayn gehargeter bobn,
Vos unter mayn shvel du host tsinish bagrobn...
Ot kumen di eydes, ot zaynen zey ale
A shleyer ikh ze fun a yidishe kale,
Ot ze ikh a shtrayml, a yidishe hitl,
Un ot iz a vayser, a heyliker kitl.*
70   Ot valgert zikh elnt a zilberner bekher
Fun velkhn mayn tate gemakht hot nokh kidesh...
Oy vey iz mir, Lite — ot zaynen, ot lign —
Azoy fil harugim: — mayn khaver, mayn bester,
Mayn shokhn, mayn korev, mayn eyntsike shvester...
Ikh veys nit tsetumlt, vos ikh volt gedarft ton,
Nor ven kh'volt itst kenen a meser a sharf ton,
A sharf ton a meser azoy vi a britve,
Volt ikh dayne merder, mayn yidishe Litve,
Di gorgls tseshnitn mit heyser nekome.
80   Nekome far koshere yidishe froyen,
Nekome far kinder un mames un tates,
Far elnte, leydike yidishe khates.
Nekome far alte farpaynikte zeydes,
Far gantse fartilikte yidishe eydes,
Vos zaynen avek tsu di shvartse akeydes
Mit heylike tfiles oyf helft nit derzogte,
Ven s'hobn zikh zeyere oygn farklogte,
Mit harbstike shkies oyf eybik farshlosn.
Un hoykh volt ikh veln atsind a geshrey ton,
90   Di velt zol derzen, di velt zol derhern,
Un demolt vet efsher azoy dokh nit vey ton,
Un s'veln nit shtikn azoy mikh di trern,
Un efsher, efsher mayn veytok vet laykhter dan vern...

Dorem Afrike (January–March 1954), 12

★ White garment in which Jewish men are buried; also worn by many on Yom Kippur.

Which lived a happy life there,
Now they are there no longer.
There spills out an empty lament,
A lamentation of crows that pick the bones
And now there all, all are missing — there is no one left
Except the murdered, the dead and piles of bones,
50   Without even Kaddish, without comfort, without mourners
My Lithuania, my homeland, how can I believe it,
That you slaughtered the Jews there in your midst,
You strangled them,
Now with your bloody fingers,
You choked them — your own children!
Your hands today are drenched with blood,
That blood you will never be able to wash away,
Your shame became extinguished within you
And your streets are rotten now with murder.

60   Here lies a bloodied woman's jacket,
Here you wear the shirts of our grandfathers,
Which you stripped from their bodies.
Here your wives wear now with impertinence,
The jewellery of my murdered grandmother,
That you cynically buried at my lintel...
Here come the witnesses, here they all are:
I see the veil of a Jewish bride,
Here I see a fur hat, a Jewish hat,
And here is a white, a holy robe.
70   Here lies in desolation a silver goblet
With which my father still made Kiddush...
Oh woe is me, Lithuania — here they are, here lie —
So many slaughtered: — my friend, my best friend,
My neighbour, my relative, my only sister...

I did not know, confused, what I needed to do,
But if I could now sharpen a knife,
Sharpen a knife like a razor,
I would cut the throats of your murderers,
My Jewish Lithuania, in burning revenge.
80   Revenge for the innocent Jewish women,
Revenge for children and mothers and fathers,
For desolate, empty Jewish shacks.
Revenge for old tortured grandfathers,
For entire annihilated Jewish communities,
That are gone to the black bindings of Isaac
With holy prayers left half unsaid,
When their eyes filled with tears,
With autumn-like sunsets forever sealed.
And now I want to scream out loudly,
90   That the world should recognize, the world should take heed,
And then maybe it would not hurt so much,
And maybe my tears would not choke me,
And perhaps, perhaps my pain would then become lighter...

Lesterung

(Fragment fun der poeme 'Ma toyvu ohalekho Yankev'.)

1   Mayn land, du bist far mir yorhunderter gelegn in geshtalt
Fun mayn farlibtn, oysgehitn, benkendikn seyfer.
Ven ikh fleg zikh derfiln elnt, oysgeshept un alt,
Un ven kh'hob oyf der velt gekukt vi durkh a shpalt,
Un s'flegt mayn harts zikh onfiln mit kine un mit eyfer
Tsu yene felker frayntlekhe, vos hobn mir a shtikl dakh
Gegebn vu nit iz avektsuleygn, oyf dervayl, mayn kop dem midn —
Fleg ikh on dir dermonen zikh, mayn heyliker tanekh,
On dir, un on mayn land un dort — on yene Yidn, —
10   Di Yidn dayne vaynmakher, un poyerim, un shmidn,
Di Yidn dayne pastekher — Yisroelim un Menashes,
Vos flegn fitern di stades tsign heymish oyf der pashe
Un hamern un gisn kiers un klezayen.
Mayn folk, kh'hob dan getrakht fun ayin takhes ayin.
Ikh hob dayn toyre doyres-lang bahaltn un gelernt.
Ikh hob gezen di alte himlen dayne oysgeshternt,
Dayn Galil, un dayn Karmel, un dem fuln Yardn.
Nor vayt bin ikh fun dir geven — oyf mayln, oyf milyardn,
Un s'iz dayn heyse erd geven far mir i kalt, i fremd:
20   Dayn flaks iz nisht gevaksn dort gerotn far mayn hemd,
Dayn broyt hot mikh a hungerikn keynmol nisht dernert.
Dayn vayn hob ikh avade nisht getrunkn fun dayn logl —
Nor tomid bin ikh umgegangn elnt un farklemt,
Un s'hobn yorn hunderter mayn benkenish fartsert,
Un dikh hob ikh shoyn oyfgehert tsu zukhn in mayn vogl.
Mayn land. On dayn amol hob ikh zikh veytikdik geklamert.
Dayn over hob ikh ayngezapt in mayne odern di harte.
Nor mid bin ikh gevorn in mayn veg oyf dir tsu vartn —
Mayn blut hot shoyn in kop bay mir di shleyfn nit gehamert,
30   Mayn kholem iz shoyn nisht geven mer bas-Yerusholayim,
Tsu shakhris hob ikh oyfgehert mayn blik tsu dir tsu vendn,
Mayn shverd hot nisht arumgegurt mit gvure mayne lendn,
Vayl ikh hob oyf a bodn zikh arayngeflantst a nayem.
Oy vey, ikh bin efsher geven farfult mit zind un vidershpenig.
Ikh hob mayn altn Got in hartsn merer nisht getrogn,
Un kh'hob zikh keyn al-kheyt fartsitert nisht geshlogn,
Ikh hob fargesn, az kh'hob oykh gehat amol a kenigraykh, a kenig,
Un in di shoyn eynzame fun ruike fartogn
Hob ikh shoyn merer nisht gezogt ma toyvu ohalekho...
40   Un du, mayn Got, host tsugezen mayn zindikn farbrekhn
Un host mir keynmol nisht dermont on dayn gebot un viln,
In tfiln-zekl hobn lang gefoylt shoyn mayne tfiln!

Blasphemy*

(Fragment of the poem 'How goodly are thy tents, O Jacob'.)

1   My land, you have lain for centuries, as a presence
From my beloved, cared-for, longed for [religious] book.
When I would feel lonely, dried out and old,
And when I looked out at the world as if through a crack,
And my heart would fill with envy and with jealousy
To those friendly people, who gave me a little shelter
Gave somewhere to lay down my tired head for a while —
Then I would think of you, my holy *Tanekh*
Of you, and of my land and there — of those Jews, —
10   The Jews your winemakers, and peasants, and blacksmiths,
The Jews your shepherds — Israels and Menashes,
Who would graze the herds of goats gently in the pasture
And hammer and cast ritual washstands and weapons.

My people, I thought then of an eye for an eye.
I kept your Torah for generations protected and learned.
I saw your ancient heavens with stars stretched out,
Your Galilee, and your Carmel, and the flowing Jordan.
Yet I was far away from you — many miles, millions,
And your hot earth was for me both cold and alien:
20   Your flax did not grow there ready for my shirt,
Your bread never nourished me, the hungering one,
Your wine I surely did not drink from your flask —
But always I wandered around alone and upset
And hundreds of years consumed my longing,
And I stopped looking for you in my wandering.

My land. With pain I clung to what once was.
I have absorbed your past into my hardened veins.
But I have become tired on my way of waiting for you —
My blood in my head the temples, no longer beat
30   My dream was no longer of Jerusalem,
In the morning I no longer turn my glance towards you,
My sword no longer girded my loins with courage,
Since I planted myself in new terrain.
Alas, I was perhaps brimful with sin and rebellion.
I no longer carried my old God in my heart,
I no longer in trepidation beat *al kheyt,*
I forgot I once also had a kingdom, a king,
And in the lonely hours of calm dawns
I no longer said *ma toyvu ohalekho...*

40   And you, my God you observed my sinful offence
And you never reminded me of your commandment and will,
The *tfiln* bag and my *tfiln* have long lain untouched.

---

* The translation used is of the version in *A shvalb oyfn dakh*, where line 51 (from *Dorem Afrike,* May–June 1965) was excluded. However, as the line is pertinent to this discussion, it is also included here.

Es hot zikh der shel-rosh badekt dort mit a grinem shiml,
Un s'iz mayn talis heyliker farshemt geblibn lign —
Un du host zikh dos tsugekukt tsu alts bay dir in himl.
Zikh tsugekukt un tsugezen, un ayngeshpart geshvign.
Un vi es volt dir glaykhgiltik shoyn keyn zakh nit gekimert,
Hostu dayn klole nisht geshikt tsu mir un nisht dayn brokhe.
Dayn khesed hot mikh eynzamen shoyn merer nisht bashiremt,
50   Nor host mayn lebn ongefilt mit groyen indervokhn.
Farvos hostu geshvign, Got, ven ikh hob zikh gematert,
Farvos hostu avekgeton fun mir dayn has un libe,
Farvos hot in mayn orem hoyz dayn shkhine nisht geflatert? —
Tsi iz mayn groyse zind aleyn geven far dem di sibe?
To vos hostu tsu yene zikh in umglik nisht dernentert,
Vos hobn tomid dikh farert mit tfiles un mit loybn,
Un vi a Got fun rakhamim, fun tsoren a farbrenter
Nisht ongetsundn mit a treyst bay zey di shvartse shoybn?
Zey zaynen dokh geven getray tsu dir durkh ale doyres,
60   Zey zaynen dokh gegangen frum in ale dayne drokhim,
Zey hobn dokh in zeyer brokh getsundn far dir menoyres,
Un bay di likht di heylike gezungen far dir shvokhim.
Zey hobn dokh zikh itlekh mol gevashn far dayn nomen,
Gefast taneysim far dir Got, vi umgliklekhe zinder.
To vos hostu akhzaryesdik fartilikt yene zomen,
Vos hobn oyfgeyn in a folk gezolt fun dayne kinder.
Du host zey, vi a pastekh, Got, dayn stade nisht gefitert.
Du host gematert zey mit dursht un nisht gegebn trinken.
Du host geshtroft zey gloybike un durkh dayn groysn tsiter,
70   Hostu aleyn zey gor gefirt tsu shekhtn in Treblinke.
Un dos iz shoyn dos tsveyte mol, vi du host zey fartilikt,
In midber hostu oysshtarbn zey alemen bafoyln,
Un itster hostu nokhamol akhzaryesdik bavilikt
Men zol di shayters onshitn mit brenendike koyln...
Iz dos a pruv geven fun dir, kedey tsu pruvn vider
Tsi s'veln dayne shklafn dikh nokh vi amol derkenen?
Derfar hostu di gaz-oyvns farfult mit mayne brider,
Un hostu dem gzar aroysgelozt — dayn stade tsu farbrenen?
Oy, Got, ot hostu shoyn gezen, vi s'iz avek tsuzamen
80   Tsum shayter-hoyfn nokhamol dayn gantser groyser kool,
Un zikh gelozn far dayn shem fartsukn fun di flamen —
Fun vanent s'hot aroysgeshpart der letster Sh'ma Yisroel

A shvalb oyfn dakh, pp. 127–29

And the *shel rosh* has become covered with a green mildew,
And my holy *talis* has lain shamefully unused —
And you observed it all from heaven.
You watched and saw it all, and stubbornly kept silent.
And as if indifferent, none of it bothered you,
You neither sent your curse to me nor your blessing.
Your grace no longer protected me, the lonely one,

50 But you filled my life with grey weekdays.
Why did you keep silent, God, while I suffered,
Why did you remove your hate and love from me,
Why did your divine presence not hover in my poor house? —
Or was my great sin alone the reason for this?
Why did you not approach them in misfortune,
Who honoured you with prayers and with praises,
And as a God of mercy, of zealous wrath
Could you not have kindled some comfort for them?
After all, they were faithful to you through all generations,

60 They went piously in all your ways,
They in their despair lit *menoyres* to you,
And at the holy candles sang praises for you.
They washed for your name's sake many times,
Fasted for you God, like unhappy sinners.
So why did you savagely destroy those offspring,
Of your children who should have developed into a people.
You have not tended them, your flock, like a shepherd, God.
You afflicted them with thirst and did not give [them] drink.
You punished them, believers, and through your great awe,

70 You yourself took them to be slaughtered in Treblinka.
And this is the second time you have exterminated them,
In the desert you ordered that they all die out,
And now you have again ruthlessly enabled
That they should pile up the pyres with burning coals...
Is this your attempt to prove once again
That your slaves still acknowledge you as of old?
Therefore, you loaded the gas ovens with my brothers,
And pronounced your decree — to burn your flock?

Alas, God, now you have seen how together they have gone
80 To the pyre-mounds once again, your whole great community,
And they let themselves be gobbled up by the flames for the sake of
Your name —

From where sighed the final *Sh'ma Yisroel*.

BIBLIOGRAPHY

I. David Fram

Archival sources

University of Texas at Austin, University of Texas Libraries, Benson Latin American Collection, *David Fram Papers* (1920s–1984): Folders 1, 2, 3, 4, 5, 6, 7, 11, 13, 17

Collected poems

Dos letste kapitl [The Last Chapter] (London: Narod Press, 1947)
——*Dos letste kapitl*, in *Efsher* [Perhaps] (London: Narod Press, 1947), pp. 85–122 <https://www.yiddishbookcenter.org/collections/yiddish-books/spb-nybc211771/fram-david-efsher> [accessed 21 December 2020]
——'Dos letste kapitl' (extract), *Dorem Afrike* (January–March 1984), 12
Efsher [Perhaps] (London: Narod Press, 1947) <https://www.yiddishbookcenter.org/collections/yiddish-books/spb-nybc211771/fram-david-efsher> [accessed 21 December 2020]; 'Efsher' (extract), *Dorem Afrike* (August 1949), 21; (extract) in *Antologye: Dorem Afrikanish. Fragmentn fun forshavetn tsu der karakteristik un zikhroynes* [South African Anthology: Characteristic Fragments and Memories], ed. by Shmuel Rozhansky (Buenos Aires: Ateneo Literario en el Iwo, 1971), pp. 199–200
Lider un poemes [Songs and Poems] (Vilna, Poland: Krejnesa, 1931)
——'Baym zeydn' [At Grandfather's], pp. 147–209; *Literarishe bleter* (1925–26)
——'Burn' [Farmers and/or Afrikaners], pp. 210–49; (extract), *Dorem Afrike* (May–June 1971), 13
——'Fareltert' [Obsolete], *Lider*, pp. 85–86.
——'Fun tate-mames Yidishe' [From Jewish Parents], p. 77; in *Antologye: Dorem Afrikanish. Fragmentn fun forsharvetn tsu der karakteristik un zikhroynes* [South African Anthology: Fragments of Research of Characteristics and Memories], ed. by Shmuel Rozhansky (Buenos Aires: Ateneo Literario en el Iwo, 1971), p. 293
——'Ikh benk' [I Yearn], pp. 89–90
——'Ikh hob gemeynt' [I Thought], p. 12–13
——'Ikh hob shoyn dem vinter, dem vinter dem tsveytn' [This Winter, this Second Winter, I have already Written], p. 11
——'In a zunikn tog' [On a Sunny Day], p. 123-32
——'In an afrikaner baginen' [In an African Dawn], p. 74; *Antologye*, p. 77
——'In tsveyen' [Twofold], p. 7
——'Mayn mame hot mir tsugeshikt a kishn' [My Mother Sent Me a Cushion], p 18
——'Mayn opfor' [My Departure], p. 14
——'Nokh vos zol ikh forn?' [Why Should I leave?], p. 24; *Antologye*, p. 18
——'Oyf transvaler erd' [On Transvaal Earth], pp. 263–74; (extract), *Antologye*, pp. 29–37
——'Reb Yoshe un zayn gortn' [Reb Yoshe and his Garden], *Lider*, pp. 91–100; *Der oyfkum: khodesh-zshurnal far literatur un kultur-inyonim* [The Rebirth: Monthly Journal for Literature and Art] (1929), n. p.

——'Shney' [Snow], p. 43

——'Tsu di shvartse' [To the Black Man], pp. 19–21

——'Vert den gringer derfun' [Where Lies the Comfort?], p. 28

A shvalb oyfn dakh: Poemes un lider [A Swallow on the Roof: Poems and Songs] (Johannesburg: Kayor, 1983)

——'Dimantn' [Diamonds], pp. 60–64; (extract), *Dorem Afrike* (September 1953), 17–18

——'Friling' [Spring], pp. 9–10

——'Ikh bin a Yid' [I am a Jew], p. 69; *Di yidishe post*, 20 May 1938, n. p.; *Dorem Afrike* (July–August 1971), 23

——'Ikh veys nisht vemen ikh zol betn' [I Do not Know Whom to Ask], p. 13

——'Lesterung' [Blasphemy], pp. 127–29; (extract), *Dorem Afrike* (May–June 1965), 3

——'Matatulu' [Matatulu], pp. 89–92; *Dorem Afrike* (December 1953), 17–19

——'Matumba' [Matumba], pp. 85–88; *Dorem Afrike* (November 1953), 16–17

——'Oyf mayn dakh hot amol gesvistshert a shvalb' [Once a Swallow Twittered on my Roof], p. 67; *Dorem Afrike* (October 1953), 6

Uncollected poems

——'Afrike' [Africa] (excerpt), *Dorem Afrike* (November–December 1978), 4

——'In Afrike' [In Afrika] (excerpt), *Dorem Afrike* (September 1983), 36

——'In Afrike' (excerpt), *Dorem Afrike* (January–March 1985), 7

——'Beyn hashmoshes' [Dusk], *Dorem Afrike* (July–September 1988), 27

——'A dertsaylung' [A Story], *Dorem Afrike* (October 1948), 9–14

——'An entfer der velt' [An Answer to the World], *Dorem Afrike* (July–August 1971), 50

——'Fun shop tsu shop' [From Shop to Shop], *Dorem Afrike* (July–September 1984), 29

——'Lider' [Songs], *Dorem Afrike* (October 1953), 6–8

——'Lider', *Dorem Afrike* (September–October 1973), 18

——'Lider', *Dorem Afrike* (July–September 1985), 21

——'Matabele' [Matabele] (extract), *Dorem Afrike* (July–August 1965), 7

——'Matabele' (extract), *Dorem Afrike* (September–October 1970), 10

——'Revrend Vilyam Skot' [Reverend William Scott], *Dorem Afrike* (December 1955), 2–3; (January 1956), 10–11; (March 1956), 4–6; (May 1956), 23–25; (June 1956), 23–25; (July 1956), 3–5

——'Undzere kedoyshim' [Our Martyrs], *Dorem Afrike* (March–April 1969), 17

Poem translations

——'In Afrike' [In Africa], trans. by Gerry Resnick, *Jewish Affairs*, 39.2 (1984), 22–23

——'Dos Letste kapitl' [The Slaughter in Lithuania] (extracts), trans. by Joseph Leftwich, *The Golden Peacock: A Worldwide Treasury of Yiddish Poetry* (New York: Yoseloff 1961, pp. 631–32

——'Dos Letste kapitl' (extracts), trans. by Joseph Leftwich, *David Fram Papers*, Folder 17, pp. 1–3, p. 15

——'Friling' [Spring], trans. by Marcia Leveson, *Jewish Affairs*, 16.2 (September 1991), 83

——'Ikh veys nisht vemen ikh zol betn' [I Do Not Know Whom to Ask] (untitled poem), trans. by Rochelle Mann, *Jewish Affairs*, 48.3 (Spring 1993), 83

——'Shney' [Snow], trans. by Jacob Sonntag, *Jewish Literary Gazette*, 6 April 1951, 2

——'Vert den gringer derfun?' [Where Lies the Comfort?], trans. by Amelia Levy in L. Goodman, 'David Fram: A Study in Growth', *Jewish Affairs*, 8.1 (January 1949), 28–31 (p. 28)

Play

——*Lili un Bliling: A vald maysele in eyn akt* [Lili and Bliling: A Forest Tale in One Act] (Grinike beymelekh: Vilnius, 1936) <https://www.yiddishbookcenter.org/collections/ yiddish-books/spb-nybc212454/fram-david-lili-un-bliling> [accessed 6 December 2020]

Prose

——'Araynfir, "In Afrike"' [Introduction, 'In Africa'], *Dorem Afrike* (July–September 1983), 37
——' "Ayndrukn vegn a bukh": *Land fun gold un zunshayn*', Y. M. Sherman' [Impressions of a Book: *Land of Gold and Sunshine*. J. M. Sherman], *Dorem Afrike* (March 1957), 19–20
——'Bagrisung fun Dovid Fram' [Greetings from David Fram], *Dorem Afrike* (July–December 1987), 36
——'A bisele vegn zikh' [A Little about Myself], in *A Shvalb oyfn dakh: Poemes un lider*, [A Swallow on the Roof: Poems and Songs] (Johannesburg: Kayor, 1983), n. p.
——'Brivn fun Dovid Fram Tsu Yidishe Shrayber, 1947–1949' [Letters from David Fram to Yiddish Writers, 1947–1949], *Di tsukunft*, 107.4 (December 2002), 5–12
——'Herman Wald' [Herman Wald], *Dorem Afrike* (March 1949), 22–23
——'Natan Berger. A poeme vegn Yohanesburg' [Nathan Berger: A Poem of Johannesburg], *Dorem Afrike* (March–April 1969), 25
——'Sekoto' [Sekoto], *Dorem Afrike* (January 1949), 19–21
——'Yerushe un hashpoes in yidishn vort-tsushtayer fun Dorem Afrike' [Heritage and Influences on the Yiddish Contribution of South Africa], in *Antologye: Dorem Afrikanish. Fragmentn fun forshavetn tsu der karakteristik un zikhroynes* [South African Anthology: Characteristic Fragments and Memories], ed. by Shmuel Rozhansky (Buenos Aires: Ateneo Literario en el Iwo, 1971), pp. 313–28

Secondary Texts

BEN-MOSHE, M., 'Fazn in Dovid Frams shafn' [Stages in David Fram's Development], *Dorem Afrike* (October 1953), 11–13
BRINMAN, Y. R., 'Dovid Fram — Lider un poemes' [David Fram — Songs and Poems], *Der veg* [The Way] (30 July 1938), 5–6
Cammy, Justin Daniel, Email to the author, 15 January 2011
DAVIMES, STEPHEN, 'Hillbrow's Yiddish Poet Drinks to Life', *Sunday Express*, 24 June 1984, n. p.
DAVIS, BARRY, 'David Fram, Yiddish Poet', *The Jewish Quarterly*, 35.4 (Winter 1988), 45–49
DE SAXE, MARIAN, 'Sing Me a Song of History: South African Poets and Singers in Exile, 1900–1990' (unpublished doctoral thesis, University of Sydney, 2010)
ESTRAIKH, GENNADY, Email to the author, 11 November 2010
FELDMAN, RACHMIEL [RICHARD], 'David Fram at Fifty', *South African Jewish Times*, 23 October 1953, n. p.
FRANKEL, HAZEL, 'David Fram: Lithuanian Yiddish Poet of the South African Diaspora, and "Illuminating Love"' (unpublished doctoral thesis, Sheffield Hallam University, 2013) <http://shura.shu.ac.uk/4914/1/frankel_david_fram.pdf> [accessed 10 November 2020]
——'David Fram: Yiddish Poet of the South African Diaspora', *Jewish Affairs*, 65.1 (Pesach 2013), 26–35
——'From the Outside Looking in: The Yiddish Poems of the Lithuanian South African Poet David Fram (1903–1988)', *Journal of Literary Studies*, 35.2 (June 2019), 20–34

——'From Steppe to Veld: The Landscape Poems of the Yiddish Poet David Fram', *Journal for Semitics*, 25.1 (2016), 235–52

——'Home and the Holocaust in Selected Paintings of Marc Chagall and Yiddish Poems of David Fram', *Soundings: An Interdisciplinary Journal*, 101.4 (November 2018), 341–59

——'Journey with Two Maps: Longing and Belonging in the Yiddish Poetry of David Fram', *The English Academy Review*, 32.2 (October 2015), 222–37

——'A Panorama of Portraits: Elements of Empathy in the Yiddish Poems of David Fram', *Literator*, 37.1 (2016), 1–10 <https:literator.org.za/index.php/literator/article/view/1262/2141>

——'Stones in the Landscape: Memory and Postmemory in the Yiddish Poems of David Fram', *European Journal of Jewish Studies*, 11.1 (2017), 148–73

GERSHATER, C., 'The Triumph of David Fram', *The Zionist Record* (30 October 1953), 5

GINSBERG, CEDRIC, Emails to the author, 29 July 2011; 23 September 2011

GOODMAN, L., 'David Fram: A Study in Growth', *Jewish Affairs*, 8.1 (January 1949), 28–31; trans. of article in *Dorem Afrike* (September 1948)

——'David Fram Turns 60', *Southern African Jewish Times*, 6 September 1963, 24

——'The Poetry of David Fram', *South African Jewish Times*, 28 November 1983, 39–40

LEVICK, W., 'Der dikhter Dovid Fram' [The Poet David Fram], *Dorem Afrike* (November-December 1978), 3–4

——'A Personal Appreciation of David Fram', *Jewish Affairs*, 36.9 (September 1983), 35–36

LEVY, ZALMAN, 'A Premier Yiddish Poet in South Africa', *Jewish Affairs*, 36.9 (September 1983), 32–35

——'Dovid Frams arayntrit in der Yiddish-dikhtung un zayn shpeterdiker gang' [David Fram's Entry in Yiddish Poetry and his Later Progress], *Dorem Afrike* (July–September 1983), 38–40

——'Der premier Yiddish-dikhter in dorem Afrike' [The Premier Yiddish Poet in South Africa], 'Lider' [Songs], *Dorem Afrike* (September–October 1973), 16–17

MILLER, ZALIA, 'A bazukh tsu Dovid Fram in Hekpoort' [A Visit to David Fram in Hekpoort], *Dorem Afrike* (January–March 1984), 9

NIBORSKI, ELIEZER, 'Dovid Fram', *Mendele: Yiddish Literature and Language*, 20.004 (11 September 2010), 1–4 <https://mailman.yale.edu/pipermail/mendele/2010-September/000420.html> [accessed 6 December 2020]

NIGER, SHMUEL, 'Naye Dikhter: Dovid Fram un Moshe Dovid Giser' [New Poets: David Fram and Moshe Dovid Giser], *Di tsukunft* [The Future] (October 1934), 615–18

RAVITCH, MELECH, 'A por khaverishe araynfir-verter' [A Few Friendly Introductory Words], in David Fram, *Lider un poemes* [Songs and Poems] (Vilna, Poland: Krejnesa, 1931), n. p.; this review also appeared later as 'Dovid Fram un zayn lider' [David Fram and his Songs], *Literarishe Bleter*, 4.403 (4 November 1932), 59

ROSENBLATT, ELI, 'Enlightening the Skin: Travel, Racial Language, and Rabbinic Intertextuality in Modern Yiddish Literature' (unpublished doctoral thesis, University of California, Berkeley, 2017)

SHABAN, ABEL, 'Dovid Fram — Dikhter un persenlekhkeyt' [David Fram — Poet and Personality], *Di Yidishe Tribune/The Jewish Tribune* (February 1931), 6

——'Tsu Dovid Fram' [To David Fram], *Dorem Afrike* (September–October 1973), 14–15

SHERMAN, JOSEPH, 'David Fram Centenary Tribute' ('"Singing with the Silence": The Poetry of David Fram'), *The Mendele Review*, 08.001 (14 January 2004), 1–17 <http://yiddish.haifa.ac.il/tmr/tmr08/tmr08001.htm> [accessed 5 December 2020]

——ed. and trans., 'David Fram at Eighty', *Jewish Affairs*, 36.9 (September 1983), 32–37

——'Literature: Yiddish and Hebrew', in *South African Jewry. A Contemporary Survey*, ed. by Marcus Arkin (Cape Town: Oxford University Press, 1984), pp. 152–8

—— 'On Publishing the New Anthology', *Jewish Affairs*, 38.9 (September 1983), 37

—— 'Singing with the Silence: The Poetry of David Fram', *Jewish Affairs*, 44.5 (September–October 1988), 39–44

—— 'South African Literature in Yiddish and Hebrew', *The Mendele Review*, 3.012 (31 August 1999), 1–11 <http://yiddish.haifa.ac.il/tmr/tmr03/tmr03012.txt> [accessed 5 December 2020]

—— 'What Balm for the Heart...? The Yiddish Poetry of David Fram (1903–1988)', *Midstream*, 52 (July–August 2006), 7–11

SHERMAN, J. M., ' "David Fram": On the Occasion of his 50th Birthday', *Jewish Affairs*, 13.3 (October 1953), 25–27

SKIKNE, MAURICE, 'The Poetry of David Fram Revisited', *Jewish Affairs*, 71.2 (2016) 85–92

STENCL, AVRAM NOCHUM, ed., 'Dovid From', in *Loshn un lebn* [Language and Life] (November 1947), 48; (August 1949), 49–50

WOLPE, DAVID [DOVID], 'Dray period in shafn fun Dovid Fram' [Three Stages in the Work of David Fram], *Dorem Afrike* (July–August 1963), 16–20

YAD VASHEM, Testimony documents (6332599, 6332600, 6332601), submitted by David Fram's nephew, Itamar Borowitz <https://yvng.yadvashem.org/index.html?language=en&s_id=&s_lastName=Fram&s_firstName=&s_place=&s_dateOfBirth=&cluster=true> [accessed 19 December 2020]

ZARAMB, S., 'The Poetry of David Fram', *The Zionist Record* (9 November 1934), 20; trans. of his article in *Literarishe bleter*, 27 (1934)

ZYGIELBAUM, FAYVL, 'Dovid Fram's 60th Birthday in Salisbury', *Zionist Record and S.A. Jewish Chronicle*, 23 August 1963, n. p.

—— 'Dovid Fram's yuvil: Tsu zayn 50stn geburtog' [David Fram's Jubilee: To his Fiftieth Birthday], *Dorem Afrike* (October 1953), 3–5

—— 'Lithuania and South Africa — Twin Theme of David Fram's Work', *Zionist Record and S.A. Jewish Chronicle* (23 August 1963), n. p.

—— 'The Yiddish Poet — David Fram: His South African Poems'. On the Occasion of his 60th Birthday, *Jewish Affairs*, 18.9 (September 1963), 19–21

—— 'Tsu Dovid Frams avekforn' [On David Fram's Departure], *Dorem Afrike* (August 1949), 22–23

II. Other South African Yiddish Poets

AISEN, SARAH, *Geklibene lider un poemes* [Selected Lyrics and Poems] (Johannesburg: Farlag fun der Dorem-Afrikaner Kultur-federatsye, 1965) <https://www.yiddishbookcenter.org/collections/yiddish-books/spb-nybc213583/aisen-sarah-geklibene-lider-un-poemes> [accessed 21 November 2020]

BENSON-RINK, LEAH, *Amol un haynt* [Once and Today], and *Oysgetunkt in trern* [Dipped in Tears] (poems) (Cape Town: Kinder, 1963) <https://www.yiddishbookcenter.org/collections/yiddish-books/spb-nybc201844/benson-rink-leah-amol-un-haynt-dertseylungen-oysgetunkt-in-trern-lider-oyf-dem-keyver-fun-a-zun> [accessed 21 November 2020] (these were published together in one volume)

FEDLER, HAYAH, *Bleter-fal* [Falling Leaves] (Cape Town: Fedler & Co., 1954), <https://www.yiddishbookcenter.org/collections/yiddish-books/spb-nybc204669/fedler-hayah-bleter-fal> [accessed 21 November 2020]

III. Abraham Sutzkever

Primary texts

SUTZKEVER, ABRAHAM, *A. Sutzkever: Selected Poetry and Prose*, ed. and trans. by Benjamin Harshav and Barbara Harshav, (Berkeley: University of California Press, 1991)
—— *Burnt Pearls: Ghetto Poems of Abraham Sutzkever*, trans. by Seymour Mayne (Ontario: Mosaic Press/Valley Editions, 1981)
—— *Di ershte nakht in geto* [The First Night in the Ghetto] (Tel Aviv: Farlag Der goldene keyt, 1979) <https://www.yiddishbookcenter.org/collections/yiddish-books/spb-nybc203216/sutzkever-abraham-di-ershte-nakht-in-geto > [accessed 21 November 2020]
—— *Di festung lider un poemes: geshribn in Vilner Geto un vald* [The Fortress Songs and Poems: Written in the Vilna Ghetto and Forest] (New York: Yiddisher Kultur Farband, 1945) <http://teachgreatjewishbooks.org/resource-kits/avrom-sutzkevers-lead-plates-rom-printers#resources> [accessed 23 December 2020]
—— "The Lead Plates of the Rom Printers"', *The Yiddish Book Center's Great Jewish Book Teacher Resources* <http://teachgreatjewishbooks.org/resource-kits/avrom-sutzkevers-lead-plates-rom-printers#resources> [accessed 20 June 2020]
—— *Lider fun yam ha-moves fun Vilner Geto, vald un vander, 1936–1967* [Poems from the Dead Sea of the Vilna Ghetto, Forest, and Wandering] (Tel Aviv: Farlag Bergen-Belzen, 1968) <https://www.yiddishbookcenter.org/collections/yiddish-books/spb-nybc213587/sutzkever-abraham-lider-fun-yam-ha-moves-fun-vilner-geto-vald-un-vander> [accessed 21 November 2020]
—— *Poetishe verk* [Poetic Works], 2 vols (Tel Aviv: Yoyvl-Komitet, 1963) <https://www.yiddishbookcenter.org/collections/yiddish-books/spb-nybc208866/sutzkever-abraham-poetishe-verk-vol-1> [accessed 9 November 2020]

Secondary texts

Nuremberg Trial Proceedings, VIII, 69th day, Wednesday, 27 February 1946, pp. 300–07, in *The Avalon Project: Documents in Law, History and Diplomacy* <http://avalon.law.yale.edu/imt/02–27–46.asp> [accessed 27 July 2020]
POLLIN-GALAY, HANNAH, 'Avrom Sutzkever's Art of Testimony: Witnessing with the Poet in the Wartime Soviet Union', *Jewish Social Studies*, 21.2 (Winter 2016), 1–34
VALENCIA, HEATHER, *Avrom Sutzkever: Still my Word Sings* (Düsseldorf: Düsseldorf University Press, 2017)
WISSE, RUTH, 'Introduction', in Abraham Sutzkever, *Burnt Pearls: Ghetto Poems of Abraham Sutzkever*, trans. by Seymour Mayne (Ontario: Mosaic Press/Valley Editions, 1981), pp. 9–18

IV. Marc Chagall

Works of art

MARC CHAGALL, *The Blue House*, 1917, oil on canvas, 66 × 97 cm, Musée d'Art Moderne et d'Art Contemporain, Liège, Belgium; *Marc Chagall: Paintings, Biography, and Quotes* <https://www.marcchagall.net/the-blue-house.jsp> [accessed 7 December 2020]
—— *Golgotha*, 1912, oil on canvas, 46.4 × 55.3 cm, Collection of Ruth O'Hara, New York
—— *I and the Village* (The Village and I), 1911, oil on canvas, 192.1 × 151.5 cm, The Museum of Modern Art, New York; *Marc Chagall: Paintings, Biography, and Quotes* <https://www.marcchagall.net/i-and-the-village.jsp> [accessed 7 December 2020]

—— *White Crucifixion*, oil on canvas, 154.3 × 139.7 cm, Art Institute of Chicago <https://www.artic.edu/artworks/59426/white-crucifixion> [accessed 7 December 2020]

—— *Yellow Crucifixion*, 1942, oil on canvas, 140 × 101 cm, Musée National d'Art Moderne–Centre Pompidou, Paris; *pneuma* <http://www.pneuma.org.uk/art/marc-chagall-the-yellow-crucifixion/> [accessed 7 December 2020]

Prose

Marc Chagall, *My Life*, 3rd edn (New York: Orion Press, 1960)

Secondary texts

Amishai-Maisels, Ziva, 'Chagall's White Crucifixion', *Art Institute of Chicago Museum Studies*, 17.2 (1991), 138–53, 180–81

Dorot, Ruth, *The Art of Time, the Art of Place: Isaac Bashevis Singer and Marc Chagall — A Dialogue* (Brighton: Sussex Academic Press, 2011)

Goodman, Susan Tumarkin, *Chagall: Love, War and Exile* (New York: Yale University Press, 2013)

Harshav, Benjamin, 'Chagall, Marc', *YIVO Encyclopedia of Jews in Eastern Europe* (15 December 2010) <https://yivoencyclopedia.org/article.aspx/Chagall_Marc> [accessed 17 December 2020]

—— *Marc Chagall: The Lost Jewish World* (New York: Rizzoli, 2006)

Kampf, Avram, *Chagall to Kitaj: Jewish Experience in 20th Century Art* (London: Lund Humphries, 1990)

Leneman, L., 'Marc Chagall wegen zeine Christus-figuren als Symbol fun Yidishe martyrertum' [Marc Chagall on his Christ-figures as Symbols of Jewish Martyrdom], *Undzer Wort* [In Yiddish], 22 January 1977, 4 (transl. by Ziva Amishai-Maisels in 'Chagall's White Crucifixion', *Art Institute of Chicago Museum Studies*, 17.2 (1991), 143

Quehl-Engel, Catherine, 'Modern Jewish Art and the Crucifixion: A Study in Appropriation', *Soundings: An Interdisciplinary Journal*, 80.1 (Spring 1997), 132–52

Trewhela, Paul, 'Chagall and the Murdered Poets', *Jewish Affairs*, 75.3 (Winter 2020), n. p. <https://www.sajbd.org/media/chagall-and-the-murdered-poets> [accessed 19 December 2020]

Wullschläger, Jackie, *Chagall: A Biography* (New York: Knopf, 2008)

V. General Secondary Sources

Aaron, Frieda, *Bearing the Unbearable: Yiddish and Polish Poetry in the Ghettos and Concentration Camps* (Albany: State University of New York, 1990)

Aciman, Andre, 'From the Other Bank', in *If Salt Has Memory*, ed. by J. Langer (Nottingham: Five Leaves, 2008), pp. 24–41

Adorno, Theodor, *Negative Dialectics*, trans. by E. O. Ashton (London: Routledge and Keegan Paul, 1973)

Aldridge, Alfred Owen, 'Biography in the Interpretation of Poetry', *College English*, 25.6 (March 1964), 412–20

Appelfeld, Aharon, *Beyond Despair: Three Lectures and a Conversation with Philip Roth*, trans. by Jeffrey M. Green (New York: Fromm Intl., 1994)

Arkin, Marcus, ed., *South African Jewry. A Contemporary Survey* (Cape Town: Oxford University Press, 1984)

Barron, J. N., and E. M. Selinger, eds, *Jewish American Poetry* (Hanover: Brandeis University Press, 2000)

Bartoloni, Paolo, *On the Cultures of Exile, Translation and Writing* (West Lafayette: Purdue University Press, 2008)

BAUER, YEHUDA, *A History of the Holocaust* (Connecticut: Watts, 1982)

BELLING, VERONICA, 'A Slice of Eastern Europe in Johannesburg: Yiddish Theatre in Doornforntein, 1929–1949', in *Place and Displacement in Jewish History and Memory: Zakor V'Makor*, ed. by David Cesarani, Tony Kushner, and Milton Shain, (London: Mitchell, 2009), pp. 169–80

—— 'Yiddish Writing in South Africa: Leibl Feldman's Radical History of Johannesburg Jewry', *Journal for the Study of Religion*, 19.2, special issue: *Echoes of Religion in Minority Literatures* (2006), 63–75

BENNETT, ANDREW, *The Author* (London: Routledge, 2005)

BIRCH, D., ed., *The Oxford Companion to English Literature* (Oxford: Oxford University Press, 2009) <https://www.oxfordreference.com/view/10.1093/acref/9780192806871.001.0001/acref-9780192806871> [accessed 9 December 2020]

BLATMAN, DANIEL, 'Bund', *The YIVO Encyclopedia of Jews in Eastern Europe* (30 July 2010) <http://www.yivoencyclopedia.org/article.aspx/Bund> [accessed 13 November 2020]

BLEICH, DAVID, 'Learning, Learning, Learning: Jewish Poetry in America', in *Jewish American Poetry*, ed. by J. N. Barron and E. M. Selinger (Hanover: Brandeis University Press, 2000), pp. 117–94

BOSWELL, MATTHEW, *Holocaust Impiety in Literature, Popular Music and Film* (London: Palgrave Macmillan, 2012)

BURGER, ARIEL, *Witness: Lessons from Elie Wiesel's Classroom* (New York: Mariner Books, 2018)

CAMMY, JUSTIN DANIEL, 'Vogler, Elkhonen', *YIVO Encyclopedia of Jews in Eastern Europe* (2 November 2010) <https://yivoencyclopedia.org/article.aspx/Vogler_Elkhonen> [accessed 3 July 2020]

—— 'Yung-vilne', *YIVO Encyclopedia of Jews in Eastern Europe* (18 November 2010) <https://yivoencyclopedia.org/article.aspx/Yung-vilne> [accessed 3 July 2020]

CARUTH, CATHY, *Unclaimed Experience: Trauma, Narrative and History* (Baltimore: Johns Hopkins University Press, 1996)

CESARANI, DAVID, TONY KUSHNER, and MILTON SHAIN, eds, *Place and Displacement in Jewish History and Memory: Zakor V'Makor* (London: Mitchell, 2009)

—— 'Introduction', in *Place and Displacement in Jewish History and Memory: Zakor V'Makor*, ed. by David Cesarani, Tony Kushner, and Milton Shain, (London: Mitchell, 2009), pp. 1–14

CLIFFORD, JAMES, 'Diasporas', *Cultural Anthropology*, 9.3, special issue: *Further Inflections: Toward Ethnographies of the Future*, (August 1994), 302–38

COHEN, NATHAN, 'Literarishe bleter', *YIVO Encyclopedia of Jews in Eastern Europe* <https://yivoencyclopedia.org/article.aspx/Literarishe_Bleter> [accessed 30 June 2020]

DRABBLE, MARGARET, J. STRINGER, and D. HAHN, eds, *The Concise Oxford Companion to English Literature* (Oxford: Oxford University Press, 2007) <https://www.oxfordreference.com/view/10.1093/acref/9780199214921.001.0001/acref-9780199214921> [accessed 8 December 2020]

EDELMANN, R., 'Ahasuerus, the Wandering Jew: Origin and Background', in *The Wandering Jew: Essays in the Interpretation of a Christian Legend*, ed. by G. Hasan-Rokem and A. Dundes (Bloomington: Indiana University Press, 1986), pp. 1–10

ESTRAIKH, GENNADY, 'Fefer, Itsik', *YIVO Encyclopedia of Jews in Eastern Europe* (6 August 2010) <https://yivoencyclopedia.org/article.aspx/Fefer_Itsik> [accessed 3 July, 2020]

—— 'Hofshteyn, Dovid', *YIVO Encyclopedia of Jews in Eastern Europe* (12 August 2010) <https://yivoencyclopedia.org/article.aspx/Hofshteyn_Dovid> [accessed 3 July 2020]

—— 'Itsik Fefer: A Yiddish "Wunderkind" of the Bolshevik Revolution', *Shofar*, 20.3 (2002), 14–31

—— *Yiddish in the Cold War* (London: Legenda, 2008)

ESTRAIKH, GENNADY, and MIKHAIL KRUTIKOV, eds, *The Shtetl Image and Reality: Papers of the Second Mendel Friedman International Conference on Yiddish* (Oxford: European Humanities Research Centre, University of Oxford, 2000)

—— eds, *Yiddish in the Contemporary World: Papers of the First Mendel Friedman International Conference on Yiddish* (Oxford: European Humanities Research Centre, University of Oxford, 1999)

EVERETT, BARBARA, 'Alphabetised', *London Review of Books*, 25 (7 August 2003), 15

EZRAHI, SIDRA DEKOVEN, *Booking Passage: Exile and Homecoming in the Modern Jewish Imagination* (Berkeley: University of California Press, 2000)

—— *By Words Alone: The Holocaust in Literature* (Chicago: University of Chicago Press, 2008)

FEFER, ITZIK, 'I Am A Jew', in *An Anthology of Modern Yiddish Literature,* trans. and ed. by Joseph Leftwitch (The Hague: Mouton, 1974), pp. 321–24; <http://teachgreatjewishbooks. org/1-poem-and-audio-recording-itsik-fefers-i-am-jew-ikh-bin-yid-1941> [accessed 16 December 2020]

—— 'Ikh bin a Yid' [I Am a Jew], in *A shpigl oyf a shteyn* [A Mirror on a Stone]: *An Anthology of Poetry and Prose by Twelve Soviet Yiddish Writers*, ed. by Khone Schmeruk (Jerusalem: The Magnes Press, 1987), 694–97

FEINSTEIN, STEPHEN C., 'Mediums of Memory: Artistic Responses of the Second Generation', in *Breaking Crystal: Writing and Memory after Auschwitz*, ed. by Efraim Sicher (Iowa: University of Illinois Press, 1998), pp. 201–51

FINKIN, JORDAN, *Exile as Home: The Cosmopolitan Poetics of Leyb Naydus* (Cincinnati: Hebrew Union College Press, 2017)

FONER, NANCY, *Across Generations: Immigrant Families in America* (New York: New York University Press, 2009)

—— 'Migration, Location and Memory: Jewish History through a Comparative Lens', in *Place and Displacement in Jewish History and Memory*, ed. by David Cesarani, Tony Kushner, and Milton Shain (London: Mitchell, 2009), pp. 131–40

GOTTHEIL, RICHARD, and THÉODORE REINACH, 'Diaspora', *Jewish Encyclopedia* <http://www.jewishencyclopedia.com/articles/5169-diaspora> [accessed 4 December 2020]

GREENSPAN, H., and OTHERS, 'Engaging Survivors. Assessing "Testimony" and "Trauma" as Foundational Concepts', *Dapim: Studies on the Holocaust*, 28.3 (2014), 190–226

GUBAR, SUSAN, *Poetry after Auschwitz: Remembering What One Never Knew*, (Bloomington: Indiana University Press, 2003)

HALL, STUART, 'Cultural Identity and Diaspora', in *Identity, Community, Culture, Difference*, ed. by Jonathan Rutherford (London: Lawrence and Wishart, 1990), pp. 222–37

HARSHAV, BENJAMIN, and BARBARA HARSHAV, *American Yiddish Poetry: A Bilingual Anthology* (Berkeley: University of California Press, 1986)

HARTMAN, GEOFFREY, ed., *Holocaust Remembrance: The Shapes of Memory* (London: Blackwell, 1994)

—— 'Introduction', in *Holocaust Remembrance: The Shapes of Memory*, ed. by Geoffrey Hartmann (London: Blackwell, 1994), pp. 1–23

HASAN-ROKEM, G., and A. DUNDES, eds, *The Wandering Jew: Essays in the Interpretation of a Christian Legend* (Bloomington: Indiana University Press, 1986)

HELLERSTEIN, KATHRYN, 'In Exile in the Mother Tongue: Yiddish and the Woman Poet', in *Borders, Boundaries and Frames: Essays in Cultural Criticism and Cultural Studies*, ed. by M. G. Henderson (New York: Routledge, 1995)

HIRSCH, MARIANNE, *The Generation of Postmemory: Writing and Visual Culture after the Holocaust* (New York: Columbia University Press, 2012)

HIRSCH, MARIANNE, and IRENE KACANDES, eds, *Teaching the Representation of the Holocaust* (New York: Modern Language Association of America, 2004)

HIRSCH, MARIANNE and LEO SPITZER, *Ghosts of Home: The Afterlife of Czernowitz in Jewish Memory* (Berkeley: University of California Press, 2010)

——'Holocaust Studies/Memory Studies', in *Memory: Histories, Theories, Debates*, ed. by Susannah Radstone and Bill Schwarz (New York: Fordham University Press, 2010), pp. 390–405

——'We Would Never Have Come without You: Generations of Nostalgia', in *Memory, History, Nation: Contested Pasts*, ed. by K. Hodgkin and Susannah Radstone (New Brunswick: Transaction Publishers, 2006), pp. 79–96

HITE, KATHERINE, 'Empathic Unsettlement and the Outsider Within Argentine Space of Memory', *Memory Studies*, 8.1 (2015), 38–48

HODGKIN, KATHARINE, and SUSANNAH RADSTONE, eds, *Memory, History, Nation: Contested Pasts* (New Brunswick: Transaction Publishers, 2006)

——'Remembering Suffering: Trauma and History', in *Memory, History, Nation: Contested Pasts,* ed. by K. Hodgkin and Susannah Radstone (New Brunswick: Transaction Publishers, 2006), pp. 97–103

HOFFMAN, EVA, 'The Long Afterlife of Loss', in *Memory: Histories, Theories, Debates*, ed. by Susannah Radstone and Bill Schwarz (New York: Fordham University Press, 2010), pp. 406–15

HOFSHTEYN, DOVID, 'In vinter-farnakhtn...' [In Winter's Dusk...], trans. by Robert Friend, in *The Penguin Book of Modern Yiddish Verse*, ed. by Irving Howe, Ruth R. Wisse, and Khone Shmeruk, (New York: Penguin, 1987), pp. 260–61

The Holy Scriptures (Jerusalem: Koren Publishers, 1989)

HOWE, IRVING, 'Writing and the Holocaust', in *Writing and the Holocaust*, ed. by Berel Lang (New York: Holmes and Meir, 1988), pp. 174–99

HOWE, IRVING and ELIEZER GREENBERG, eds, *A Treasury of Yiddish Poetry* (New York: Holt, Rinehart and Winston, 1969)

HOWE, IRVING, RUTH WISSE, and KHONE SCHMERUK, eds, *The Penguin Book of Modern Yiddish Verse* (New York: Penguin, 1987)

HUNGERFORD, AMY, 'Teaching Fiction, Teaching the Holocaust', in *Teaching the Representation of the Holocaust*, ed. by Marianne Hirsch and Irene Kacandes (New York: Modern Language Association of America, 2004), pp. 180–91

HUNT, L., *Inventing Human Rights: A History* (New York: Norton, 2008)

JOCKUSCH, LAURA, 'Justice at Nuremberg? Jewish Responses to Nazi War-Crime Trials in Allied-Occupied Germany', *Jewish Social Studies*, 19.1 (2013), 107–47

KAPLAN, BRETT ASHLEY, *Landscapes of Holocaust Postmemory* (New York: Routledge, 2011)

——*Unwanted Beauty: Aesthetic Pleasure in Holocaust Representation* (Urbana: University of Illinois Press, 2007)

KASSOW, SAMUEL, 'Shtetl', *YIVO Encyclopedia of Jews in Eastern Europe* (18 October 2010) <https://yivoencyclopedia.org/article.aspx/Shtetl> [accessed 23 July 2020]

KATZ, DOVID, *Words on Fire: The Unfinished Story of Yiddish* (New York: Basic Books, 2004)

KEARNEY, RICHARD, *On Stories* (London: Routledge, 2002)

KIRSHENBLATT-GIMBLETT, BARBARA, and JONATHAN KARP, eds, *The Art of Being Jewish in Modern Times* (Philadelphia: University of Pennsylvania Press, 2008)

KLIER, JOHN 'Pale of Settlement', *YIVO Encyclopedia of Jews in Eastern Europe* (14 September 2010) <http://www.yivoencyclopedia.org/article.aspx/Pale_of_Settlement> [accessed 21 November 2020]

KOTLERMAN, BER, 'South African Writings of Morris Hoffman: Between Yiddish and Hebrew', *Journal of Semitics*, 23.2i (2014), 569–82

KRONFELD, CHANA, 'Murdered Modernisms: Peretz Markish and the Legacy of Soviet Yiddish Poetry', in *A Captive of the Dawn: The Life and Works of Peretz Markish (1895–1952)* (Oxford: MHRA and Maney Publishing, 2011), pp. 186–206

KRUTIKOV, MIKHAIL, 'Raysn: The Belarusian Frontier of Yiddish Modernism'. A Festschrift in Honor of David Roskies, *In geveb* (June 2020), 1–11 <https://ingeveb.org/articles/raysn-the-belarusian-frontier-of-yiddish-modernism> [accessed 18 November 2020]

——'Yiddish Literature: Yiddish Literature after 1800', *YIVO Encyclopedia of Jews in Eastern Europe* (29 June 2016) <https://yivoencyclopedia.org/article.aspx/Yiddish_Literature/Yiddish_Literature_after_1800> [accessed 3 July 2020]

——'Yiddish Studies from a New Perspective', trans. by Saul Noam Zaritt, *In geveb* (December 2015), 1–3 < https://ingeveb.org/articles/yiddish-studies-from-a-new-perspective > [accessed 18 November 2020]

KUGELMASS, JACK, and JONATHAN BOYARIN, eds and trans, *From a Ruined Garden: The Memorial Books of Polish Jewry*, (New York: Schocken Books, 1983)

——'Introduction', *From a Ruined Garden: The Memorial Books of Polish Jewry*, trans. by Jack Kugelmass and Jonathan Boyarin (New York: Schocken Books, 1983), pp. 1–19

KULBAK, MOYSHE, 'Raysn' [Byelorussia], in *The Penguin Book of Modern Yiddish Verse*, ed. by Irving Howe, Ruth Wisse, and Khone Schmeruk, trans. by Leonard Wolf (New York: Penguin, 1987), pp. 388–93

LaCAPRA, DOMINIC, *Writing History, Writing Trauma* (Baltimore: John Hopkins University Press, 2001)

LANDSMAN, ANNE, *The Devil's Chimney* (Johannesburg: Ball, 1997)

LANG, BEREL, 'Introduction', in *Writing and the* Holocaust, ed. by (New York: Holmes and Meir, 1988), pp. 1–16

——ed., *Writing and the Holocaust* (New York: Holmes and Meir, 1988)

LANGER, JENNIFER, ed., *If Salt Has Memory* (Nottingham: Five Leaves, 2008)

——'Introduction', in *If Salt has Memory*, ed. by Jennifer Langer (Nottingham: Five Leaves, 2008), pp. 9–23

LANGER, LAWRENCE, *Admitting the Holocaust* (Oxford: Oxford University Press, 1996)

LANGFIELD, M., 'Lost Worlds: Reflections on Home and Belonging in Jewish Holocaust Survivor Testimonies', in *Place and Displacement in Jewish History and Memory*, ed. by David Cesarini, Tony Kushner, and Milton Shain (London: Mitchell, 2009), pp. 29–42

LANSZMANN, CLAUDE, *Shoah: An Oral History of the Holocaust* (New York: Pantheon, 1985)

LEISER, BURTON (Berel), 'Der Berditchever Rov', *Mendele: Yiddish Literature and Language*, 07.136 (20 January 1998) <http://www.columbia.edu/~jap2220/Arkhiv/vol07%20(1997–8)/vol07136.txt> [accessed 22 December 20]

LEFTWICH, JOSEPH, ed., *An Anthology of Modern Yiddish Literature* (The Hague: Mouton, 1974)

——ed., *The Golden Peacock: An Anthology of Yiddish Poetry* (London: Robert Anscome, 1939)

——ed., *The Golden Peacock: A Worldwide Treasury of Yiddish Poetry* (New York: Yoseloff, 1961)

LEVESON, MARCIA, 'Introduction', in Vincent Swart, *Collected Poems*, ed. by Marcia Leveson (London: Donker, 1981), pp. 7–24

LEVITT, LAURA, *American Jewish Loss after the Holocaust* (New York: New York University Press, 2007)

LEVY, ZALMAN, 'Der afriker in der higer literatur' [Africa in Local Literature], *Dorem Afrike* (October 1957), 17–19

LEWINSKY, TAMAR, *Displaced Poets: Jiddische Schriftsteller im Nachkriegdeutschland, 1945–1951* (Göttingen: Vandenhoeck & Ruprecht, 2008)

LIPPHARDT, ANNA, 'Yiddish after the Holocaust: A Case Study', *Europa Ethnica*, 3–4, special issue on Jewish Diaspora (2011), 80–87

LIPTZIN, SOLOMON, *The Maturing of Yiddish Literature* (New York: David, 1970)

LYOTARD, JEAN-FRANCOIS, *The Differend: Phases in Dispute* (Manchester: Manchester University Press, 1988)

MCEWAN, IAN, 'Only Love and then Oblivion', n. p. <https://www.theguardian.com/world/2001/sep/15/september11.politicsphilosophyandsociety2> [accessed 23 December 2020]

MITCHELL, W. J. T. ed., *Iconology: Image. Text. Ideology* (Chicago: The University of Chicago Press, 1986)

—— *The Language of Images* (Chicago: The University of Chicago Press, 1980)

MOSS, KENNETH, Emails to the author, 3, 4, and 5 January 2001

NEMEROV, HOWARD, 'On Poetry and Painting, with a Thought of Music', in *The Language of Images*, ed. by W. J. T. Mitchell (Chicago: The University of Chicago Press, 1980), pp. 9–14

NOVERSHTERN, AVRAHAM, 'Kulbak, Moyshe', *YIVO Encyclopedia of Jews in Eastern Europe* (19 August 2010) <https://yivoencyclopedia.org/article.aspx/Kulbak_Moyshe> [accessed 3 July 2020]

OMER-SHERMAN, RANEN, *Diaspora and Zionism in Jewish American Literature* (Hanover: Brandeis University Press, 2002)

PETERSON, NANCY J., *Against Amnesia: Contemporary Women Writers and the Crises of Historical Memory* (Pennsylvania: University of Pennsylvania Press, 2001)

POLLIN-GALAY, HANNAH, *Ecologies of Witnessing: Language, Place and Holocaust Testimony* (New Haven: Yale University Press, 2018)

POLSKI, HYMAN, *In Afrike* [In Africa] (Johannesburg: Pacific Press, 1952)

PRAGER, LEONARD, *Yiddish Culture in Britain: A Guide* (Frankfurt a. M.: Lang, 1990)

RADSTONE, SUSANNAH, and BILL SCHWARZ, *Memory: Histories, Theories, Debates* (New York: Fordham University Press, 2010)

ROSEN, ALAN, 'Yiddish and the Holocaust', *In geveb* (August 2015), 1–3 <https://ingeveb.org/chapters/yiddish-and-the-holocaust> [accessed 17 August 2018]

ROSEN, JONATHAN, 'Forward and Back: A Journey Between Worlds', in *Who We Are: On Being and Not Being a Jewish Writer*, ed. by Derek Rubin (New York: Schocken, 2005), pp. 249–66

ROSENTHAL, ERIC, *Encyclopaedia of Southern Africa*, 4th edn (London: Warne, 1967)

ROSKIES, DAVID, *Against the Apocalypse: Responses to Catastrophe in Modern Jewish Culture* (Cambridge, MA: Harvard University Press, 1984)

—— *The Jewish Search for a Usable Past* (Indiana: Indiana University Press, 1999)

ROTHBERG, MICHAEL, *Traumatic Realism: The Demands of Holocaust Representation* (Minneapolis: University of Minnesota Press, 2000)

ROWLAND, ANTHONY, *Poetry as Testimony: Witnessing and Memory in 20th Century Poetry* (New York: Routledge, 2013)

ROZHANSKY, SHMUEL, ed., *Antologye: Dorem Afrikanish. Fragmentn fun forshavetn tsu der karakteristik un zikhroynes* [South African Anthology: Characteristic Fragments and Memories] (Buenos Aires: Ateneo Literario en el Iwo, 1971)

RUBIN, DEREK, ed., *Who We Are: On Being and Not Being a Jewish Writer* (New York: Schocken, 2005)

RUBIN, STEVEN J., 'Poets of the Promised Land', in *Jewish American Poetry*, ed. by J. N. Barron and E. M. Selinger (Hanover: Brandeis University Press, 2000), pp. 197–215

SCHERMAN, RABBI NOSSEN, ed., *The Complete ArtScroll Machzor: Yom Kippur* (New York: Mesorach Publications, 1986)

SCHERMAN, RABBI NOSSEN, and RABBI MEIR ZLOTOWITZ, eds, *The Complete ArtScroll Machzor, Rosh Hashanah* (New York: Mesorah Publications, 2001)

SCHIFF, HILDA, ed., *Holocaust Poetry* (New York: St Martin's Press, 1995)

——'Introduction', in *Holocaust Poetry*, ed. by Hilda Schiff (New York: St Martin's Press, 1995), pp. xiii–xxiv

SCHWARZ, JAN, REVIEW OF *Choosing Yiddish*, in *Journal of Jewish Identities*, 8.1 (January 2015), 201–05

—— *Survivors and Exiles: Yiddish Culture after the Holocaust* (Detroit: Wayne State University Press, 2015)

SHAIN, MILTON, and RICHARD MENDELSOHN, eds, *Memories, Realities and Dreams* (Johannesburg: Ball, 2000)

SHERMAN, JOSEPH, 'Between Ideology and Indifference: The Destruction of Yiddish in South Africa', in *Memories, Realities and Dreams*, ed. by Milton Shain and Richard Mendelsohn (Johannesburg: Ball, 2000), pp. 28–49

——ed., *From a Land Far Off: A Selection of South African Yiddish Stories* (Cape Town: Jewish Publications, 1987)

——'Introduction', in *From a Land Far Off: A Selection of South African Yiddish Stories*, ed. by Joseph Sherman (Cape Town: Jewish Publications, 1987), pp. 1–15

——'Serving the Natives: Whiteness as the Price of Hospitality in South African Yiddish Literature', *Journal of Southern African Studies*, 26.3 (September 2000), 505–21

—— *Yiddish after the Holocaust* (Oxford: Boulevard Books, 2004)

SHERMAN, JOSEPH, and OTHERS, eds., *A Captive of the Dawn: The Life and Works of Peretz Markish (1895–1952)* (Oxford: MHRA and Maney Publishing, 2011)

SHMERUK, KHONE, ed., *A shpigl oyf a shteyn* [A Mirror on a Stone]: *An Anthology of Poetry and Prose by Twelve Soviet Yiddish Writers* (Jerusalem: The Magnes Press, 1987)

SHNEER, DAVID, 'An Introduction. *My Name is Now*: Peretz Markish and the Literature of the Revolution', in *A Captive of the Dawn: The Life and Works of Peretz Markish (1895–1952)*, ed. by Joseph Sherman and others (Oxford: MHRA and Maney Publishing, 2011), pp. 1–15

SHREIBER, MAEERA, 'The End of Exile: Jewish Identity and its Diasporic Poetics', *PMLA*, 113.2 (1998), 273–87

SICHER, EFRAIM, ed., *Breaking Crystal: Writing and Memory after Auschwitz* (Urbana: University of Illinois Press, 1998)

——'The Holocaust in the Postmodernist Era', in *Breaking Crystal: Writing and Memory after Auschwitz*, ed. by Efraim Sicher (Urbana: University of Illinois Press, 1998), pp. 297–328

——'Introduction', in *Breaking Crystal: Writing and Memory after* Auschwitz, ed. by Efraim Sicher (Urbana: University of Illinois Press, 1998), pp. 2–16

SIMON, J., 'Jewish Identity in Two Remote Areas of the Cape Province: A Double Case Study', in *Place and Displacement in Jewish History and Memory: Zakor V'Makor*, ed. by David Cesarani, Tony Kushner, and Milton Shain (London: Mitchell, 2009), pp. 114–28

STARCK-ADLER, ASTRID, 'Multilingualism and Multiculturalism in South African Yiddish', *Studia Rosenthaliana*, 36: *Speaking Jewish — Jewish Speak: Multilingualism in Western Ashkenazic Culture* (2002–03), 157–69

——'Old Home vs Land of Opportunity: Interrogating "Home" and "Exile" in Rakhmiel Feldman's *Trayers* [Tryers]', *Jewish Affairs: Literature*, 52.3 (Spring 1997), 79–84

——'South African Yiddish Literature and the Problem of Apartheid', *Jewish Affairs*, 65.1 (Pesach 2010), 6–12; first published, trans. by Karen-Anne Durbach, in *Jewish Affairs*, 49.2 (Winter 1994), 39–45.

——'These Two Autobiographical Books are my Identity Document: David Wolpe', in *Selves in Question: Interviews in Southern African Auto/Biography*, ed. by Judith Luther Coullie and others (Honolulu: University of Hawai'i Press, 2006), pp. 357–65

STONEBRIDGE, LINDSAY, and RACHEL POTTER, 'Sands of Sorrow: Rights, Refugees and the Impasse of Empathy', Transnational Holocaust Memory Conference, Leeds, U.K.,

January 2015 <https://britishjewishstudies.org/2014/10/06/transnational-holocaust-memory-26–27-january-2015-at-the-university-of-leeds-united-kingdom/> [accessed 23 December 2020]

—— 'Writing and Rights', *Critical Quarterly*, 56, special issue: *Writing and Rights* (2014), 1–16

SWART, VINCENT, *Collected Poems*, ed. by Marcia Leveson (London: Donker, 1981)

TOKER, LEONA, 'Folk Theodicy in Concentration Camps: Literary Representations', in *Knowledge and Pain*, ed. by Esther Cohen and others (New: Rodopi, 2012), 197–214

VAN VOREN, ROBERT, *Undigested Past: The Holocaust in Lithuania* (New York: Rodopi, 2011)

WAGNER, PETER, *Icons — Texts — Iconotexts: Essays on Ekphrasis and Intermediality* (New York: De Gruyter, 1996)

—— 'Introduction: Ekphrasis, Iconotexts, and Intermediality — the State(s) of the Art(s)', in *Icons — Texts — Iconotexts: Essays on Ekphrasis and Intermediality*, ed. by Peter Wagner (New York: De Gruyter, 1996), pp. 1–42

WEINREICH, MAX, *History of the Yiddish Language*, 2 vols (Yale: Yale University Press, 2008)

WEISSMAN, GARY, 'Questioning Key Texts: A Pedagogical Approach to Teaching Elie Wiesel's *Night*', in *Teaching the Representation of the Holocaust*, ed. by Marianne Hirsch and Irene Kacandes (New York: Modern Language Association of America, 2004), pp. 324–37

WELLEK, R., and A. WARREN, *Theory of Literature* (London: Penguin, 1949)

WIESEL, ELIE, *Night* (New York: Farrar, Straus and Giroux, 2006)

WIEVIORKA, ANNETTE, 'On Testimony', in *Holocaust Remembrance: The Shapes of Memory*, ed. by Geoffrey Hartman (London: Blackwell, 1994), pp. 23–32

WIMSATT, W. K., and M. C. BEARDSLEY, 'The Intentional Fallacy', in *The Verbal Icon: Studies in the Meaning of Poetry*, ed. by W. K. Wimsatt (Kentucky: University Press of Kentucky, 1982)

WIRTH-NESHER, HANA, 'Modern Yiddish Literary Studies: A Shifting Landscape', *Poetics Today*, 35.3 (2014), 211–24

—— 'Tradition, the Individual Talent, and Yiddish', *In geveb*, (December 2015), 1–8 <https://ingeveb.org/articles/tradition-the-individual-talent-and-yiddish> [accessed 1 December 2020]

WOLPE, DAVID, 'Yidishe literatur in Dorem Afrike' [Yiddish Literature in South Africa], *Dorem Afrike* (December 1956), 21–23

ZALKIN, MORDECHAI, 'Panevėžys', *YIVO Encyclopedia of Jews in Eastern Europe* (14 September 2010) <https://yivoencyclopedia.org/article.aspx/Panevezys> [accessed 23 July 2020]

ZEMEL, CAROL, 'Diasporic Values in Contemporary Art: Kitaj, Katchor, Frenkel', in *The Art of Being Jewish in Modern Times*, ed. by Barbara Kirschenblatt-Gimblett and Jonathan Karp (Philadelphia: University of Pennsylvania Press, 2007), pp. 176–92

INDEX

Lightning Source UK Ltd.
Milton Keynes UK
UKHW031332020622
403853UK00001B/31